Borders

Borders

Frontiers of Identity, Nation and State

**Hastings Donnan
and
Thomas M. Wilson**

Oxford • New York

First published in 1999 by
Berg
Editorial offices:
150 Cowley Road, Oxford, OX4 1JJ, UK
70 Washington Square South, New York, NY 10012, USA

Berg is the imprint of Oxford International Publishers Ltd.

Library of Congress Cataloging-in-Publication Data

A catalogue record for this book is available from the Library of Congress.

British Library Cataloguing-in-Publication Data

A catalogue record for this book is available from the British Library.

ISBN 1 85973 241 0 (Cloth)
1 85973 246 1 (Paper)

Typeset by JS Typesetting, Wellingborough, Northants.
Printed in the United Kingdom by Biddles Ltd, King's Lynn.

For Peter, Hannah, Lucy and Kate

Contents

List of Maps and Figures

Maps

Figures

Acknowledgements

Thanks are due to the following for permission to quote from unpublished work: Henk Driessen, Lindsay French, Michael Kearney, Bill Kelleher, Paul Nugent and Mary Margaret Steedly. We are also grateful to Jonathan Benthall and the Royal Anthropological Institute of Great Britain and Ireland for permission to reprint a figure from an article by Sandra Wallman which first appeared in *Man*, Vol. 13, 1978. And at Berg we owe a special debt to Kathryn Earle who kept us on the straight and narrow, a path difficult to follow in the study of borders.

Preface

This book is intended to be read as an introduction to the burgeoning literature on borders. In the following pages, we outline the history of the anthropological study of borders, and trace its connections to cognate disciplines, before reviewing a wide range of ethnographic case studies to suggest how a focus on borders can illuminate our understanding of nation and state – until relatively recently two curiously neglected topics in anthropology.

Our principal aim is to introduce the student of anthropology to a topic – international borders – which has increasingly captured the intellectual and popular imagination, though we also hope that students of other disciplines will find something of value in our effort to outline what anthropology in particular can bring to its study. Often this value lies, as in other areas of anthropological research, in the fine-grained ethnography that anthropologists collect – in this case about how people experience the nation and state in their everyday lives at international borders. We therefore make extensive use of case material, for it is in the richness of these examples, we believe, that the vitality or otherwise of wider collectivities is effectively revealed. If we have a theoretical course to follow, it is one which worries about the connections between these local border studies and the wider polities of which they are a part; in other words, one which claims that much can be learnt about the centres of power by focusing on their peripheries.

We came to this book from long-standing personal experiences of, and involvement with, borders, and openly recognise that the border between Northern Ireland and the Irish Republic, near which we both live, influences our perceptions of borders elsewhere, playing a part in our initial and continuing interest in the anthropology of international borders worldwide. This experience is undoubtedly reflected in our interests and approach. As we write, in July 1998, the Irish border has once again become the focus of tension, underlying and aggravating other schisms and boundaries which have too often so violently divided all those who live in Northern Ireland. In such circumstances, it is difficult not to emphasise the urgency and immediacy of such politicised boundaries and their frequently terrifying consequences over other boundaries which are perhaps of a more or wholly symbolic kind. This 'bias' is certainly reflected in what follows.

Other anthropologists have come to the study of borders from other directions. Some from their personal experience as migrants or descendants of migrants, some from experience of crossing the borders of sex or gender, and yet others from a desire to break down the borders between different disciplinary and literary or artistic traditions. In fact, by the mid-1990s borders had become such a buzzword that it was difficult to imagine a field or an experience to which the term could not be or was not being applied. It was truly in danger of being both everywhere and nowhere. We could not possibly deal with all of this literature here, though where it touches on our central concern with international borders we do try to refer to it.

Our initial excursion into this field took the form of organising a conference on state boundaries in the Irish border town of Carlingford in 1992. Many of the topics raised at this conference, such as migrant labour, ethnic and national identity, the gendering of borders and border conflict inevitably resurface in the pages that follow.

Hastings Donnan and Thomas M. Wilson

Introduction: Borders, Nations and States

> There has always been a tension between the fixed, durable and inflexible requirements of national boundaries and the unstable, transient and flexible requirements of people. If the principal fiction of the nation-state is ethnic, racial, linguistic and cultural homogeneity, then borders always give the lie to this construct.
>
> Horsman and Marshall, *After the Nation-State*

Borderlands are sites and symbols of power. Guard towers and barbed wire may be extreme examples of the markers of sovereignty which inscribe the territorial limits of states, but they are neither uncommon nor in danger of disappearing from the world scene. In Northern Ireland the relatively dormant security apparatuses on the Irish border remain, despite the rhetoric of a Europe without frontiers and the negotiations between the British and Irish states and a variety of political parties and paramilitary groups in the Northern Irish peace process. Observation towers, security gates, concrete pillboxes and helicopter pads appear and disappear overnight, testament to the adaptability of the state. In fact, the resilience of the physical power of the state is one of the dominant themes in the lives not only of those who live and work at the Irish border but also of the peoples of the borderlands of the world. But while the negotiation of state power is a central motif in any narrative or image of the world's borderlands, it is certainly not the only one. In this book we explore some of the ways in which these signs of military might must compete with, and in some cases accommodate, other forms of power in the borderlands of nation-states. We examine how an anthropological focus on international borders can illuminate the role of border identities and regions in the strengthening or weakening of the nation-state, an institution synonymous with the creation and exercise of political power, but one experiencing the twin threats of supranationalism from above, and ethnonationalism and regionalism from below. Through this review we hope to place the anthropology of borders firmly within the anthropological analysis of the relations of power between and among nations and states.

We take as our starting point that anthropologists have much to contribute to an understanding of the transformations in nations and nationalisms in the world today. Attention to these changes is timely and appropriate. It has become increasingly apparent over the last decade that as some states cease to exist, others come into being, and that allegedly new forms of nationalism are both creating and destroying traditional borders, thereby setting in motion the forces of war, racism and the mass movement of refugees. Many of these developments have been claimed by the other social sciences as their domain, yet few recent studies of nationalism by political scientists, sociologists, geographers and historians deal adequately with the cultural aspects of international borders, the frontiers with which they are associated, and the physical and metaphorical borderlands which stretch away from the legal borderlines between states. This book seeks to place general anthropological studies of border communities and border cultures within the wider social science of borders, nations and states. At the same time, it seeks to problematise the role of culture within other disciplines' investigations of international borders and frontiers, in an effort to provide a fuller picture of the historical, ethnic and nationalist forces which sustain a variety of identities in the borderlands of modern nation-states.

Old and New Borders, Nations and States

On one level, our focus on the anthropology of international borders is a reflection of the many and startling changes which the world has undergone since 1989. A list of these world transformations is now something of a cliché, but is nonetheless a compendium of such radical change in global politics, economics and social relations that it is worth repeating. The fall of the Berlin Wall, the most famous symbol of the border between two competing world systems, heralded the end of the Cold War, the disintegration of the Soviet empire and state, and the reawakening of long quiescent nation-states, as well as the creation of some new ones in Europe and Asia. The dissolution of Yugoslavia was the spark to another twentieth-century Balkans conflict, a series of ethnonationalist wars which overshadow all processes of nation- and state-building in the region. The Gulf War, which marked a so-called New World Order of American, Arab and European cooperation, followed so closely on almost a decade of Iranian and Iraqi conflict that the effects on the sovereignty of small and large states alike in that part of the world are still unfolding. The European Community, an intergovernmental association of twelve states which worked towards a common internal market, has become, since the Maastricht Summit of 1992, the European Union (EU), a group of fifteen states seeking monetary and political union and the establishment of rights, entitlements and protections for its 'European' citizens. The EU's success, coupled with the major advances in economic performance in the Asian Pacific Rim, stimulated similar moves in the western hemisphere, leading to the North American Free Trade Agreement, an economic arrangement among the United States, Mexico and Canada, which will have far-reaching social and political effects, not least in the borderlands of those three countries. And the accords in the Middle East and

Northern Ireland have given hope to people around the world that a 'peace process' can lead to lasting solutions to the problems of ethnic and nationalist strife.

As a result of these and other changes, in all of the continents, the number of states in the world has risen at a rate not seen since the heady days of the dissolution of the Great Empires after the two world wars. The membership of the United Nations has grown to today's total of 185 states. As a necessary complement to this, the number of borders between states has grown apace, resulting in no fewer than 313 land borders between nation-states. Along with the growth in numbers of states and their borders comes a redefinition of their structure and function. However, some of these changes do little to increase communication and cooperation between nations. The transformations of the post-1989 world have brought with them a rise in the number, type and intensity of border disputes. These include conflicts between states over their supposed sovereign territory (for example, between Iraq and Kuwait, Armenia and Azerbaijan, Ethiopia and Eritrea, Israel and Lebanon, Greece and Turkey, Serbia and Bosnia and Croatia), cross-border ethnic conflict (in such areas as Nagorno-Karabakh, Zaire and Rwanda, Greece and Albania, Ireland and the United Kingdom, Palestine and Israel, Serbia and Albania), regional contests over self-determination and nationhood (for example, among the Chechens, the Kurds, the Basques, the Irish, the Sikhs and the Quebecois) and local, regional and national efforts to support or to curb the cross-border movement of refugees, immigrants, illegal workers, smugglers and terrorists (perhaps most notably at the US–Mexico border and at the many external borders of the EU).

In fact, border wars have been a long-standing if not necessary component to the processes of nation- and state-building in the post-imperial age, and have not only inspired their protagonists to greater nationalist endeavours but have fired the imaginations of people everywhere who sympathise with the rights of minority nations and small states to rule themselves. Such border wars are too numerous to list them all here, but we might mention as examples the impact which the conflicts in Korea, Vietnam, Laos, Cambodia, India, Pakistan, China, the Belgian Congo, Nigeria and Biafra, Chad, Mozambique, South Africa and Israel have had on the balance of power, both in the world and in the regions in which they took place.

Borders no longer function as they once did, or at least not in every respect. Globalisation of culture, the internationalisation of economics and politics, and the decline in Cold War superpower and satellite hostilities have apparently resulted in the opening up of borders and the relaxation of those state controls which limited the movement of people, goods, capital and ideas. Scholars debate the extent and the depth of these border transformations, which seem to fly in the face of numerous examples of international borders which have been made stronger and more impenetrable. This book explores some of these debates in ways that make them more relevant to anthropological concerns, and it presents arguments regarding the role which culture plays in the social construction and negotiation of these borders.

One thing is clear. Changes in the structure and function of international borders, whether they be world-wide or restricted to one state, reflect major changes in the strength and resilience of the nation-state, and in the variety of social, political and economic processes long thought to be the sole or principal domain of the state. State borders in the world today not only mirror the changes that are affecting the institutions and policies of their states, but also point to transformations in the definitions of citizenship, sovereignty and national identity. It is our contention, moreover, that borders are not just symbols and locations of these changes, which they most certainly are, but are often also their agents. It is not surprising that the concept of transnationalism, which has become central to many interpretations of post-modernity, has as one of its principal referents international borders, which mark off one state from another, and which sometimes, but not as often as many people seem to suppose, set off one nation from another. However, these borders, structures of the state themselves, are constructed by much more than the institutions of the state which are present there, or of which the border's framework is a representative part, as in customs, immigration and security forces. Borders are also meaning-making and meaning-carrying entities, parts of cultural landscapes which often transcend the physical limits of the state and defy the power of state institutions.

Nations and the 'Great Fiction'

There are many definitions of 'border', 'frontier' and 'boundary' in the social sciences, and almost as many research designs for their study. The anthropological approach to international borders which we advocate in this book entails the study of power in and between nations and states, including the ways in which versions of that power are enhanced or growing, or diminished or declining, with particular reference to border cultures and identities. In this and subsequent chapters we consider how the state is subverted in its borderlands, how borderlanders are often victims of the abuse of power, and sometimes agents or the sources of state power, and how the state's borders may be strengthened, in the face of the so-called processes of globalisation, internationalisation and supranationalisation.

Almost all that occurs in the everyday lives of people in the modern world can and does occur in its borderlands. This makes borderlands interesting to social scientists, but not necessarily special. However, *some things can only occur at borders*. This is because of the function of borders in the relations between states, and because of the role played by borders in the origin and development of states, a role which they may continue to play in the future. Moreover, many features peculiar to borders are significant to their respective nations and states, both historically and today. We are not alone in recognising that borders have character-istics that differentiate them from other areas in states, and that border people are part of social and political systems unlike most others in their respective countries. Like Adeyoyin (1989: 378), we assume that 'border regions as socio-cultural systems are a living reality. They are . . . characterized by an inner coherence and unity which is essential to their nature'.

Martínez has suggested that five key processes help to shape the 'borderlands milieu' (1994b: 8–14; see also 1994a: 10–25). *Transnationalism* is the process whereby borderlanders are influenced by, and sometimes share the values, ideas, customs and traditions of, their counterparts across the boundary line. This is partly a function of their peripheral location in their states, which, together with their unique local culture and shared economic relations with other border communities, gives them a sense both of political and social *separateness* and *otherness,* i.e. of being culturally different from core or majority populations in their 'national societies'. Martínez also recognises that borders are areas of *ethnic conflict and accommodation,* due in large part to their cultural heterogeneity and their role as areas of immigration. But perhaps most predictable of all, borders are places of *international conflict and accommodation* unlike any others in their respective states, precisely because of their geographical location, the structures and agents of the state present there, and the aforementioned cultural characteristics which set most borders apart from more homogeneous, developed and powerful zones in the state.

These special characteristics of borderlands correspond to those identified by Malcolm Anderson (1996a: 1–3). To Anderson, borders (he uses the term 'frontiers') are both institutions and processes. As institutions, they mark and delimit state sovereignty and rights of individual citizenship. As processes, borders have a number of functions. They are instruments of state policy, although the state's policies may be enhanced or impeded by the degree to which it exercises actual control over the border and its people. Anderson also recognises that borders are markers of identity, and have played a role in this century in making national identity the pre-eminent political identity of the modern state. This has made borders, and their related narratives of frontiers, indispensable elements in the construction of national cultures. This important role of the border, in the creation and the mainte-nance of the nation and the state, is one reason why borders have also become a term of discourse in narratives of nationalism and identity.

Anthropology may be the best placed of the social sciences to examine some of the least studied and understood phenomena of international borders, namely border cultures and identities (sometimes called border 'mentality' by our colleagues in other academic disciplines; see, for example, Rumley and Minghi 1991a). To do this, anthropologists must return to a topic long studied by the discipline, but one which has proved mercurial and exasperating to many of the scholars who have immersed themselves in its study. Ethnicity, and its correlate, national identity, is a fundamental force found at all borders, and it remains the bedrock of many political, economic and social activities which continue to befuddle the institutions and agents of the state, in the borderlands and in metropolitan centres of power and influence. As the geographer Ilidio do Amaral (1994: 17) remarked when considering the present condition and future of international boundaries:

> Even in Western Europe, the home of the ideal homogeneous nation-state, ethnic divisions are readily apparent in regional and nationalist political activity. Conflicts whose origins stem from the multi-ethnic compositions of the state are the most difficult with which governments have to contend, and their severity can be great enough to threaten the territorial integrity of the state. Therefore, the ideas about the role of ethnicity need to be reconsidered in a new light.

Ethnicity and national identity pose threats to many states today, as they have in the past and will in the future, precisely because ethnic groups and nations have as one of their defining characteristics a perceived and essential relationship to a real, i.e. historically recognised, territory, or to a homeland to which they can only aspire. We define nations as communities of people tied together through common culture, who have as their pre-eminent political goal the attainment of some form of independence, autonomy or devolution. Nations can be distinguished from ethnic groups by their political role in a state, and by their political goals. Ethnic groups are often – we go so far as to venture most often – minority nations within states which are dominated by one or more majority nations, or within which some form of political autonomy is all but impossible for the members of the minority. Most such ethnic groups are in fact ethnically tied to nations elsewhere, but this does not prescribe their actions within the state in which they are a minority. Minority nations in a state may have as their principal political objective such things as the avoidance of ethnic strife, an active role in party politics, the attainment of wealth and prestige, and/or assimilation in a variety of ways. These behaviours do not preclude their affiliation or ascription to a nation elsewhere, whether that nation be just over the border, as among ethnic Hungarians who reside in all of Hungary's neighbouring states, or among Mexican-Americans, or be found in much more distant locales, as among the Armenian diaspora. In fact, whether self-ascribed or imposed by the wider society, the vast number of ethnic groups have a national identity as the cultural cement which binds them together, and their nationalism is linked in varying degrees to a past, present or hoped-for future national territory and nation-state sovereignty.

Affiliations such as these are based on what can be called the 'great fiction' of world politics, which has guided the actions of poets, priests, peasants and patriots since the nineteenth century, namely, that all nations have the right, if not the destiny, to rule themselves, in their own nation-state, on their own territory. Yet not all nations have been able to achieve this. States have a number of internal structural requirements. There are simply not enough natural resources, territory or wealth around to give every nation a star role as a nation-state. Said differently, there is too much power in the hands of too few to allow minority nations to achieve the type and degree of independence to which such gilded terms as 'self-determination' continue to inspire. This has become especially apparent in one area of the world which, because of its history of nations and states, and its current role in the redefinition of traditional relations between borders and states, is of particular concern to us in this book. 'In Europe, events since 1918 . . . have proved the bankruptcy of the idea of every ethnic nation forming its own state' (do Amaral 1994: 20).

Much recent scholarship in the social sciences has debated the future of the nation-state, particularly in the context of such 'threats' as multinational corporations, supranational trading blocs and political entities, globalisation of culture and society, and the perceived demise of imperialism and other forms of nationalistic enterprise (for an excellent review of these scholarly debates, see Milward 1992). Not surprisingly, much of this debate centres on Europe, birthplace of both the nation and the state, and where the European Union is both a symbol and an agent of the changes which may befall the states of the world in the future. And it is Europe that provides supportive case material for both sides in the debate: both for the view that the nation-state may be losing political and economic competencies, such as agricultural, fiscal and foreign-policy making, to the elites and institutions of an integrating Europe, and for the view that the reports of the nation-state's demise may be premature. In fact, it has been persuasively argued that the nation-state may be reconfiguring itself in Europe today, and is certainly not losing ground to either supranationalism or to the globalising pressures of consumer culture and capitalism. Michael Mann boldly concludes that the 'Western European weakenings of the nation-state are slight, ad hoc, uneven, and unique' (1993: 116) and that 'The nation-state is . . . not in any *general* decline, *anywhere*. In some ways, it is still maturing' (1993: 118, emphasis in original). Other scholars, however, contend that the nation-state is experiencing a crisis. But even if the states of Europe have been surrendering areas of national sovereignty to the European Union, they have done so in what Milward believes is a successful attempt to rescue themselves after the debacle of this century's wars, and to resist the pressures of integration on their own structures and power. Milward also stresses the importance of national identity and notions of popular sovereignty to the successful rescue of the European state. 'That the state by an act of national will might pursue integration as one way of formalizing, regulating and perhaps limiting the consequences of interdependence, without forfeiting the national allegiance on which its continued existence depends, appears to be confirmed by what we know of public opinion about the [European Union] in the member states' (Milward 1992: 19). Although empirical studies of national and European identities and the relationships between them are few, there is growing evidence from throughout the Union that European identity, regardless of the intentions of Eurocrats, cannot displace the national as the paramount political belonging.

If the fate of the European nation-state is in question, then it seems fair to us to query the future of the international borders of Europe. Are they too withering away, or proudly withstanding any attacks launched against them from within and without? Borrowing from Milward, can we say that the rescue of the European nation-state within the European Union has meant the rescue of nation-state borders as well? And what would this mean to the borders and the people who live at and use them? While much research in political science, sociology, geography, economics and law has been at Europe's borders (see, for example, Strassoldo and Delli Zotti 1982; DeMarchi and Boileau 1982b; Anderson 1996a; O'Dowd and Wilson 1996), little of this work deals with issues of identity and ethnicity. A review of the state of the art in border studies in Europe (Strassoldo 1989: 383–4) shows that the 'new' type of European border study, i.e. that conducted since the 1960s, has eschewed earlier legal and geographical models, which concentrated on conflict and were laden with statist ideological perspectives, in favour of focusing less on the problems of the state *per se* and more on integration, socio-economics and the problems of border peoples. These new border studies have been fostered by local, regional and European organisations and have been 'policy-orientated'. Regrettably, however, few such studies have been based on 'empirical, broadly social, research' (Strassoldo 1989: 386).

This situation has begun to change. In the following chapters we consider examples of empirical research at borders in Europe, North America, Africa and Asia. We use this case material to ask whether in the midst of the transformations affecting states, states are able to maintain or extend their already considerable power. But even more important given the concerns of this book, we ask which aspects of border cultures thrive, if any, in spite of the restrictions of the state, which elements of border life exist because of the relative impermeability or porosity of their borders, and how do ethnic and national identities find meaning, if not strength, at the periphery of their states, in the face of the centralisation of power?

We focus throughout the book on anthropological research in communities which live along state borders, whose members have social and political networks which are sometimes extremely small and local, and which sometimes stretch across the globe. Such networks are the very substance of border life, while border life is itself an essential ingredient in the history, myths and legends of every state. Regardless of the problems associated with the role of nations and ethnic groups in the definition of the state, it is clear that all so-called 'international' borders are the places where states meet, and where the leaders and institutions of the state must negotiate with their counterparts in neighbouring states. Although the structures of the state at international borders are often static, the negotiations of political and economic actions and values (a theme to which we shall return in chapter six) among the agents and organs of the state, wayfarers, and those who live at the border are continuous and dynamic.

Old and New Anthropological Perspectives

If on one level this book must explore international borders because of the recon-figuration of nations and states in the geopolitical environment of post-1989, on another level our focus on the anthropology of borders is a reflection of changes in anthropology and the social sciences over much the same period. During this time anthropologists have increasingly probed new ways of theorising the conditions and practices of modernity and postmodernity. Much of this theorising has sought to liberate notions of space, place and time from assumptions about their connection to the supposedly natural units of nation, state, identity and culture. These new theories regard space as the conceptual map which orders social life. *Space* is the general idea people have of where things should be in physical and cultural relation to each other. In this sense, space is the conceptualisation of the imagined physical relationships which give meaning to society. *Place*, on the other hand, is the distinct space where people live; it encompasses both the idea and the actuality of where things are (Gupta and Ferguson 1992; Keith and Pile 1993; Hastrup and Olwig 1997). The dialectical relations between a people's notions of space and the political and economic conditions of their places are at the core of anthropological interest in accounting for cultural disjuncture, displacement and distress, which to many anthropological and other theorists are integral conditions of post-modernity. In order to understand the forces that have transformed modernity, with its apparent fragmentation of culture in conceptualisation and lived experience, many anthrop-ologists have rethought the concept of culture itself.

Contemporary anthropology does not accept the culture concept uncritically. As Clifford suggests (1988), the predicament of culture in anthropology today is similar to the predicament of culture in the world around us. Part of the problem of culture for anthropologists is in the determination of its boundaries. Although anthropologists often assume that local cultures are partial elements in wider cultures, they just as often treat cultures at these levels as limited and concrete objects in their own right. This problem of bounding culture is compounded by the notion that cultures of disjuncture and difference are still seen to provide maps of meaning and charters for action among peoples who no longer can rely on the unity, homogeneity and protection of discretely bounded nations, communities, states, identities and territories. In short, although some anthropologists underplay culture as the matrix in which social life finds meaning and substance, culture is still seen by many people to provide exactly what these anthropologists have decided for them is no longer there.

The real predicament of culture for anthropologists is not that the usefulness of the concept of culture as an analytical tool is at an end. Rather, it is precisely because it, like the concepts of nation and identity, is recognised by most people to be a charter for behaviour, a marker of social membership, a matrix for changing meanings and relations, and a metaphor for the values and actions of everyday life that the discipline must continue to examine human life through its lens. Culture encompasses both imagined and lived experience, and it provides unity, continuity and boundedness in the spaces, places and times of modernity and postmodernity.

As we noted above, the problems of defining the boundaries between cultures in the postmodern world has been a growing concern for cultural anthropologists (see, for instance, Hannerz 1996). So many social groupings are now qualified by prefixes such as 'post', 'trans', 'supra', 'inter' and 'meta' that it seems everyone in the field is either attempting to theorise the social practices and meanings integral to these formations, or are trying to keep up with the social practices and meanings of the theorisers. How to understand has become confused by some anthropologists with what and who to understand. Thus, attempts are made to create new vocabularies capable of articulating conceptual and analytical frameworks for studying people who are no longer as constrained by the boundaries of nation and state as they once were (Basch et al. 1994).

It is clear that the cultural interstitiality on which much anthropology focuses today genuinely reflects the experiences of many of the groups of people anthropologists study, groups which are characterised as no longer occupying discrete spaces or as having discrete cultures. These people, often labelled transnationals, are compelled or choose to cross a wide range of geopolitical and metaphorical borders. Refugees, migrants, workers, criminals, soldiers, merchants and nomads cross and create many boundaries in their movements through their and other people's spaces and places. Even as they problematise the relationship, however, anthropologists must not forget that many of these people themselves still believe in the essential correspondence between territory, nation, state and identity, a correspondence in which each element is assumed to be an integral part of naturally occurring and bounded units. And even if some transnationals have lost this belief, they must nevertheless deal with those who still hold it. The state, which epitomises the belief in the homology between culture, identity, territory and nation, is a structure of power. Boundary making and breaking within and between states is a political act which can be seen to support or oppose that structure. Borders may serve as useful metaphors for understanding the rootlessness of many populations today, but this should not obscure the fact that everyone lives within or between the boundaries of nation-states, and these boundaries are always more than metaphorical.

Border Cultures

Regardless of the clear connection between culture and most definitions of the nation, as well as the oft-presumed relationship of nation to state, there has been a relative dearth of research on the cultural construction of interstate borders. In fact, it is our impression, as noted above, that culture is the least studied and least understood aspect of the structures and functions of international borders. Border studies in the social sciences have tended to focus on the historical and contemporary conditions of nation- and state-building, and the related themes of sovereignty, diplomacy and security. Although scholars in a variety of fields have recognised the role of culture in the creation and maintenance of borders and borderlands, few have directly tied culture to their analyses of statecraft at, across and as the result of borders. There are notable and important exceptions, of course. In political science, Anderson (1996a) recognises that cultural landscapes transcend political ones in border regions. O'Dowd has led a sociological research team which has set out to examine different forms of Irish and British society and culture as they influence policy making and its reception in the Irish border region (O'Dowd and Corrigan 1995, 1996; O'Dowd et al. 1995). Martínez (1994a) and Sahlins (1989, 1998) have examined the historical role of local, regional and national cultures in the creation and negotiation of the US–Mexico and the French–Spanish borders respectively. Nugent and Asiwaju (1996) have compiled a number of historical and geographic perspectives on culture, space and place at African borders. These and other social scientists, many of whose works we discuss in chapter three, are aware of the importance of understanding the role of culture in the establishment and development of international borders. Many other scholars, however, when tracing the evolution and present conditions of national boundaries, have concentrated on the formal arrangements between states, which often do not take into account the needs, desires and other realities of the people who live at those borders, as well as the cultural significance of the borders to people in more distant metropolises.

It is our contention here that culture is important to the study of international borders in a number of fundamental ways. First, it is a determining factor in states' diplomatic arrangements which establish borders. Culture continues as a force in all subsequent deliberations between the states, especially as these deliberations reflect political and economic conditions in the borderlands. Second, local and regional cultures in borderlands are not just reactive agents. In their proactive role they affect policy formation, representation and reception, at the borders and elsewhere. In fact, our emphasis on culture at borders is a reminder that state policies which encourage cooperation or conflict along international borders not only involve many aspects of 'national' life, in terms of state administration, economics and politics, but they involve just as much of a commitment from the regions and localities that straddle the borderline. Third, all border communities and the larger economic and political entities of which they are a part have cultural frontiers which they continually negotiate. Because nations and states have political and cultural frontiers which entail regular and often sharply contested negotiations to mark their limits, border communities are implicated in a wide range of local, national and international negotiations. A focus on border cultures is one way to identify and analyse the networks of politics, economics and society which tie individuals and groups in border regions to others, both inside and outside their own countries.

In an anthropological sense, border culture functions at two overlapping and inextricable levels. Culture ties the people and institutions of the international borderlands to people and institutions within their own states *and* to those very far away. It is in this sense that we speak of cultural landscapes which transcend political borders. Such landscapes are defined by the social interactions which construct them. They cannot be inferred or deduced from a knowledge of the political and economic structures of the states at their borders. The size and extent of the networks that link border people to others, including those who cross borders on their way elsewhere, those in positions of power in state centres, and those who may never even see the border but whose decisions affect life there, are matters of empirical research. So too are the lives of people who live and work at borders, some of whom do so *because* of the very existence of the border. Their lives are part of border cultures, ways of life and forms of meaning which they share only or principally with other borderlanders, on the same or the other side of the legal state demarcation, the borderline. In this way, too, local border cultures almost always transcend the limits of the state, calling into question yet again the lack of fit between national culture and state sovereignty and domain.

We believe that anthropology provides the best way to study border cultures. Anthropological research, utilising its methodology of long-term residential and participative fieldwork, as well as the range of other social science methods, places economic, political and social institutions and actions within wider contexts of meaning and behaviour and, in so doing, demonstrates how border communities and structures are linked to more encompassing and perhaps more powerful social and political formations.

The anthropology of border cultures does this in several ways. Anthropologists provide the data to explore the cultural bases to ethnic, racial and national conflict at international borders, a task made all the more urgent by the resurgence of ethnic and nationalist violence at many of the world's borders. Border research may thus serve to help policy makers, government leaders and others to understand the local and regional factors which push or pull refugees, migrants and illegal labourers across borders. The policy impact of a wide range of immigration, tax, trade and health laws are often first felt amongst border populations, leading us to suggest that the field of applied anthropology has much to do and learn in the borderlands of the world.

Perhaps foremost among all of the anthropological tasks at borders, however, is the investigation and interpretation of the symbolic aspects of the state. Border-lands are often the first or the last areas of the state that travellers see. Ever since the creation of modern nation-states, borders and their regions have been extremely important symbolic territories of state image and control. Yet border cultures are not constructed solely by national centres. The investigation of the symbolic reveals the cultural characteristics that local people use to define their membership in local, regional, national and supranational entities. Ultimately, anthropological research on border cultures contributes to our knowledge of identity formation, maintenance, adaptation and disintegration. Conversely, anthropology's ability to explicate the roles of national, ethnic, gender, sexual, religious and class identities in border areas is one way to demonstrate the importance of culture in the mapping out of the progress of nations and states in the modern and postmodern worlds, and their continuing power over the imagination (for examples of how anthropologists can provide insight into border identities, see Wilson and Donnan 1998b).

A focus on border cultures thus allows us to engage issues of nation and state by generating data on how these are routinely lived and experienced by ordinary people. By their very nature, international borders highlight ambiguities of identity as people move through interactions based on, for example, citizenship, nationhood and membership in a local community. An examination of such shifting contextual manipulations of identity can reveal much about how the structures of state power manifest themselves in people's daily lives. The 'meeting' between 'state' and 'people' is often particularly visible in border regions, and the identification of the traces left by each upon the other, by drawing attention to relations of power, may help to right a recent tendency to over-emphasise the symbolic in the anthropology of relations between local communities, ethnic groups and nations. In fact, most state borders have been places where people's interaction on the one hand with the forces of the state, with its top-down notions of national culture, and on the other hand with peoples across the borderline, who are in their own contest over their 'national' culture, have helped to fashion distinctive national societies and cultures (see, for example, Douglass 1998; Sahlins 1998).

Although there is a risk of essentialising a notion such as 'border cultures', we believe that there are sufficient grounds for looking at borders generically (cf. Martinez 1994a: xviii; Thomassen 1996: 46). Such a focus looks at states at the extremity of their power, at places where 'national cultures' mix and clash. Border areas are places where nations (i.e. populations who believe that because of shared culture and a common past they share the present and a common political future) must and do deal with two or more states. Nations can end at or cross these borders, but in either case those who have experience of these areas must confront the realities of state control which facilitate or constrain the likelihood of transborder movement. This book is organised around the twin themes of viewing border cultures first as windows on nationalism and the state, and, second, as ways of documenting and understanding multiple cultural identities, in the midst of great world social, political and economic change.

Some Definitions in the Anthropology of Borders

The study of borders in anthropology has been patchy. One international border, that between the United States and Mexico, has enjoyed a long and sustained anthropological interest (for a critical review of the literature on this region, see Alvarez 1995). Yet with few exceptions, this literature has had little impact outside of North America, and even there has figured more prominently in research on Mexican and Mexican–American life than in anthropology generally. We trace the history of the anthropology of borders in chapter two, but note here with surprise not only the relative lack of comparative study of international borders in anglophone anthropology, but also how so few problematise or even review issues of identity, nation and state.

This relative dearth of anthropological research on nation and state at international borders is surprising in a number of ways. Most anthropologists cross international, regional and provincial borders to reach their field research sites, and are thus made aware of the political, economic, legal and cultural difficulties which such barriers present both to travellers and residents. Furthermore, the social science of international borders has embraced the interpretative analysis of the historical and cultural construction of nations (see chapter three). Also, as mentioned above, the increasing attention to symbolic boundaries has led many anthropologists to question their definitions of community and culture, and the ways these concepts match with political–legal administrative institutions such as wards, boroughs, constituencies, towns, cities, counties, provinces, states and supra-nations (see Donnan and Wilson 1994a).

We recognise that something that should make border regions attractive as research locales for the study of nationalism, ethnicity, illegality and conflict may actually be something that prevents ethnographers from conducting border field studies. Governments often do not like foreign scholars, or national scholars from their own metropolitan centres, nosing around disputed borders, especially if the governments fear security breaches. Anthropologists may also encounter difficulties in securing funding, because of the administrative problems of obtaining approval to conduct research in two or more states. When compounded by the problems of completing years of training, often in two languages and in two sets of 'national' scholarly literatures, the research difficulties give one pause. One other factor which makes anthropological research at international borders difficult is that borders are too readily recognised and accepted in a people's or a nation's daily life (Prescott 1978:13). As such they are often unproblematic, if not invisible, to many people, and thus evade the anthropological gaze.

Such difficulties must be overcome if anthropology is to contribute to the wider comparative social science of nations and states on the role of culture in power relations. One goal of this book is to encourage just such a contribution by stimulating anthropological interest in international border research. To achieve this, however, we must be clear on a few important definitions.

Over the last decade 'borders' and 'borderlands' have become increasingly ubiquitous terms in the work of a wide range of academics and intellectuals including journalists, poets, novelists, artists, educationalists, literary critics and social scientists (see, for example, Chambers 1990; Eyre et al. 1990; Giroux 1992; Hart 1991; McMaster 1995). But while this convergence of interest might indicate agreement about a topic of importance and significance, the terms are used in so many different ways as to suggest that it is not one topic but many. Social scientists occasionally claim precision, though even they employ a range of terms – border, borderland, border zone, boundary, frontier – which sometimes pass as synonyms and at other times identify quite different phenomena.

In anthropology, where 'borders' have acquired a new significance in the wake of recent theoretical developments (see, for example, Rosaldo 1989), it is likewise possible to identify a number of meanings for the term 'border', from its referent as a line in the sand to its use as a metaphor for the cultural and other 'borderlands' of postmodernity. We explore these more fully in the next chapter. For the moment it is enough to reiterate that our concern in this book is with state borders, and to outline what many people believe state borders should be and should do, before providing our definition of borders.

State borders secure their territories, which are the repository of their human and natural resources. These territories may also have strategic and symbolic importance to the state. Borders are signs of the sovereignty and domain of the state, and are markers of the peaceful or hostile relations between a state and its neighbours. They are also a means of maintaining state control over the movement of people, goods, wealth and information, all of which must be deemed acceptable to the state in order to cross its borders. Thus borders are both structures and symbols of a state's security and sovereignty. They are historical and contemporary records of a state's relations with other states, with its own people, and with its own image. In our definition, borders have three elements: the juridical borderline which simultaneously separates and joins states; the agents and institutions of the state, who demarcate and sustain the border, and who are found most often in border areas but who also often penetrate deeply into the territory of the state; and frontiers, territorial zones of varying width which stretch across and away from state borders, within which people negotiate a variety of behaviours and meanings associated with membership in their nations and states (see Wilson and Donnan 1998a: 9). As features of the borders of all modern nation-states, these frontiers are territorial in nature, which distinguishes them from the metaphorical frontiers of identity so prominent in much contemporary postmodern analyses.

Culture as Power

This book examines the cultures to be found along and across international borders, because it is here that we can see most clearly how the cultural landscape qualifies the political and economic realities of the power of the state and international capital. We must be careful, however, not to let the images and metaphors of frontiers and borders blur our view of the politics of both anthropology and the borderlands themselves. As Heyman cautions, in regard to the US–Mexico border, 'It is . . . when the border is condensed to an image, and when this image symbolizes wide-ranging political or theoretical stances, [that] understanding of the border becomes reductive and delocalized' (1994: 44). The recent interest in theorising the border-lands of identity, in urban and rural centres and peripheries everywhere, may seem on the surface to be especially relevant at the politico–territorial borderlands, but it does not take us very far unless we also examine how state power is situated in place, space and time. Although images of frontiers and international borders may further the intellectual pursuit of other metaphorical borderlands of self and group identity, they may indicate a superficial and exploitative use of these borders as metonyms, as plot devices necessary for the furtherance of the narratives of identity elsewhere, in an anthropological equivalent to Hitchcock's 'McGuffin' (the thing, event, or moment in the story which gets the plot started, but which is irrelevant to the narrative once it gets going).

Borders are not just good places to study symbolic boundaries; they are places of specific cultural relations which are based on particular temporal and spatial processes, which have been and continue to be significant to their attached and associated nations and states. We need only examine state and supranational policies, as they are received, perceived and implemented at international frontiers, to see the value of the related concepts of culture and border. And it is in the exercise of state power, in which no two states are equal, regardless of the equality of sovereignty which their border posturing suggests, that borderlands take on signifi-cance beyond the frontiers themselves.

The politics of national frontiers are simultaneously bounded, by the state's territorial control, and fluid, brimming over into the next state and inwardly moving to influence national centres of cultural and political dominance. While 'border cultures' are metaphorical images of the state of culture in anthropological discourse today, their fixed nature in space and time may help us also to understand the culture of the state, where power is much more than representational. The study of culture is the study of power relations. The border cultures examined in the follow-ing chapters are those of transient people and displaced communities, as well as those of the border peoples whose physical distance from the centres of sovereignty is no measure of the power they may hold in locality and nation. We suggest that culture may still serve as the link between the anthropologies of power and meaning, among those who believe in the fixity of nation, state and identity, and those who are adrift in space, place and time.

In the next chapter we examine the development of diverse viewpoints in the anthropology of borders and boundaries, before comparing, in chapter three, perspectives on borders to be found in other scholarly disciplines. Subsequent chapters review how anthropologists have studied the cultural relations of power among borders, nations and states. Chapter four examines rituals and ethnicity; chapters five and six explore economic relations, which sometimes subvert the state, and often create conditions of differential power and value; and chapter seven reviews the border constructions of the politics of the body. We conclude in chapter eight with a discussion of the contemporary crisis of the nation-state, and consider some ways in which an anthropological concern with culture and power may enable anthropologists to contribute to wider debates in the scholarship of borders, nations and states.

–2–

Borders and Boundaries in Anthropology

The new frontier is no longer distinguished by space alone. The people on it no longer merely face one another in a struggle for a common culture for their interactions. Rather, the frontier is marked by the cultural selectivity of peoples and interest groups in a world in which variety is rapidly swelling, not ebbing. The frontier is all around us.

Bohannan, 'Introduction' in *Beyond the Frontier*

This chapter examines the growing body of literature on the anthropology of 'borders' and 'boundaries'. It identifies the different approaches which anthropologists have taken to each of these concepts, and points out that while they have sometimes conflated them, at other times they have been careful to draw a distinction.[1] Some anthropologists have been primarily interested in the social boundaries which order social relations and mark membership in collectivities, others in the cultural boundaries which separate different worlds of meaning, and yet others in boundaries whose principal characteristic is that they are marked in geopolitical space. Of course, these three elements – the social, the cultural and the territorial – are not necessarily mutually exclusive. They may distinguish different types of boundary but they need not; they may, in fact, be aspects of a single boundary. In this chapter, we identify three dominant patterns of usage or emphasis in recent anthropological research on borders and boundaries, each of which is marked to some extent by an associated body of literature. An obvious danger of any such categorisation is that it risks over-emphasising the differences and separation between the categories. As we shall see, some of the work we consider seeks to

---

1. 'Border' has ranked high among the major buzzwords of the 1990s. Part of its power has been the many contexts of use to which it lends itself. Borders can be identified almost everywhere and at every level of society and culture. But this is also a potential disadvantage, for it risks, of course, losing its focus. We do not pretend to be arbiters of terminological usage, but we do think that some sorting out is long overdue, of approach and focus of study if not of terminology. It is almost a quarter of a century since the potential confusion generated by different usages of 'border' and associated terms was first remarked upon (see Blacking 1975; Hannerz 1975). In this chapter, we retain the terminology of the literature and case studies discussed, but only in order to avoid entanglement in repeated terminological clarifications. Nevertheless, we should be clear that these usages do not always match our own definitional prejudices, which we have set out in chapter one.

problematise the relationship between social and cultural boundaries.[2] Some also seeks to problematise the relationship between the social, the cultural and the territorial.

Anthropologists were not always interested in boundaries, or at least not in the sense used in recent years. Early anthropological concern with society as a functioning organic whole meant that anthropologists were interested in boundaries chiefly as a device to define and delimit the 'edges' of their subject matter. Several generations of British social anthropologists in particular sought to isolate for study populations which could in some sense be regarded as socially and culturally discrete. 'Boundaries' were of interest only in so far as they enabled 'closure' of the research population; what was of real interest was not the boundary itself or relations across it, but the practices, beliefs and institutions of those it encompassed. It was believed that cultural diversity could be explained by geographical or social isolation and that the best way to analyse such diversity was to study the separate cultural worlds of which it was composed. The result was a body of influential work produced by the structural–functionalists on, for instance, the 'Tallensi' and the 'Tiv', studies which, together with work on a few dozen other 'tribes', have become the classics of the discipline. Even as recently as the 1970s, 'bounding' one's study area in this way was a pressing concern for many intending fieldworkers, though ways were being sought to transcend its limitations (cf. Gluckman 1964).

Of course, there were theoretical perspectives which potentially threatened to subvert this approach by directing attention to relations across rather than within these culturally bounded wholes. The diffusionists, for instance, were interested in how certain traits had apparently transcended cultural barriers and had been communicated from one culture area to another (cf. Rosaldo 1989: 228n). Acculturation theory similarly sought to address relations across cultural boundaries (see Bohannan and Plog 1967). But by mid-century the diffusionists were all but discredited, and by and large it was the structural–functional approach, and subsequently its offspring, the 'community study', which dominated research. By the late 1960s this had slowly begun to change, partly in response to the increasing mobility of peoples whom anthropologists had hitherto studied as cultural isolates, and who were now gradually being released from the colonial grip and were experiencing industrialisation and urbanisation. The boundaries of the study group could now no longer or so easily be traced in geographical space, but had shifted to the cities of the rapidly decolonising world, where members of different groups were increasingly being thrown together. A new set of perspectives emerged, necessarily more conscious of and sensitive to a world where people of varied

---

2. The emphasis on 'social organisation' is evident in the titles of some of the chief exemplars of this pattern: Barth's *Ethnic Groups and Boundaries: The Social Organization of Culture Difference* and Cohen's *Belonging: Identity and Social Organisation in British Rural Cultures.*

backgrounds and experiences came into contact. The boundaries between these people thus themselves became of interest.

The history of the theoretical development of British social anthropology and American cultural anthropology could therefore be characterised as marked by a discernible shift of focus: from an interest in what a boundary encompasses to an interest in the boundary itself. No one has perhaps done more to put boundaries on the anthropological map than Norwegian anthropologist Fredrik Barth, and it is to his work, and to that stimulated by his insights, that we now turn.

Social and Symbolic Boundaries

In 1969 Barth published *Ethnic Groups and Boundaries: The Social Organization of Culture Difference*, an edited collection of essays which set out to address 'the problems of poly-ethnic organization' (1969: vii), or what happens when different cultural groups come into contact. In his introduction to this collection, Barth questions the value of a view that sees the world as divided up into social collectivities which correlate neatly with discrete and discontinuous cultures. Instead, for Barth, ethnic groups are socially constructed, made up of individuals who strategically manipulate their cultural identity by emphasising or underplaying it according to context. People may cross the boundaries between groups should they find it advantageous to do so, and may maintain regular relations across them, but this does not affect the durability and stability of the boundaries themselves. Cultural emblems and differences are thus significant only in so far as they are socially effective, as an organisational device for articulating social relations.

We do not intend to elucidate here the many different insights generated by Barth and his colleagues in their short collection of essays, but it will be useful to summarise some of the salient points they make about ethnic boundaries. Above all, Barth argues that ethnic groups cannot be understood in terms of long lists of 'objectively' identified cultural attributes. People may stress some cultural traits in their dealings with other groups but ignore others, and we cannot predict these in advance. Instead, it is much more productive to view ethnic groups as an 'organizational type'; as categories in which membership is based on self-ascription and ascription by others. As long as individuals themselves claim membership in a particular ethnic category, and are willing to be treated as such by others, they express their allegiance to the shared culture of this category however that shared culture might be signalled. From this perspective, the boundary between categories becomes the critical focus for investigation: how and why are such boundaries maintained in the face of personnel flows and systematic relations across them? What sorts of rules structure behaviour at and across boundaries in such a way as to allow those boundaries to endure? Ethnic groups are not simply the automatic by-product of pre-existing cultural differences, but are the consequences of organisational work undertaken by their members who, for whatever reason, are marked off and mark themselves off from other collectivities in a process of inclusion and exclusion which differentiates 'us' from 'them'. The pressing question as far as Barth is concerned, therefore, is why inter-group boundaries are sharply marked even as people cross them and even as the cultural differences between the groups change.

Barth's observations clearly challenged existing wisdoms and his suggestion, in a phrase which has been widely cited since, that the critical focus of investigation should be 'the ethnic *boundary* that defines the group, not the cultural stuff that it encloses' (Barth 1969: 15, emphasis in original) set the agenda for much subsequent research. Judith Okely (1983), for example, explicity employs Barth's insights to illustrate how Traveller-Gypsies in Britain maintain a distinct identity in the face of continuing and regular contact with the non-Gypsy, or Gorgio, population. Some Gypsy cultural traits, such as pollution beliefs, are employed as symbols of identity, while others are not, and important traits may change over time and be replaced by others. Moreover, Okely argues, even though some aspects of Gypsy culture resemble aspects of the wider society, this cultural overlap with the Gorgio population does not necessarily weaken Gypsy identity, nor the Gypsy–Gorgio boundary. Indeed, Gypsy beliefs should not be seen independently of the wider society, 'mainly because they create and express symbolic boundaries between the minority and majority' (1983: 78). Okely thus directs our attention to the importance of viewing any boundary from both sides, from both within and without, a point developed by Sandra Wallman (1978), who considers several possible analogies for describing how social boundaries are always the outcome of a two-sided process. Following Yehudi Cohen (1969), a boundary might be seen as a balloon which responds to changes in internal and external air pressure. While this is helpful in so far as it emphasises how the size, quality and significance of a boundary can vary through time, it does not allow for the possibility, to which Barth initially alerted us, that boundaries may be crossed without threatening their existence. The more permeable teabag, Wallman (1978: 205) suggests, might therefore be a better if more prosaic image with which to visualise the relationship. Wallman's point here in invoking such analogies is that we must never forget that a boundary occurs only as a reaction of one system to another, and is thus necessarily oppositional, having two sides.

But according to Wallman, boundaries also have two kinds of meaning. The first is structural or organisational, by which she means that a social boundary 'marks the edge of a social system, the *interface* between that system and one of those contiguous upon it' (Wallman 1978: 206, emphasis in original). This interface is between two systems of activity, of organisation, or of meaning and, following Douglas (1970), is liable to be characterised by ambiguity and danger. At the same time a boundary also has significance for the members of these systems. Its second meaning, therefore, refers to how it marks members off from non-members and

	IDENTITY	INTERFACE
INSIDE (us)	We identify 'us' in opposition to 'them'. We use the boundary for our purposes, according to our need(s) at this time/in this context.	The border around the familiar, the normal, the unproblematic.
OUTSIDE (them)	'They' identify themselves by contrast to the rest of us. They use the boundary for their purposes.	The beginning of another system. Performance, appearance, activity, social or symbolic structure is different.

Figure 2.1 Wallman's four-part social boundary matrix (Wallman 1978: 207)

acts as the basis by which each can be identified. For Wallman, all social boundaries thus do not just have two sides, but are characterised by an interface line between inside and outside, as well as by an identity line between 'us' and 'them' (cf. Ross 1975). 'The *interface element*', she continues, 'marks a change in what goes on. The *identity element* marks the significance given to that change and expresses the participants' relation to it' (Wallman 1978: 207, emphases in original). These elements are arranged by Wallman across a four-part matrix, as illustrated in Figure 2.1.

Although Wallman is chiefly interested in elucidating processes of 'race' and ethnicity in England, she identifies a number of potentially productive lines of inquiry for the study of social boundaries more generally. Any social boundary, she argues, must be seen as a consequence of the various possible relationships between identity and interface on both sides of itself. Because so many different factors can influence the social meaning of difference, and can shift the point of interface between one system and another, a range of questions must be asked of each element:

What *kind* of resource is this boundary? What is it used *for*? In which (and how many) contexts is it relevant? What is its status in historical or situational time? For whom is it an asset, for whom a liability? With what other differences is it congruent or associated? What meaning does it have on the other (outer) side? (Wallman 1978: 208, emphases in original).

All of these questions draw attention to the relational nature of social boundaries and to the way in which they, and the manner in which they are marked, may alter through time. This issue of the marking of boundaries and their meaning has been subject to systematic investigation by Anthony Cohen in an influential series of books (1982a, 1985, 1986a, 1987). Cohen was led to a focus on boundaries by his dissatisfaction with the analytical inadequacy of classical sociological and anthropological notions of 'community' which stressed structure or morphology as its defining feature. A community exists, Cohen insists, only by virtue of its opposition to another community. The notion is thus relational, implying both similarity and difference, and the best place to study the everyday practices of exclusion and inclusion is at a community's boundary. The debt to Barth is both obvious and openly acknowledged.

Cohen is interested in understanding the importance of community in people's experience. He is consequently interested in what the boundary means to people or, as he puts it, with 'the meanings they give to it' (A. P. Cohen 1985: 12). These boundaries are constructed by people in their interactions with others from whom they wish to distinguish themselves but, unlike the markers of national boundaries, we cannot objectively determine in advance what the distinguishing features of these symbolic boundaries will be, nor exactly where the boundaries will be drawn. Moreover, they may mean different things to different individuals, both to those on opposite sides of a boundary as well as to those within it. In fact, boundaries recognised by some may be invisible to others (A. P. Cohen 1985: 13). The task of the researcher, therefore, is to uncover these boundaries and the meanings they are given, for only in this way can we grasp what 'belonging' to a community involves. With this emphasis on people's own experiences of boundaries and their perceptions of them, Cohen would seem to be principally concerned with what Wallman earlier called the 'identity element' of a boundary.

In Britain at least, which is the focus for Cohen and the contributors to his two edited collections (1982a, 1986a), the symbolic marking of community boundaries has become increasingly important as the significance of the structural parameters of community have weakened or disappeared. Cohen argues that ties of locality, kinship and class have all been transformed as technological advances in communication have swept local diversity under a carpet of cultural homogeneity and as local communities have become ever more tightly bound to the wider political and administrative structures of the state. What remains distinctive about locality and community, therefore, is not their structural differentiation from other similar entities, which is both difficult to discern and has slowly been eroded, but their *sense* of difference and distinctiveness. Community difference and identity now reside less in the structures which once seemed to underpin them than in the minds of the people who express them. Consequently, it is in symbolism, rather than in structure, that we must 'seek the boundaries of their worlds of identity and diversity' (A. P. Cohen 1986b: 2). This insight that structural boundaries have given way to symbolic boundaries is shown by contributors to be applicable whatever the scale of boundary in question, from the boundaries inside households (Bouquet 1986) to the boundaries between different ethnic collectivities (McFarlane 1986). Cohen's framework thus claims to be all-encompassing, applicable to boundaries at whatever level of social organisation is being studied.

At the same time, however, Cohen indicates that structure does matter. He recognises that it is insufficient to focus only on the intricacies of relations within a local boundary, and argues that any local collectivity must be viewed in context of the wider societal relationships and entities of which it forms a part. He thus endeavours to show how experience of one can mediate the meaning of the other: how wider political and economic forces impinge upon locality and vice versa (see A. P. Cohen 1982a: 12). However, what this often comes down to, as Banks (1996) and others have pointed out, is an argument about the ways in which external forces can be manipulated to symbolic advantage at the local level: how a harbour blockade as an 'extra-local' event is used by Shetland fishermen to articulate local difference and solidarity (A. P. Cohen 1982b) or how centrally formulated government policy can be made 'grist to the symbolic mill of cultural distance' and boundary marking (A. P. Cohen 1986b: 17). This tendency to focus on the 'inside' is exacerbated by the fact that much of the ethnography presented by Cohen and his contributors draws upon research among peripheral minorities. The result is, as several critics have remarked, that one side of the boundary between localities and the structures beyond has tended to receive rather more attention than the other (see, for example, Banks 1996: 148). '[E]conomic, political and informational ties to the complex state systems of the British Isles' are recognised as 'present[ing] powerful constraints' on the articulation of local identities (A. P. Cohen 1982a: 12), and thus on the way in which boundaries are drawn, but it is the manner in which the former are absorbed by the latter that is the principal subject of analysis.

Similar criticisms have been levelled at Barth. As we have seen, Barth, too, emphasises that boundary making involves both self-ascription and ascription by others. But he too tends to focus on one side rather than the other, emphasising internal identification rather than external constraint and the shaping influence of wider structures, such as those of class and the state (see, for instance, Asad 1972). However, as Jenkins points out, it is important to distinguish 'between two analytically distinct processes of ascription: *group identification* and *social categorization*. The first occurs *inside* the . . . boundary, the second *outside* and across it' (1997: 23, emphases in original). Jenkins argues that Barth and Wallman (and, one might add, Cohen) elide this distinction in their assertions that 'ethnicity depends on ascription from *both* sides of the group boundary'. As a result, they minimise the relative power relations upon which 'categorisation' especially depends, underplaying the fact that members of one group may be able to impose their categorisations on the members of another group. By recognising that some groups may be better able than others to make their categorisations stick we give greater theoretical centrality to relationships of domination and subordination, as Jenkins

(1997: 23) notes. We shall see that some of those who focus on state boundaries attempt to build this dimension into their analyses.

Geopolitical and State Boundaries

State boundaries obviously entail a mapping out in geographic space and recognition in international law. They mark the limits of sovereignty and of state control over citizens and subjects, limits which may be upheld by force or by the threat of force. Because of this, they have a tangible and visible quality less evident of symbolic boundaries. They are 'objective', or at least have an objective dimension to them, rather than 'subjective' (cf. A. P. Cohen 1985: 12). Some scholars therefore refer to them as *real* borders in a shorthand attempt to distinguish them from symbolic boundaries which have no necessary territorial equivalent. This can be misleading, for whatever else state boundaries might be they are obviously also cultural and symbolic. Moreover, symbolic boundaries are no less 'real' for not being physically marked, since they are clearly real in their consequences. Nevertheless, while geo-political territorial boundaries are necessarily always also cultural and symbolic, it is worth recalling that the reverse is not true, and that cultural and symbolic boundaries do not always have a spatial dimension.

State boundaries have not been subject to systematic scrutiny by anthropologists to the same extent as have symbolic boundaries. They have therefore not been so heavily theorised by them. By and large, this has been left to other disciplines, such as political science and political geography, as we examine in chapter three. This is not because anthropologists have failed to conduct field research at inter-national boundaries. Nor is it because anthropologists have been wholly unaware of or uninterested in the ways in which state boundaries can impinge upon their subject matter. Rather, it is because their questions have, until recently, led them in other directions. Even where a state border has figured in the lives of those studied by anthropologists, it has rarely been problematised as a primary focus for empirical investigation or theoretical reflection. Although Needham, for instance, considered it sufficiently important to contextualise his analyses of Purum society by mentioning its proximity to the Indo–Burma border, he remained thoroughly preoccupied by other considerations (see, for example, Needham 1958, 1962). Goody (1970) too, driven by the pressing issues of the day, focused on the 'inheritance frontier' between matrilineal and patrilineal groupings rather than on the border between Ghana and Upper Volta near which he worked. And where 'frontier', 'state' and 'border' are more explicitly considered, as in Leach's (1960) 'The frontiers of "Burma"', it is to show how such European concepts do not always straightforwardly apply elsewhere.

In much of the literature we consider in this section, the borders themselves appear chiefly as a backdrop to some other line of inquiry. They are often no more than an analytically distant presence with a vague influence on whatever the topic in hand; at worst, they are merely part of the obligatory 'scene-setting', their study relinquished to political scientists and geographers. As a result, we are compelled to approach them obliquely, by stealth and subterfuge rather than directly. From the perspective of this book, then, the history of the anthropological study of state boundaries might be said to be a history of missed opportunities.[3] It has certainly been unsystematised, with few of those who have worked and written about state and sub-state or regional borders citing the work of others who have made similar studies. In this respect, the study of these borders is in marked contrast to the clear intellectual genealogising and cross-referencing characteristic of the study of symbolic boundaries outlined in the previous section and typical, as we shall see later, of a 'postmodern' reading of borders.

This omission is particularly striking in the case of the first four authors we consider. All four were associated in one way or another with the University of Manchester. One called his book 'Frontiertown', the other three published books which mention 'borders' in their titles.[4] Three of them carried out their field research within five years of each other in the 1950s, two of these – Abner Cohen and Ronald Frankenberg – while based in the Department of Social Anthropology at Manchester whose Head, Professor Max Gluckman, wrote introductions to their monographs, and the third – Rosemary Harris – while a student at the Queen's University of Belfast (but who, with Gluckman's encouragement, published her book with Manchester University Press[5]). The fourth – Myron Aronoff – carried out his research in the 1960s, again while based at the University of Manchester and again under Gluckman's patronage and supervision. Given these connections, we might seem here, in hindsight, to have an embryonic 'school' of border studies. But it does not appear to have been recognised as such at the time, since none of these authors cross-references the work of the others, nor does Gluckman draw

3. In his review of anthropology's overall contribution to the scholarship of the US–Mexico border, which was then and still is the most studied state border, Ellwyn Stoddard concluded that while anthropology, of all the social sciences, has the methods and skills most appropriate to borderlands research, it nonetheless had done little to support contemporary comparative study of that border and, perhaps because of its biases, had actually impeded the 'scientific research of Mexican-Americans' there (1975: 52).

4. *Village on the Border: A Social Study of Religion, Politics and Football in a North Wales Community* (Frankenberg 1957); *Arab Border-Villages in Israel: A Study of Continuity and Change in Social Organization* (A. Cohen 1965); *Prejudice and Tolerance in Ulster: A Study of Neighbours and 'Strangers' in a Border Community* (Harris 1972).

5. Gluckman was general editor of the series in which Harris's book appeared and is mentioned by Harris (1972: vi) in her acknowledgements as having 'steadily insisted that I must publish an account of Ballybeg'. It is interesting to note that Anthony Cohen was also connected with Manchester University, although his contribution came much later: he was lecturer in sociology and in anthropology there, and also published much of his work with Manchester University Press.

any connections between them in his introductory essays. The pressing theoretical concerns of the period clearly led in other directions, and it is the cross-cutting ties which constrain conflict that provide a unifying theme for these monographs. The potential theoretical interest of a common focus on state and regional borders is thus left hanging, as a loose theoretical thread that needs tying.

Despite the title, Frankenberg (1957) actually makes curiously little mention of the border in his *Village on the Border*. It is not even listed in the index. None the less, he does note how social relations in the Welsh village in which he worked bear the imprint of the nearby English–Welsh border, both historically and in the present. Local relations in the village of 'Pentrediwaith' are insidiously inflected by the border, whose historical legacy can be traced in the divisions among villagers which Frankenberg recorded during his fieldwork. Although more complex in practice, the inhabitants of 'Pentre' are categorised locally as 'insiders' (Pentre people) or 'outsiders'. These two categories map crudely onto a number of other oppositions, such that insiders are generally associated with the Parish Council and are generally wage-earners, Welsh-speaking and Nonconformist ('Chapel'). In contrast, outsiders are associated with the Bench, and are self-employed, English-speaking and Anglican ('Church'). This twofold divide has the further overtones of, respectively, the distinction between tenant/labour on the one hand and landlord/capital on the other, a distinction which itself derives from and recalls the historic border between England and Wales (Frankenberg 1957: 11–12). Local conflict thus always threatens to escalate into a question of nationality. Only cross-cutting linkages (of kinship, common residence and common social and economic interests) help to keep this threat in check: 'open and continuous breach is not possible. If it did occur it would place in conflict not only friends but different members of the same family. Thus "national" divisions are at village level modified by the face-to-face character of village society' (Frankenberg 1957: 18). In short, the divisions to which the nearby regional border draws attention and which it underscores are domesticated by the exigencies of the daily round at the local level. Such is the reality of everyday life for Frankenberg's residents in the 'village on the border'. Frankenberg thus does tell us that the border is significant, but not perhaps to the extent that the book's title might lead us to expect.

Not surprisingly, Frankenberg looked for inspiration to some of the compelling studies of his day: to studies of tribal Africa carried out by the generation of British social anthropologists of the time, and particularly to the work of those from his own institution, the University of Manchester. Indeed, the chief interest of Frankenberg's book as far as Gluckman is concerned, and as he remarks in his introduction, 'lies in its application of ideas developed in the study of tribal society to a community in Britain' (Gluckman 1957: 7). Frankenberg's juxtapositions are indeed interesting and insightful, and might still be read with benefit by those with an interest in British rural society. But at the same time his selection of comparative theoretical work is revealing: might one not have supposed that a work nominally interested in a 'border village' would make at least passing reference to, for example, Frederick Jackson Turner's (1977 [1920]) frontier thesis and the subsequent elaboration of this thesis by a succession of critics, to Kroeber's (1953) reflections on boundaries and frontiers in his introduction to North American culture areas, to Lattimore's (1968 [1956]) article on the 'frontier in history', or even to the Chicago School's discussion of city boundaries and urban zoning (for instance, Park, Burgess and McKenzie 1967 [1925])? Given what we said earlier about the 'bounding' of tribal studies in the British social anthropological tradition, the importing to Britain of insights from tribal ethnography was hardly likely to encourage the inclusion of such work.

Harris's study of an Irish border village, 'Ballybeg', fares only slightly better on these measures. There are a couple of entries under 'border' in the index, but still no mention of Turner, Lattimore or Park nor any sustained attempt to include mention of the border between Northern Ireland and the Republic as any more than a backdrop to the analysis. Nevertheless, it is a backdrop which Harris stresses is highly significant:

> the border certainly exerted a definite influence on the pattern of social relationships in the area. Most vitally, perhaps, it crystallised the opposition to each other of Catholic and Protestant . . . The border, close physically and omnipresent psychologically, brought into sharp contrast not only those actually separated by it but those separated because their opinions about it were opposed (Harris 1972: 20).

Harris thus makes it abundantly clear that Ballybeg's proximity to the border can intensify local feelings of prejudice and antagonism. Indeed, because of the border's impact on Ballybeg the reader is advised to be wary of assuming that what was true of it was also true of other areas in Northern Ireland (1972: vii); the influence of the border may have made it unrepresentative. But though Harris thereby identifies the border's pivotal significance for Ballybeg, her analytical objectives lie less in elaborating this point than, like Frankenberg, in showing how conflict in a polarised society – this time divided between Catholic and Protestant – is restrained by cross-cutting personal relationships and the norms which apply to them. As a result, the border itself remains largely just off the theoretical stage, impinging on the play of life in Ballybeg but external to it, and thus taken for granted rather than made the subject of a generalising or comparative analysis. In our experience and research, however, it is clear that the border in Northern Ireland today is never taken for granted in communities situated near it, precisely because it functions as a structure and symbol of differentials in status, power and politics.

Abner Cohen (1965) is less content to leave the border as a backdrop to his study of social change and continuity in the Arab villages of 'The Triangle' between

Israel and Jordan. Cohen sets out to explain why an indigenous and ancient form of political organisation based on patrilineal descent – the *hamula* – should suddenly re-emerge as a significant political force in the late 1950s when its importance had been steadily declining over the previous hundred years. The *hamula* had been the dominant form of political organisation in the early nineteenth century, its solidarity underwritten by the maintenance of a joint estate and by a high proportion of endogamous marriages. At the end of the British Mandate in Palestine in 1948 this system had all but broken down and had been replaced by 'class' divisions based on socio-economic status. These cut across historical allegiances to *hamula*s, greatly weakening their political efficacy. After the establishment of the Israeli state, and by the time of Cohen's fieldwork in 1959, the situation had changed again. The wealthy families which for much of the century had dominated village life by forging a cross-*hamula* 'alliance' no longer found it so easy to exercise their power. As their opponents consolidated in patrilineages to challenge them, so their own agnates rallied round, resulting in a renewed emphasis on patriliny as the basis of political action. It is Cohen's contention that the Israel–Jordan border is the key to understanding the dynamics of this historical cycle.

Cohen argues that this revival of an old, indigenous political form in response to contemporary circumstances is a consequence of a constellation of economic and political conditions which he refers to as 'The Border Situation'. The border situation which emerged at the end of the 1948–9 Palestinian war was to change life dramatically for the Arab villagers of the Triangle. According to Cohen (1965: 9–18), four main components characterised the border situation after the armistice boundaries had been drawn up in 1949: (i) some families were cut off from their land and kin in what were their parent villages only a few miles away in Jordan and with which, prior to 1949, relations had been intense; (ii) Triangle villages were now suddenly isolated from Arab national organisation which had emerged during the Mandate; (iii) villagers became increasingly incorporated within the framework of Israeli society from which they derived economic advantage; and (iv) the area now became of great strategic importance. In short, though these Arab villages were not of the Israeli state they were, nevertheless, clearly in many ways a part of it, 'caught between . . . two opposing fronts, because they happen to be near the border' (A. Cohen 1965: 16).

Much of Cohen's book is concerned with documenting how the resurrection of *hamula* politics was a reaction to these border-specific conditions: for instance, the hold of the 'class'-based cross-*hamula* elite was weakened as rich families were cut off from some of their land and as the Israeli economy opened up new sources of income for all villagers. For Cohen, the border is thus more than a backdrop; it creates the very conditions of everyday life for these Arab villagers and as such is at the heart of his explanation. Cohen is quite explicit about the analytical centrality of the border: 'The reality of the border is thus thrust upon the

Triangle villages ... [Hostility at the border] ... has become a major factor underlying the social organization of these villages, and cannot therefore be treated as a temporary, or abnormal, phenomenon any longer, nor can it be regarded as just an "intruding factor" in village society' (A. Cohen 1965: 17).

While its theoretical foundation has been radically critiqued (Asad 1975), of the four Manchester border monographs Cohen's is perhaps the most stimulating for the modern border scholar. Although writing about the same country – Israel – and out of the same theoretical stable – Manchester – Myron Aronoff (1974) does little to advance Cohen's reflections on borders, and surprisingly does not even cite them. In *Frontiertown*, his monograph on the politics of community building in a new town in the Negev Desert, Aronoff has two main concerns: the first of these, which once again explicitly acknowledges the intellectual debt to Gluckman (Aronoff 1974: xiii, 12), is to examine the role of political strife and cross-cutting loyalties in the creation of community cohesion; and the second is to explore the links between local and national political organisation. Although Frontiertown is 'close to the Jordanian border' (Aronoff 1974: 41), the border itself is rarely mentioned. Instead, the focus is firmly on the relationships between local-level political organisation in this border community and the ministries, organs and agencies of the Israeli state. Aronoff does not make it clear if the Jordanian border's proximity gives any specific inflection to these relations other than to impart to them a sense of urgency and strategic significance. Nevertheless, while the presence of the border itself at times seems almost incidental, Aronoff's emphasis on the state does usefully alert us to the interdependency between local-level politics and wider political structures. In this particular case, as Aronoff (1974: 17) tells us, the outcome of this relationship for Frontiertown provides a striking example of 'the primacy of national over local interests'. As we shall see later, this need not always be the outcome where border politics are involved.

In fairness, we note that none of these four anthropologists sets out to examine border life specifically. Rather, their aim was to demonstrate the value of Gluckman's insight that community cohesion can be generated, and radical cleavage prevented, by cross-cutting conflicts of loyalty and allegiance. In this they were no different from a number of other ethnographers trained in Manchester at the time. It is not even clear from their work if they selected a border area for study because they thought it a potentially rich location for researching competing loyalties. Yet by selecting such a field site these ethnographers could be said to have laid the foundation for current border studies. All of them noted the significance of proximity to a border for the communities they studied, and while only Cohen was to explore this influence systematically, each recognised it to varying degrees. Although not specifically focused on culture, nation and state at international borders, their work nevertheless showed the value of localised studies for the understanding of how cultural landscapes are superimposed across social and political divides.

Almost a decade after Cohen's book, John Cole and Eric Wolf (1974), two American anthropologists, published *The Hidden Frontier*, a study of 'ecology and ethnicity' in the Italian Tyrol. This time the field site had been explicitly chosen because of the fact that, historically, it had been partitioned and repartitioned, and had been left, in the 1960s when the study was carried out, with a population whose ethnic attachments allowed Wolf to pursue the issues which interested him: such as, why ethnic and nationalist loyalties so often seem to transcend class loyalties and ties of formal citizenship (Cole and Wolf 1974: 4). Abner Cohen, of course, had raised similar questions. In fact, the two studies share a number of interests in common. Like Cohen, Cole and Wolf set out to explore how what happens at the local level can challenge or confirm developments in the 'larger system'; as in *Arab Border-Villages*, they were thus 'interested in the transformations of local . . . political alignments in relation to the promptings of market and nation-building' (Cole and Wolf 1974: 4). Furthermore, in both studies these transformations take on their particular urgency because they occur at the politically sensitive margins of the state; and (again in both studies) among ethnic minorities incompletely incorporated into the national body or resistant to it. It is puzzling, then, that Cole and Wolf do not refer to *Arab Border-Villages* or build explicitly upon its insights, especially when they were obviously aware of Cohen's other work (they cite his later book, *Custom and Politics in Urban Africa*, published in 1969). Again this seems to be an example of the apparently non-cumulative nature of border studies during this period and, indeed, of its lack of any real theoretical or methodological core.

The main focus of *The Hidden Frontier* is on two villages in northern Italy, only a mile or two apart but located in the separate Italian Provinces of Alto Adige and Trentino. Before the First World War these provinces, and the two villages, had been integral parts of the Austrian 'Tyrol', but were transferred to Italy by the peace settlement in 1919. Alto Adige, which was German-speaking, was cut off from the German-speaking Tyrolese who remained a part of Austria to the north, and to whom there remained a strong allegiance. The residents of Alto Adige now became an ethnic minority within Italy, and resisted attempts at incorporation by the Italian state under whose control they now found themselves.[6] In contrast, Trentino, which was Romance-speaking and which even when under Austrian domination had been seen as part of Italy, was welcomed back into the fold and quickly integrated into the Italian nation. Although briefly reunited under the Third

---

6. The border region of Friuli in north-eastern Italy – Holmes (1989) – bears some potentially interesting similarities to the Italian Tyrol: before the First World War both had been under Habsburg control and both had their borders extended at the end of the war, resulting in the incorporation into Italy of a large German-speaking minority. Consideration of the issues raised, however, are subordinated to Holmes's main aim of elaborating the concept of peasant-worker society.

Reich, the Tyrol was again partitioned at the end of the Second World War. This dashed any hopes of future reunification for the German-speakers of Alto Adige, who now sought some form of accommodation to the new Italian Republic at the same time as they continued to defend themselves against social and cultural encroachment by the Italians (see Cole and Wolf 1974: 270–1, 272). This remained the situation at the time of fieldwork.

Cole and Wolf trace the impress of these dramatic events on life in the villages of St Felix (German-speaking) and Tret (Romance-speaking). What particularly interested them about the South Tyrol was the durability of this cultural frontier long after the political borders of state and empire had shifted. National boundaries had clearly survived the demise of state boundaries, and remained important to everyday routine. Despite the many similarities between these villages, especially those arising from living in a shared mountain environment, each had followed a different political and cultural course since the settlement of 1919. Distinguished, among other things, by their rules of inheritance and the political and ideological consequences of these rules, villagers played down their differences from one another in everyday encounters, yet once in company of their own were quick to resort to ethnic stereotypes to explain the actions of the others. Cole and Wolf (1974: 281) thus reiterate Barth's (1969) observation that ethnic boundaries may be maintained despite relations across them. Their major contribution, however, and of principal interest to the present discussion, was in showing how we must move beyond purely local influences to understand and explain this process.

Here, then, we have an example of where ethnic boundaries arise as a result of, and are sensitive to, the rise and demise of state boundaries. One can only be understood with reference to the other. In this respect Cole and Wolf could be said to represent the coming together of a symbolic boundary focus with a political economy perspective which attempts to situate local boundary making within wider historical and political processes. *The Hidden Frontier* was innovative in combining these perspectives, and as such stands as an early exemplar of what a border study can be like, offering a sophisticated mix of ethnographic fieldwork, historical documentation and political–economic approach. By introducing a political econ-omy perspective to Barth's emphasis on symbolic boundaries, Cole and Wolf effectively marked an important transition in the anthropological study of boundaries and heralded the beginning of a new form of inquiry. However, since much of the more recent literature forms the basis of our book, and is discussed in detail later, we do no more here than provide a brief sketch of how the field subsequently developed (see also Donnan and Wilson 1994b).

From the 1970s onwards, anthropologists began to use their field research at international or interstate borders as a means of widening perspectives in political anthropology to encompass the formal and informal ties between local communities and the larger polities of which they are a part. We have already seen how Aronoff

(1974) used a border field site as a means of focusing on nation and state building in Israel, and other anthropologists did likewise for other regions of the globe (on Africa and India see, respectively, Kopytoff 1987; Pettigrew 1994). Some studied border areas as a way of examining how proximity to an international border could influence local culture (Douglass 1977; Heyman 1991; Kavanagh 1994) or could create the conditions which shape new rural and urban communities (Alvarez 1991; Price 1973, 1974). Others focused on the voluntary and involuntary movement of people across borders as traders, migrants and refugees (Alvarez 1994; Alvarez and Collier 1994; Hann and Hann 1992; Hansen 1994; Malkki 1992). Yet others concentrated on the symbols and meanings which encode border life (James 1979, 1988; Lask 1994; Lavie 1990; Shanks 1994; Stokes 1994). Regardless of theoretical orientation or locale, however, most of these studies have focused on how social relations, defined in part by the state, transcend the territorial limits of the state and, in so doing, transform the structure of the state at home and in its relations with its neighbours.

This new anthropological interest in how local developments can have an impact on national centres of power and hegemony was partly influenced by historical analyses of localities and the construction of national identities (see, for example, Sahlins 1989), and recalls Cole and Wolf's insistence on the need to view the anthropology of borders as historical anthropology. As the South Tyrol case so clearly shows, borders are spatial and temporal records of relationships between local communities and between states. Ethnographic explorations of the intersection of symbolic and state boundaries have salience beyond anthropology because of what they may tell us of the history of cultural practices as well as the role of border cultures and communities in policy-making and diplomacy. We shall see some examples of this later. But for the moment it is enough to note the growing importance of a border perspective in political anthropology, a perspective in which the dialectical relations between border areas and their nations and states take precedence over local culture viewed with the state as a backdrop. What we must do now is examine the last of the three main ways in which we suggest that 'border' has recently been used by anthropologists: as a metaphor for the cultural borders of the contemporary cosmopolitan world.

It is important to note that this last pattern of use partly grew out of experience of the US–Mexico border and to which, therefore, it is in a sense organically linked. The US–Mexico border is the only state border to have generated a sizeable body of scholarly work from many different disciplinary perspectives. Anthropologists too have made their contribution, though in the 1950s and 1960s much of their work, like that outlined above, used the border to frame the study rather than integrating it as a variable in the analysis. As elsewhere, it is only more recently that the wider political and economic context has featured in analyses of the US–Mexico border, where the issues of underdevelopment, transnationalism, and the globalisation of power and capital, among other aspects of culture, increasingly concern the growing number of historically informed and wide-ranging ethnographic accounts (for an overview, see Alvarez 1995). Some of this work has followed broadly in the tradition of Cole and Wolf and, as we shall see later, has examined the historical and contemporary intersections of state and symbolic boundaries in, for instance, the creation of a proletarianised and disenfranchised labour force (see, for example, Heyman 1991; Kearney 1998a; chapters five and six, this volume). But much of it has taken a somewhat different course, and has pursued instead a line of inquiry which recruits the 'border' as an image for what happens when two or more cultures meet. It is to this latter work that we now turn.

Cultural and Postmodern Borderlands

We have indicated that the use of the term 'border' as an image for the juxtaposition of cultures is closely tied to anthropological and other social scientific research at the US–Mexico state border. But the ubiquity of the term as a metaphor in current academic discourse has many other sources too. Debates about the intellectual common ground across the disciplinary boundaries of subjects such as literature, anthropology and political science, discussions initiated by previously marginalised intellectuals such as women, and debates about ethnic, class and gendered identities and about sexual orientation have, for instance, all found the border metaphor helpful (cf. Lugo 1997: 44) and have contributed to its visibility by using it in the titles of books and conferences. The current fascination with borders and border crossings thus extends far beyond anthropology into literary theory, cultural studies, media studies and beyond (see, for example, S. Gupta 1993; Pratt 1992). The borders concerned exist at many different levels, and may be cultural, social, territorial, political, sexual, racial or psychological, while the notion of 'border crossings' is similarly varied and is just as likely to be used to refer to cross-dressing or the synthesising of cinematic genres as it is to refer to traversing state lines.

The border-as-image entered into anthropology largely through the work of those dissatisfied with the classic anthropological view of culture which emphasised patterns of meaning that are shared and consensual. Such a view, it is suggested, barely countenances the possibility of change, inconsistency and contradiction. Advocates of attempts to rethink this conventional view of culture were sometimes those who had had direct experience of cultural inconsistency and contradiction in their own lives, such as those who questioned prevailing norms of sex and gender and those who belonged to ethnic or other minorities. The American anthropologist Renato Rosaldo grew up as a Chicano in the United States. Speaking Spanish to his father and English to his mother, Rosaldo was acutely aware of the 'mundane disturbances that so often erupt during border crossings' (Rosaldo 1989: 29). Yet the cultural perplexities of his everyday life were not easily accommodated by the conventional anthropological concept of culture, an inadequacy which propelled him and the many others who similarly sought to understand cultural disjuncture to devise new strategies for studying both the interstices between cultures and the differences within them. For Rosaldo, the notion of 'borderlands' is central to this project:

> For social analysis, cultural borderlands have moved from a marginal to a central place. In certain cases, such borders are literal. Cities throughout the world today increasingly include minorities defined by race, ethnicity, language, class, religion, and sexual orientation. Encounters with 'difference' now pervade modern everyday life in urban settings . . . Borderlands surface not only at the boundaries of officially recognized cultural units, but also at less formal intersections, such as those of gender, age, status, and distinctive life experiences (Rosaldo 1989: 28–9).

According to Rosaldo, social analysis must reorient itself to the study of such borderlands, which 'should be regarded not as analytically empty transitional zones but as sites of creative cultural production that require investigation' (1989: 207–8, 1988: 87).

In his review of the literature on the anthropology of 'borderlands', Alvarez (1995: 448) is careful to point out that the term refers not just to the region adjacent to a state border, but also to the 'multiple conceptual boundaries involved – the borderlands of social practices and cultural beliefs in a contemporary global context'. In this new formulation, Alvarez stresses, borderlands evoke the geopolitical and the metaphorical, the literal and the conceptual. As we shall see later, some scholars are concerned about the loss of focus this would seem to involve, and though Alvarez's review does not say as much itself, it too communicates an ambivalence about such extended usage.

Nevertheless, in a paper on Mexican long-haul trucking, written with George Collier, Alvarez broadly follows this extended conceptualisation of 'borderlands'. For Alvarez and Collier (1994), 'borderlands'

> refer not just to the physical spaces at the conjunction of national frontiers, but to the sites that can potentially be found anywhere where distinct cultures come together in interaction without losing their differences. In our analysis of northern Mexican trucking, the Los Angeles wholesale markets are as much a 'borderland', for the way they juxtapose and confront Anglo and Mexican ways of doing business, as the actual U.S.-Mexico frontier that Mexican truckers cross through Tijuana (1994: 607).

Alvarez and Collier compare northern and southern Mexican truckers to show how participation in alien markets stimulated by the North American Free Trade Agreement (NAFTA) will be as much driven by cultural styles of doing business as by economic motives. There are clear differences in entrepreneurial style between the two groups of truckers. The northern truckers develop inter-personal networks of patronage, trust and reciprocal obligation while the highland Maya truckers in the south rely on a more corporatist organisation and ideology. In both cases, however, the goal is the same: to develop new opportunities for trade by reconfiguring foreign markets along ethnic lines (cf. Strating 1997). This both enables the truckers to gain a foothold where alien cultural styles predominate and opens the market to other kinds of commerce for the truckers' compatriots. This is precisely what Alvarez and Collier (1994: 624) tell us happened in Los Angeles, where Mexican traders took over the Seventh Street Market as existing traders moved out to alternative market facilities elsewhere in the city. In this analysis, then, the 'borderlands' extend far beyond the national boundary, and refer to cultural encounters in California's wholesale trade.

As Heyman (1994) has pointed out, Alvarez and Collier's account of borderlands in Los Angeles draws directly on an understanding of social and economic relations at the state border between the United States and Mexico. The borderlands which they describe in the wholesale markets seem to share some of the socio-political processes characteristic of borders between states; namely, both involve 'differential access to formal channels of power' (Heyman 1994: 50). It is this, according to Heyman, which makes the extended image of borders seem apt in this instance. We learn something only 'when we extend fairly specific analytical insights from one "border" denotation to another' (Heyman 1994: 50). Scholars critical of applying a metaphorical notion of borders to all forms of cultural encounter thus hesitantly concede that there is potentially something to be gained by such a comparison, but only as long as the 'borders' compared share processes that transcend the similarity of image. However, this is not always the case.

Roger Rouse's (1991) analysis of the Mexican wage labourers who migrate from Aguililla in southwest Michoacán to Redwood City in the San Francisco Bay region of California provides a good example of a study where 'border' is used as an image with little or no analytical reference to the US–Mexico border itself. Most of Rouse's migrants find work as dishwashers, gardeners, hotel workers or child minders. However long they stay in California, most of them retain strong ties with Michoacán, and there is much movement of people and goods back and forth between the two locations. As a result, Rouse (1991: 14) suggests, Aguilillans now constitute a single community across a variety of sites, each with its own history, language, political system and cultural code. They inhabit a world which shows few signs of synthesis or homogenisation and where competing cultural forms can be managed only by developing skills of 'cultural bifocality'. Such a world is usefully conceptualised, Rouse argues, as a 'border zone', for it bears striking similarities to the sense of cultural fracture and confrontation which often colours life at state borders like that between the United States and Mexico. It is '[t]ies such as those between Aguililla and Redwood City, places two thousand miles apart, [that] prompt us to ask how wide this [U.S.-Mexico] border has become and how peculiar we should consider its characteristics' (Rouse 1991: 15). Cyclical migration, Rouse (1991: 17) proposes, has resulted in a proliferation of such border zones right across the United States and these zones are a good example of what, following Rosaldo (1988: 85, 1989: 212), he refers to as the 'implosion of the Third World into the First'.

Heyman is very critical of Rouse's use of the border image, chiefly because Rouse does not attempt to identify any strong analytical connection to state border processes. For Rouse, the image is apposite simply because the migrants he studied crossed the international state line, and because they must manage two worldviews in their lives. As with Rosaldo (1989: 207), borderlands and border zones exist everywhere for Rouse because cultures are not homogeneous. Such images can be seductive, and Heyman cautions vigilance against being carried away by the rhetoric. By falling for this metonymic usage, he suggests, our understanding of the border becomes reductive, and risks leaving power out of the picture (Heyman 1994: 46).[7]

Heyman is certainly right to point to how the 'cultural' has been so strongly emphasised by those who find the 'borderlands' image a powerful device for evoking the postmodern condition. Gupta and Ferguson, for example, see the borderlands as a place of 'incommensurable contradictions', a zone of cultural overlap characterised by a mixing of cultural styles:

> The term does not indicate a fixed topographical site between two other fixed locales (nations, societies, cultures), but an interstitial zone of displacement and deterritorializa-tion that shapes the identity of the hybridized subject. Rather than dismissing them as insignificant, as marginal zones, thin slivers of land between stable places, we want to contend that the notion of borderlands is a more adequate conceptualization of the 'normal' locale of the postmodern subject (Gupta and Ferguson 1992: 18).

From this perspective, the borderlands become the crucible within which a new politics of identity is being forged. Gloria Anzaldúa's (1987) *Borderlands/La Frontera* is one of the most widely cited examples of this process and potential. Anzaldúa's borderlands are at once physical, psychological, sexual, class and racial, and are firmly rooted in conditions at the state border between the United States and Mexico where, she says, the 'lifeblood of two worlds [merge] to form a third country – a border culture' (1987: 3). Her project is to cross the conceptual lines of class, gender and ethnicity and thereby to challenge the traditional hegemonies

---

7. Such arguments recall earlier exchanges between Asad and Barth, as well as some of the concerns expressed by Cole and Wolf. They clearly echo in the field of 'border studies' wider theoretical concerns in anthropology over the relative prominence to be given to 'culture' and 'power'.

of patriarchy and subordination by the US nation-state. 'Caught between Mexican tradition and Chicana existence, Spanish and English, sexual domination and choice, the United States and Mexico, Anzaldúa remakes the border and the conceptual understanding of the boundaries of life' (Alvarez 1995: 460). Much recent writing by natives of this border region has similarly attempted to expose the 'multiple subjectivities' of borderland life by describing how those who live there draw strategically on multiple repertoires of identity (for instance, see Behar 1993; see also Hicks 1991; and the essays in Welchman 1996).

Many others too have used these notions of the border zone and borderland to address contemporary processes of diaspora and displacement. In 'Blow-Ups in the Borderzones' Smadar Lavie (1992) has analysed the agonising and relentless search for identity which typifies the work and lives of two categories of intellectual in Israel – the 'Palestinian citizens of Israel' and the 'Arab-Jews' or Mizrahim – categories which, following Shohat (1989) and in an effort to reflect the region's particular history of colonisation, Lavie collectively refers to as 'Third World Israelis'. These intellectuals find themselves in exile among the Ashkenazi (the 'First World') elite of Haifa and Tel Aviv, yet equally perceive their return 'home' to their natal villages as an exile from exile. As one of them put it: 'I'm living on a fence – one foot here, one foot there, always trying to close my legs' (Na'im 'Araidi, cited in Lavie 1992: 84). By referring to *blow-ups* Lavie draws attention to the *explosion* of identities which characterises postmodern borderlands – explosion in the sense both of proliferating and fragmenting identities – as well as to how the dilemma of negotiating identity is *magnified* there. As with Anzaldúa, the borderlands Lavie has in mind are those between 'Nation' and 'Empire'; her intellectuals must continually strive 'to articulate the locus and the process of the intersections where Arab and European, Palestinian and Israeli, Mizrahi and Ashkenazi, clash and merge' (Lavie 1992: 90).

From the perspective of these scholars the borderland is simultaneously a zone of cultural play and experimentation as well as of domination and control. The 'borderzone is not just a dangerous space, but a festive one, because of the creative energy liberated by the common struggle of resistance' (Lavie 1992: 93). It is a liminal space, an 'experimental region of culture' (Turner 1982: 28), whose appeal is 'the access artists have to many languages (discourses) from different communities' (McMaster 1995: 82). This fusion of registers in the border-crossing, which Hannerz (1997) has referred to as 'culture+culture', is ultimately empowering, at least for Anzaldúa and apparently also for Lavie's intellectuals. But it need not always be so. Contrary to Gupta and Ferguson's optimistic prediction of hybridity, it is not in fact clear that a hybrid identity or subjectivity is the happy result of meetings at the border. At least some evidence indicates otherwise. Many Mexican migrants, for example, are caught in a world where cultural play is the least of their worries and where their subjectivity remains strongly Mexican (Heyman 1994:

47). Rabinowitz (1994) has similarly argued that borderland encounters in Israel have deepened the rifts between Israeli and Palestinian identities rather than produced a synthesis, and the same is arguably true of Catholic and Protestant identities at the Irish border (see also Feldman 1995: 241).

In this section we have briefly considered the work of those who suggest that 'border' be metaphorically extended to all situations characterised by contradiction and contest in the light of critics who challenge this metaphorical approach for distracting attention from the 'real' problems of state borders and from issues of power. In a sense, of course, borders are always metaphors, since they are arbitrary constructions based on cultural convention. Yet, 'far from being mere abstractions of a concrete reality, metaphors are part of the discursive materiality of power relations' and as such 'can serve as powerful inscriptions of the effects of political borders' (Brah 1996: 198). Although 'border positionality does not *in itself* assure a vantage point of privileged insight into and understanding of relations of power', despite what some of the writers considered above might imply, it does 'create a space in which experiential mediations may intersect in ways that render such understandings more readily accessible' (Brah 1996: 207, emphasis in original). The two approaches need not, therefore, be as far apart as their advocates sometimes imply. In fact, they often influence each other, a productive coming together upon which we seek to draw throughout this book.[8]

The 'Borderlands Genre'

In this chapter we have suggested that three reasonably distinct but mutually interacting streams characterise the anthropological study of borders and boundaries. In such an account there is perhaps a tendency to over-systematise, and to succumb to the temptation to reconstruct rival intellectual genealogies with the possibly misleading benefit of hindsight.[9] Differences may have been stressed at the expense of similarities, edges emphasised rather than overlap. Yet as we have tried to show, it is this very overlap that has been so thoroughly exploited by those writing in what Alvarez has called the 'borderlands genre', whose borderlands lie not just

---

8. Although we draw on both bodies of literature, we should be clear that research which uses the borderland metaphor to clarify the deterritorialised identities of postmodern life is not our main concern here. Only when these identities are linked in concrete ways to the experiences of living at or crossing state borders, and of managing the various structures of the state which establish microborders throughout the state's domain − such as in airports, floating customs and immigration checks, post and passport offices, armed service installations and internal revenue institutions − do we incorporate them into the discussion.

9. This may be particularly true of our account of anthropological research on geopolitical borders, the ethnography of which, as we noted, has been patchy, under-theorised, and so far largely unsynthesised.

between different classes, genders or ethnicities but between academic disciplines and between different perspectives within a single discipline. Developments in this theoretical borderland have been rich and stimulating. The work done there has captivated our imaginations. At the same time, the terms of its discussion have become 'blurred in popular [academic] usage' (Alvarez 1995: 448), the potential overlap between different 'borders' sometimes being used as a stylistic device to imply resonances and connections not always demonstrated or warranted. However engaging these explorations are, therefore, we must be careful that style does not succeed over substance, and that analysis is not sacrificed to image.

In our view, then, all three approaches considered here are valuable components of an anthropology of international borders, but only as long as we keep sight of the ways in which they differ and of how some minimise the role of the state and the nation, and even the geopolitical border, in their efforts to be fashionable or persuasive. Indeed, in this book we specifically draw attention to the confluence of symbolic and politico–jural boundaries between nations and states, showing how the juxtaposition of competing perspectives in an anthropology of borders can be analytically rewarding. In this sense our book might be read as a modest attempt to integrate seemingly divergent trends in the anthropological study of power and culture, trends which sometimes seem to be at loggerheads. Such trends are also to be found in our sibling disciplines in the social sciences and humanities, the subject of the next chapter.

—3—

Other Approaches to Borders,
Nations and States

It would be futile to assert that an exact Science of Frontiers has been or is ever likely to be evolved: for no one law can possibly apply to all nations or peoples, to all Governments, all territories, or all climates. The evolution of Frontiers is perhaps an art rather than a science, so plastic and malleable are its forms and manifestations.

Lord Curzon of Kedleston, *Frontiers: The Romanes Lectures*

Over the course of this century social scientists and historians have increasingly looked at international borders as one way to understand changing relations between nation, state and territory. Wars and peace-making have often been the stimuli for such inspections. This was especially true at the ends of the two world wars, which were the most important periods of state and border construction up to the relatively peaceful perturbations which marked the demise of the Soviet empire and the liberation and creation of a score of states in Eurasia after 1989. The comparative study of borders was spurred on by a variety of forces before this most recent period of nation-state formation and dissolution. The Europeanising processes of the European Union (EU), which led to the Single European Act of 1986, created new conditions of governance for regions and states within the EU. The changing role of the United States in the world economy also transformed some of its relationships with its southern neighbour, Mexico, changes which had important consequences for their mutual border regions and people. The full effects of post-imperialism and post-colonialism were becoming evident to a new generation of Asians and Africans, some of whom were the first to be born in their recently independent nation-states. Scholars thus began to focus on state borders as a way to study the changing national and international dynamics of territory, sovereignty and identity.

In so doing, social scientists readily problematised trans-frontier economic, legal and political systems (see, for example, Anderson 1982a), but often neglected trans-frontier cultural systems. This is partly the result of different disciplinary attentions, but also partly a methodological problem. The symbolic constructions of the boundaries to international border cultures are often extremely significant signs of regional and national identity, but yet are among the most difficult to discern.

Nevertheless, cross-border cultures are as important and vital as cross-border economic cooperation and political negotiation. Over the last decade or so this has become increasingly accepted by scholars of border studies, who have attempted to build multifaceted analyses of border localities and border regions using a variety of methods and theories culled from the spectrum of social sciences and humanities (see Asiwaju and Adeniyi 1989, for the most comprehensive set of empirical and theoretical essays on borders in general and African borders in particular; see Paasi 1996, for an example of a border study rich with insight gleaned from a variety of scholarly disciplines). One way in which interdisciplinary and multidisciplinary approaches to border studies have proceeded has been through the conception of borders and their regions as 'systems', worthy of study in their own right and not just as the peripheries of states and their institutions, or as the outer wrapping of state societies. As Stoddard suggests in his review of the evolution of the scholarly study of the US–Mexico border in the period 1970–82, this border

> was conceptualized as one system (i.e. a *single culture* spanning the national boundary) which had been created from an interpretation of cultural, economic, social, political and kinship linkages so necessary for successful articulation of border activity on a day-to-day basis. This distinct border culture also revealed the vast number of informal transborder networks which tied border institutions together in a highly interdependent symbiotic relationship. By the end of the decade, other scholars, quite independently were conceptualizing the Borderlands [between Mexico and the US, and elsewhere] in similar terms (1989: 414, emphasis in original).

Scholars, journalists, business people and government leaders have begun to recognise that an understanding of the complex world represented in a border system demands combinations of methods. However, such recognition hardly mitigates the strong disciplinary approaches to border studies which have evolved over the post-war years, and even earlier.

To frame our perspective on the anthropology of border cultures, we review some other ways of doing border studies, focusing particularly on how geography, history, political science and sociology have tackled issues of territory, sovereignty and identity, key concerns in all scholarly perspectives on borders, nations and states.

Geography and Border Landscapes

The one inescapable fact regarding international state borders is that they all have territory, they all *are* territory. This is perhaps the one indisputable element in their definition, wherever they are found. As an academic discipline geography has been drawn to the study of the spatial dimension to borders, and to the ways in which territory and topography, among other aspects of the physical environment, interrelate with the social, economic, political and cultural conditions of nations and states. To a geographer, the study of a border like 'the study of any area involves the totality of the elements which, when combined, give character to *place*' (Gildersleeve 1976: 19, emphasis in original). International borders are the places which mark the physical limits to state power and they are the spatial expression of states' political organisation and territorial divisions.

Political geography has been the sub-field which has been most associated with border studies since just before and after the First World War, when geographers attempted to understand why and where state boundaries were drawn, and to describe and classify these borders in such terms as good, bad, artificial and natural (Minghi 1969 [1963]: 140–2). By the Second World War the emphasis in political geography had 'shifted from the criteria by which a boundary is drawn, to the functions which it performs' (Minghi 1969 [1963]: 146). Central to this changing perspective was the recognition that international borders are the contact points between territorial power structures and not just demarcations of national sovereignty. 'Viewed in this manner, the position of a boundary, when observed over time, could become an index to the power relations of the contending forces on either side' (Minghi 1969 [1963]: 145). The evolution of geographical border studies thus proceeded from the categorisation of the form of international borders to their many functions, from the perception of borders as static elements in state relations to the view that they are dynamic structures and areas in a variety of power relations within and between states. In this way, a border provides a window on a political system, on the interplay between state political systems, and on the role of states in shaping the border landscape (Kasperson and Minghi 1969a: 77–8).

Borders as we have defined them in chapter one are divided up by geographers into the related concepts of 'boundaries' and 'frontiers', both of which are seen to separate territories that are subject to different sovereignty. As Prescott stipulates in his monumental work on *Political Frontiers and Boundaries* (1987), boundaries are the *lines* which demarcate state territory, and in most places they have superseded *frontiers*, which were zones of varying depth which marked either the political division between two countries or the division between the settled and uninhabited areas within a country. According to Prescott, 'there is no excuse for geographers who use the terms "frontier" and "boundary" as synonyms' (1987: 36). He goes on to define *border* as the areas adjacent to the boundary, which 'fringe' it (1987: 12), while the *borderlands* refers to 'the transition zone within which the boundary lies' (1987: 13–14).

Although there still remains considerable overlap and confusion about these terms, even within Prescott's own definitions (for example, when does the border merge into the borderlands, and can a state have an external frontier with its neighbour if it has an agreed boundary, even if it does not control all of its citizens, residents and resources within its boundary?), it is clear from this perspective why states would want to establish precise boundaries and eliminate the ambiguities of external and internal frontiers. States seek to delineate their land and sea boundaries in order to acquire territory for their human and material resources and to guarantee their internal and external security (1987: 24). But as states establish clear, if not stable, boundaries, the role of these boundaries in relation to their states also evolves. Since the 1940s geographers have analysed three types of such change: evolution in definition, evolution in position, and evolution in the state's role and functions at its boundary (Prescott 1987: 63). The former involves the negotiations between states regarding the original terms, conditions, administration and placement of the boundary. The second evolution refers to the changes in the borderline over time, as a consequence of states' relations and the forces at work globally. The last type of evolution concerns the state's structures at a boundary. As Prescott concludes (1987: 80), 'the only function of a boundary is to mark the limits of sovereignty'. This function also evolves, reflecting the transformation in a state's relations with other states at its boundaries, and this entails changes in customs, immigration and security arrangements.

The definitions put forward by Prescott are not without difficulty, principally because they are guided by statist political concerns, and do little to acknowledge the alternative interests of economy, society and culture, which Prescott correctly recognises as major facets of boundary and frontier. 'The factors that encourage co-operation or conflict along international boundaries and the consequences that follow from policies connected with these two activities involve many aspects of national life. These aspects include strategy, administration, economics, politics, and culture. No single discipline deals exclusively with this field of scholarship' (Prescott 1987: 8). This state of affairs cannot and should not prevent any one discipline from attempting to incorporate as many theoretical and methodological perspectives as possible in its efforts to understand the dynamics of border cooperation and conflict. One of the goals of this book is to elucidate anthropological attempts to achieve this. Geographers have also been active in their efforts to synthesise a variety of viewpoints in the evolution of their political geography of borders.

One way in which geographers have attempted to evade the pitfalls of the simple description and categorisation of borders, in order to recognise and understand the dialectical relations between boundaries and the physical and human environments which shape them, and which in turn are shaped by them, is through the analysis of *border landscapes*. As Rumley and Minghi (1991a: 2) conclude in an essay published almost thirty years after Minghi's important review article of 1963, political boundaries have long been of interest to geographers because they are the clearest link between geography and politics. Boundaries are the expression of the spatial limits of state power, the manifestations of political control, and indicators of changes in political power within and between states. However, while the importance and definition of boundaries are relatively unquestioned in geography, 'the specific definition of border areas as opposed to boundaries as the objects of analysis remains unclear in much of the literature' (Rumley and Minghi 1991a: 2). Case studies and theories of border landscapes should provide a way forward, enabling geographers to transcend the limits imposed on their boundary studies due to the emphasis on the structures and functions of the state at the borderline itself.

Border landscapes, those areas contiguous to the state boundary which are moulded by the human and physical environment, including the boundary itself, and which in turn shape the environment, have been distinguished by four main research themes (Prescott 1987: 161–73; see also Rumley and Minghi 1991a: 3). The first of these research themes sees the boundary as an element of the cultural landscape, and includes a consideration of the form and function of state and other institutional structures along the borderline. The second looks at how the boundary influences the economic and demographic landscape which stretches away from the boundary on either or both of its sides. The third type of border landscape study examines the impact of the boundary on the attitudes of border inhabitants, while the fourth approach explores the effect of the boundary on national policies. In Prescott's view, these last two research themes do not specifically involve the cultural landscape, though they most certainly would be of concern and interest to an anthropologist.

Although this is an impressive set of themes, it has not led to a major break-through in the role and importance of geographical border studies within the discipline of geography more generally, nor has it had much influence outside the discipline. According to Minghi (1991), this may be due to the continuing emphasis on boundaries and on the conflict and tensions between nations and states that exist at them. The case study approach in political geography, which was well established in the 1960s, tended to fall into set categories, such as the study of disputed areas, boundary changes, the evolution of boundaries, boundary delimita-tion and demarcation, exclaves and tiny states, maritime boundaries, disputes over natural resources, and internal boundaries (Minghi 1969 [1963]). But this research was overly descriptive and classificatory, was not interested in the recognition and understanding of social and political process, and lacked concern with the develop-ment of border landscape theory (Rumley and Minghi 1991a: 3–4). As a result, the geographical concept of border landscapes has had less impact than it might within the discipline, and has been all but ignored by other social scientists (Rumley and Minghi 1991a: 1).

After a generation of such border studies, there has recently been a number of calls for a reorientation by border landscape geographers to wider comparative and theoretical concerns (cf. Herzog 1990; House 1982; Minghi 1991; Rumley and Minghi 1991a, 1991b). In this new border geography, there is more consideration of border landscapes as the product of economic, political and cultural processes, and more of a comparison between border areas and their contiguous populations and state territories. These geographers have also recognised that 'too little concern has been given to conceptual developments in the other social sciences which might have some relevance to an understanding of border landscapes' (Rumley and Minghi 1991a: 4).

The turn in geography away from the study of state boundaries to the investigation of action, agency and process within border landscapes, tied to a range of institutions and peoples removed from the boundary and border area, reflects work which has been conducted in a variety of disciplines over the years, but which has also not been very influential outside those disciplines. Ladis Kristof pointed out in 1959 that geographers and political scientists should not use the terms 'frontier' and 'boundary' as synonyms because the latter refers to the territorial limit to a modern state, while the former denotes the process of expansion of a political entity, and is derived from a political concept which has existed since the Roman Empire (1969 [1959]). Etymologically, 'frontier' was the front, the foreland, of the hinterland, the motherland, the core of the state, kingdom or empire. 'Thus the frontier was not the end . . . but rather the beginning . . . of the state; it was the spearhead of light and knowledge expanding into the realm of darkness and of the unknown' (Kristof 1969 [1959]: 127). In this sense, a frontier is not the beginning of a state which is encountered when one is entering it from the outside. It is the agent of the state's continual expansion; it is at the forefront of a state's role with its neighbours. As a result, boundaries and frontiers are different things, and may tell us much about the structure and function of international borders as we have defined them in chapter one, which in our usage incorporates both the borderline (or boundary in geographical terms) and the frontier (or border area or landscape). For Kristof (1969 [1959]: 127–9) frontiers are *outer-oriented*, with their attention directed to those areas of friendship and danger which exist beyond the state. Boundaries on the other hand are *inner-oriented*. They neither denote nor connote relationships. They are the physical manifestation of the sovereign limits of state territory and power. The frontier is the product as well as the agent of *centrifugal forces*, while the boundary is the manifestation of *centripetal forces*. Frontiers are *integrating factors* because they are zones and ways of life which allow outsiders to adapt to the behavioural patterns of the state, and enable people from within the state to have an orderly transition to the places and people beyond the boundary. The boundary, however, is a *separating factor*. It does not exist to enable assimilation or integration; it is there to divide populations and political bodies. The boundary functions to distinguish the insiders from the outsiders, and to control rather than to interact.

In these ways we might see the geographical study of boundaries as the individual or comparative analysis of a state's territory, institutions, power and functions.

Boundaries can be compared one to the other as the symbols and reality of the physical extent of the state, as social and political facts, with form and function different in minor details but similar in most major ways. Frontiers, however, are phenomena of history (Kristof 1969 [1959]: 129). They cannot be isolated from their particular historical circumstances because they are the products of historical forces which cannot be duplicated, and which in most cases are older than those entities which are framed by the modern boundaries of nation-states. While geographers have wrangled with the spatial dimension to the definitions of borders, and their roles in nation and state relations, in part in an effort to construct the beginnings to a comparative study of boundaries and frontiers, other disciplines have sought similar goals but have looked at borders from a different perspective, such as the temporal.

History and Borderlands

Frontiers figure prominently in the history of nations. Perhaps the most influential scholarly study of a frontier has been Frederick Jackson Turner's essay on 'The Significance of the Frontier in American History', which was first read before the American Historical Association in Chicago in 1893. Turner's 'frontier hypothesis' was that 'the existence of an area of free land, its continuous recession, and the advance of American settlement westward explain American development' (Turner 1977 [1920]: 3). Although largely discredited now, it became one of the most debated problems in American historiography and has influenced scholars in many disciplines worldwide for a century, in part because of its geographical and techno-logical determinism and its attempt to link space and time to the formation of a national character. But for us this hypothesis serves as an example of the ironic situation that while there has been an emphasis on borders and frontiers in some of the historical scholarship of nations and states, there has also been a relative dearth of historical studies of borders, border peoples and borderlands as motive forces in the development of those nations and states. In this section we do not seek to review the historiography of international borders, but to provide a glimpse into the changes which are occurring among historians who seek to reframe the questions asked of borders and borderlands in the comparative study of ethnicity, nationalism, regionalism and international relations.

Frontier histories owe much to the conception of a frontier as a front or vanguard of the nation. In this view, frontiers have their primary importance in what they do and what they say about the ontology of the nation and/or its state. But beyond concluding that all nations have histories which valorise their political and geograph-ical frontiers, and that all states have developed or evolved boundaries which mark the extent of their power and domain, historians (and others) now question how to mould the unique case studies which result from these perspectives into a framework for comparison, generalisation and theory building. As Martínez (1994a) points out in his insightful history of the US–Mexico borderlands, borders share functional commonalities with other borders worldwide because they are there to regulate, prevent and control the economic, political and social interactions between people in both states. This simultaneous role as national limit and transnational conduit is affected by similar global and regional conditions. 'For example, cross-boundary relationships and the movement of goods and people are driven by international trade, interdependence, and migrations, processes that are duplicated widely throughout the world' (Martínez 1994a: 5). But border peoples and regions are much more than these relationships, and they often play a more important role in the history of their nations and states than many studies suggest. There is a growing trend in historical studies to eschew the traditional view of borders as seen from the centre in favour of a new view of borders from the perspective of a state's periphery, from the borders themselves (Baud and van Schendel 1997: 212). Such efforts, to be found in Asiwaju and Adeniyi (1989), Baud (1992, 1993, 1994), Derby (1994), Martínez (1994a), Nugent and Asiwaju (1996), Sahlins (1989), and van Schendel (1993), seek 'to redress the imbalance of "state-centered" studies' (Baud and van Schendel 1997: 235), and to discover which social forces originate in borderlands along with the effects they have had both locally and beyond the borderlands.

To achieve this, historians have not only had to problematise the spatial and temporal dimensions to this new kind of border study, but they have also had to redefine the focus of each case study in order to recognise and understand the differences as well as the similarities between borders. This new history of borders is in fact a history of *borderlands*, the region bisected by the boundary line between states, which in comparative perspective is presumed to encapsulate a variety of identities, social networks, and formal and informal, legal and illegal relationships which tie together people in the areas contiguous to the borderline on both of its sides. This concept of borderlands is analogous to geographers' border landscapes and it essentially provides the same function in history as landscape does in geography, which is to focus on the border region and its people as active partici-pants in their state, and as important forces in their nation's and state's relationship to their territories. As Baud and van Schendel (1997: 235) indicate in their review of the history of borderlands, while much has been written on how states deal with their borderlands 'historians have paid much less attention to how borderlands have dealt with their states. As a result, borderlands have been represented as far more passive and reactive than is warranted. The study of borderlands assigns an active historical role to borderlands and their population.' Borderlands in recent historical scholarship are placed at the centre of study, and a focus on them is seen as a productive way to generate meaningful comparisons with other borders and states, in an effort to develop equivalent descriptive categories and workable theories.

The US–Mexico borderlands provide a particularly fertile arena in which to examine the tensions between border people and institutions, including their identities, organisation and world views, and their hegemonic state structures, particularly in the United States. Between 1930 and 1974 historians of this border viewed it as a frontier, and concentrated on its explorers, economic development, missionary activity, armies and fortifications, administrative structures and role in international relations (Almaráz 1976: 10). Martínez has been at the forefront of those historians who seek to develop models of borderlands to facilitate their comparison regionally and globally. We have already mentioned, in chapter one, the concept of the 'borderlands milieu', which Martínez (1994a: 10) based on his study of the US–Mexico border, but which he suggests might be a useful way to approach the study of borderlands elsewhere. This milieu can be affected by many cross-border and national factors, which can be grouped in such a way as to produce a typology of borderlands interaction (1994a: 6–10). *Alienated borderlands* are those where routine cross-border exchange is prevented due to tensions and animosity between their respective states and/or border populations. This situation may be the result of ethnic, religious, nationalist or economic dispute, but, whatever the cause, day-to-day contact across the borderline is minimal if it exists at all. *Coexistent borderlands* are present when neighbouring states reduce tensions to a manageable level, and modest cross-border interaction occurs. *Interdependent borderlands* involve a symbiotic relationship between border regions in adjacent countries. There is a binational economic, social and cultural system at work between the two border regions, and perhaps between their states, but a number of policies retain state separation at the boundary. *Integrated borderlands* have no barriers to the flow of goods and people, and the two border regions and their respective states enjoy a relationship of equality, trust and respect. Martínez's contribution to the historical study of the US–Mexico borderlands and to borderlands in general is significant for his efforts to create tools whereby borders might be compared cross-culturally and internationally, especially because he goes beyond the description and categorisation of borderlands to explore in detail the social, political, economic and cultural conditions of everyday life there. He does this in ways which show that although the form of borderlands interactions and international state relations may be similar, only immersion in the economic and social history of borderlands localities will enable the observer to understand the types and experiences of border people.

Other historians have also made contributions to general theorising about borders, while still others have carried out studies of borders which contribute to theories of nationalism and state formation. Peter Sahlins's examination (1989, 1998; see also Douglass 1998) of the Cerdanya region of the Spanish–French border has been an influential work both in history and in other fields like anthropology and sociology. The Cerdanya, a valley region bifurcated by the state border between France and Spain at the eastern end of the Pyrenees, is distinguished by the rare occurrence of a small exclave of sovereign Spanish territory, the town of Llívia, remaining on the northern side of the border, surrounded by sovereign France, only kilometres from the rest of the Spanish state. Sahlins's book examines the emergence of the relationships between territory and identity in the Cerdanya over the last three centuries from the triple perspective of the two states and local society. Although ethnically Catalan, the people of the French and the Spanish Cerdanya have been affected as residents and citizens of two evolving states in both similar and dissimilar ways by the border, since the border was established between the two countries in the Treaty of the Pyrenees in 1659. They were clearly swept up in the processes of state consolidation and the creation of the two national identities which were the projects of those states. But Sahlins's study goes beyond the provision of a case study of state and national impact at the local levels of the Cerdanya borderlands, to examine the role of the borderlands in the negotiation and demarcation of the borderline itself, the states' definition of national territory and identity, and the evolution of various types of local and Catalan identity in the two Cerdanyas. According to Sahlins (1989: 8), in the Cerdanyan borderlands

> both state formation and nation building were two-way processes at work since at least the seventeenth century. States did not simply impose their values and boundaries on local society. Rather, local society was a motive force in the formation and consolidation of nationhood and the territorial state. The political boundary appeared in the borderland as the outcome of national political events, as a function of the different strengths, interests, and (ultimately) histories of France and Spain. But the shape and significance of the boundary line was constructed out of local relations in the borderland.

Sahlins's study of this borderland gives perhaps the best example of how one region, with shared culture but divided between two states, has avoided passivity in the evolution of its respective states and national cultures, all the while retaining a distinctive identity within these wider hegemonic structures. The complexity of their situation, which it must be stressed is a complexity more to the observer of borders and nations than it is to the Cerdans who live it, is enhanced when one considers that Catalan identity is also a national one, as demonstrated in autonomous province status for Catalunya within Spain, and international renown as a progressive region in the European Union. Sahlins shows that there is no intrinsic, inherent, nor necessary relationship between territory, identity and sovereignty. Borderlands are places where these converge in ways which must be interrogated, in order to discover the role which culture plays in wider processes of state and national politics, economics and society.

In the French–Spanish–Catalan borderlands, notions of identity, territory and politics evolved together in the modern era, along horizontal and vertical axes between the locality and the nation, and the periphery and centres of two states and one ethnic region. This gives us one glimpse of how to place border studies in history and the social sciences within wider theoretical frames. The analysis of culture and identity has in fact become a major theme in historical studies of borderlands, precisely because of the tensions residing in states' attempts to impose national culture on all of its localities, and the ambivalence border regions often experience as they are both pushed away from national centres, as part of the centrifugal forces of being the state's frontier with non-national others, and pulled in by the centripetal forces of the borderlands and state centres across their border-line. Because of their transborder and transnational linkages, these border cultures are often treated suspiciously by states and their agents, many of whom believe in the traditional view of the convergence of state, nation, identity and territory.

None of these concepts are as uncomplicated as many old theories and stereo-types suggest, however, for borderlands are and have been spatially and temporally dynamic. For example, borders rarely match the simplicity of their representation on maps, which are themselves tools of control and order. In some countries today, mapmaking is still controlled by the military, maps of border areas are not freely available to the public, and on these maps the national territory is greater than the territory the country in fact holds (Baud and van Schendel 1997: 222).

The meanings which local and more distant populations attach to borders change over space and time. To understand the evolution of borderlands, and to facilitate their international study in ways which can recognise their unique characteristics while placing them in a framework which allows regional or universal comparison, Baud and van Schendel (1997: 223–4) suggest utilising the metaphorical concept of the life cycle, which enables us to scrutinise embryonic, infant, adolescent, adult, declining and defunct borderlands. However, in order for this or any other model of borderlands to act as a basic strategy of comparison, it must take into account the various factors of world, regional, national and local events and processes, which may result in certain systemic similarities and differences among borderlands in different continents. An effort such as this might need to marry the spatial and temporal contexts to borderlands development. 'The impact of a particular world historical transformation (world time) on social change in borderlands must be related to the developmental phases of the states concerned (state time), as well as the stages of the life cycle in which individual borderlands find themselves (border-land time)' (Baud and van Schendel 1997: 236).

As a discipline, history has increasingly looked at borderlands as social or cultural systems which often transcend the state boundary, and which have been active in the construction of their nations and states, and not simply the passive entities which older studies have suggested. It places borderlands in their spatial and temporal contexts in order to investigate the evolving relations between territory, identity and sovereignty, which have also been the concern of political science and sociology, the subjects of our next sections.

Political Science and Border Regions

Culture has not been a principal focus of political science analyses of power, territory and politics at international borders, though culture's role in facilitating cross-border political and economic cooperation, as well as its place in the definition, recognition and behaviour of ethnic groups, key elements in the origin and evolution of state borders, have become important parts of recent political scholarship. This naturally reflects the evolution of political science as a discipline, particularly since the 1970s, but it also indicates a turn in the study of politics to concerns with history, locality, ethnicity and regionalism. Political science analyses of international borders in the 1990s have also increasingly turned to the investigation of state and supranational policy in all of its forms, including the role of local actors in national and international policy-making.

As in other disciplines, political science research at the US–Mexico borderlands serves as an excellent example of general developments in the field of the politics of international borders, though the comparative and cross-border study of the political system here did not begin in earnest until the 1960s (Bath 1976). Even then, and continuing into the 1970s, most borderlands studies of politics focused on political culture and socialisation, particularly in regard to political efficacy and participation. This emphasis on political culture (cf. Almond and Verba 1963, 1989) borrows heavily from structural–functional theories of sociology and anthropology. Political culture refers to the attitudes and values which enable individuals and groups to be socialised into the ways of their political system, thereby enabling it to perform its necessary functions. Unlike other studies of culture, most notably that of anthropology, culture in this sense is but one element in the definition and reproduction of a political system. Culture is not the means to describe and analyse the total system of social, political and economic relations.

The particular forms that the studies of political participation, mobilisation and integration took on at the US–Mexico border did not properly address the borderlands as a cross-border system, although they paid lip service to it. In fact, most analyses of border political culture were done by sociologists, anthropologists, economists and philosophers (Bath 1976: 58). They were also marked by a lack of attention to non-Mexican Americans in the borderlands, and an over-emphasis on border political culture, especially on the southern side, as it related to national culture and character (Bath 1976: 59). Nevertheless, the exploration of Mexican and Mexican-American political values and actions at the border is an early example of ethnicity as a factor which gives character to the borderlands, binds communities to each other across the borderline, and which provides some of the foundation to the US–Mexico border being considered as a regional system, tied in various ways to national centres.

One thing that was missing in most of these US–Mexico borderlands studies was the examination of many of the practical aspects of cross-border cooperation, especially in terms of policy formation and implementation (Bath 1976: 56). Today this is no longer the case in the political studies of the US–Mexico borderlands, as the economies, societies and polities of the two countries become more integrated through the processes entailed in NAFTA. In Europe there has always been greater attention paid in political science to the policy implications of boundary making, in particular in those places where there have been boundary disputes before and after the two world wars (cf. Tägil et al. 1977), and after the recent transformations in Central and Eastern Europe. Since the late 1970s, in fact, researchers in the borderlands of Europe have attempted to distance themselves from static models which looked at one side of borders from the viewpoint of national metropolitan centres. As Coakley (1982) reminded all scholars of borderlands, ethnicity has been as important a determinant as history and international relations in the evolution of borders in Western Europe, where culture continues to be at least as significant as territory for any understanding of nations, states and their borders. Yet regardless of how appropriate such reminders have been, culture has continued to take a back seat to economics, government and administration in political studies of Europe's borderlands.

The chequerboard dimension to the formation and in some cases dissolution of European states and borders over this century is one reason why there has been a focus in the continent on the allocation of territory, the delimitation of international boundaries, and their demarcation through a variety of natural and man-made features. However, other factors have been at work in the evolution of political studies of borders in Europe since the 1970s. The European Economic Community became the European Community (EC) and then the European Union (EU), in the process growing from six to fifteen states, encompassing 350 million residents, most of whom have been called 'citizens' of the EU since 1995. There has been a proliferation of new internal borders within European states, in line with a growing interest in each state in devolving governmental powers to regions and provinces. Economic integration has been increasingly achieved, as symbolised in the EU's 'Europe without frontiers', which marked the removal of political barriers to the free movement of goods, services, people, ideas and capital between member states. This opening up of internal borders has been matched by a strengthening of the EU's external borders, in part as a response to the changes in the world economy which have obviated the need for most European countries to import labour from outside, while most of the traditional labour-exporting countries in Asia and Africa have been faced with conditions that have stimulated emigration for work.

As a result of all of these forces, political studies of European borderlands have tended to concentrate since the 1970s on *border regions*, a notion which in some ways resembles both geography's border landscapes and history's borderlands.

These regions, which are territorial units marked off from their surroundings and with some sense of their own identity (Tägil 1982), are important to political analyses because of their proximity to the international boundary, as well as because of their fluctuating relationship to various state and national centres. Moreover, border regions in Europe today have new salience because of the overlapping and extremely important processes of centre and periphery relations, internationalisation, increased state centralisation or internal state devolution and de-centralisation, and cross-border cooperation and conflict (Tägil 1982: 31).

Many of the important changes which the political study of borders have undergone, both in Europe and more widely, can be traced in the works of Malcolm Anderson, arguably the most influential scholar in the contemporary political science of international borders. In 1982 Anderson (1982b) introduced a revisionist set of European border studies by noting that boundary disputes were no longer significant features of European politics, the majority of struggles for political autonomy had only minor transborder implications (Northern Ireland excepted), and the effects of economic and social marginalisation which many frontier (the term which Anderson uses for the three aspects of borders which we delineated in chapter one) regions feel are common to other peripheral regions in European states (Anderson 1982a: 1–2). Nevertheless, his essay and the collection which it begins are chiefly dedicated to examining the political problems which beset frontier regions in Europe, a concern which he has pursued until today.

The biggest problem faced by frontier regions in the early 1980s seemed to be the unchanging nature of international borders in general, particularly when compared with sub-national borders, i.e. the new and in some cases revitalised provincial and regional borders within states. Perceived to be unchanging, international borders remained peripheral in the eyes of policy-makers and scholars alike. Anderson concluded that the economic lifeblood of these border regions had to rest in transfrontier cooperation, in the myriad ways in which border regions have been tied to their counterparts across the international boundary in the past, continue to be so involved, and hope to enhance. But while economic cooperation is a feature of all densely populated border regions in Western Europe, the economic problems each region faces are tied to the difficulties of providing political, legal and administrative structures to organise the cooperation, because 'there is no common legal or institutional form for this co-operation' (Anderson 1982a: 3). Although Anderson was aware of the economic, historical and cultural contexts to political cooperation across borders, and in fact was one of the earliest proponents of more research into the role of culture in such activities, his real interest lay in the politics of border regions, in particular in the institutional frameworks which allowed orderly and predictable forms of international cooperation.

According to Anderson, the politics of transfrontier cooperation are worthy of note for several reasons (1982a: 7–8). Cross-border cooperation gives citizens of one country a say in the affairs of their neighbouring country, although their right to express such a view is often unclear. The territorial dimension to this cooperation is also often unclear because the boundaries of the transfrontier regions, i.e. those national regions participating in a somewhat formal arrangement with other such regions in their country and elsewhere, are often drawn differently. Depending on the real or perceived parity of the cross-border relationships, and influenced by the border region's relationship with its central government, the state might intervene in aid of its region. Because many people in border regions work and play across the borderline, and often have business interests and property in the other state, they are frequently participants in the formal and informal politics of that state. As a result, complex political alliances emerge, wherein the connections between the juridical institutions of states and local and regional political practices are often unclear (Anderson 1982a: 9–10). This obviously has consequences for the relationships between citizens and regional, state and international bodies, especially in their roles in constructing notions of territory and sovereignty.

By 1996, when Anderson published *Frontiers*, in which he reviews historical and theoretical perspectives on international borders worldwide, his position on borders had shifted from a largely statist perspective to one more focused on the frontiers themselves. In this view, frontiers are both institutions and processes (Anderson 1996a: 1). As institutions, frontiers provide a range of boundaries which are important to states, including the real and symbolic enclosure of territory and citizenry, as well as the boundaries necessary for the definition and maintenance of a variety of groups, and perhaps even for individual self consciousness (cf. A. P. Cohen 1994; Vereni 1996). At the very least, it is clear that 'all frontiers have a psychological component' (Anderson 1996a: 3). Thus, frontiers are both signs and agents of identity, and identities themselves are central ingredients in the construction of frontiers as dynamic fields of social, economic and political relations. As processes, frontiers are also multidimensional (Anderson 1996a: 2–3). Frontiers are instruments of state policy. Government policies at frontiers, and government policies regarding frontiers, are in place to promote the national interest. However, the policies and practices of governments are limited by the amount of real political control they have over state frontiers. International relations at the end of the millennium are increasingly based on the ways in which power and sovereignty are shared, diluted, pooled and dispersed in the course of dealing with trade, crime, terrorism and the global provision of services. Moreover, frontiers are not only markers of national identity, but also of ethnic, racial, gender, sexual and regional identities, among others, making them both a conduit for discourse and a term of discourse (see also Wilson and Donnan 1998a). The meanings people ascribe to national frontiers change through time, in the context of the political event, and depending on the statuses and identities of the people concerned.

Although Anderson's *Frontiers* ranges far and wide in comparative and empirical scope, it is significant that it highlights the role of identities in understanding international borders, as well as the role borders play in shaping identities such as ethnic, local, class, religious and linguistic (1996a: 5). This emphasis, we suggest, reflects intellectual processes in political science which have parallels in the other scholarly disciplines reviewed in this chapter. Over the years, political scientists in general have often given a lead to scholars interested in the development of nations and states, especially in the ways these have been 'built', 'formed', 'constructed' and 'imagined'. The precise and once presumed fit between nation, state and territory is being challenged in political science as in other disciplines, through concepts such as border regions, borderlands and border landscapes. Like other scholars, political scientists are having to grapple with the proliferation of identities in a post-industrial and globalising world, one in which the meanings of national and ethnic identity, and their relations to territory and sovereignty, are no longer the self-evident givens that they were once taken to be.

In contemporary border studies political scientists deal not only with the interpretive side of new political symbols and discourses, but continue to be interested in the material practices of power and politics. One of the principal ways in which the themes of border regions, cross-border cooperation and regionalism have been sustained in these studies has been through their role in public policy formation. This was one of the areas which was identified in the 1970s as a potentially critical new development for the discipline in its approach to the US–Mexico border (Bath 1976: 56). It was a call echoed by political scientists working elsewhere, to the degree that cross-border policy and political practice, including the identification, description and analysis of the factors that hinder and enhance all formal institutional and all informal behavioural ties which constitute and affect such activities, have become the biggest focus in the politics of borders. A few examples should suffice. Research in politics at borders has involved the examination of policies dealing with the environment (Baker 1996), transportation and communication (Letamendía et al. 1996), immigration and other border controls (Butt Philip 1991), policing crime and terrorism (Anderson and den Boer 1994), and regional development, including those regions that transcend state borders, sometimes even at external borders of wider supranational bodies (Scott and Collins 1997). These references are only a small sample of the proliferation in political analyses of studies of institutions, administration and policy at international borders. Of some significance to our argument, however, is the fact that most of these studies most contextualise, if they do not specifically problematise, the roles of culture and identity in almost every aspect of the policy process. As Anderson has indicated recently (1996b: 21), national and regional frontiers in the EU are now being reconfigured as 'instruments of cultural defence'.

Border regions are places of identity and policy-making, and political scientists, like geographers and historians, have become part of the wider theorising about what culture can tell us about the role of borders in the changing relationships among identity, territory and sovereignty. Culture continues to be a secondary, albeit important, focus in much of this literature. We now move on to our consideration of border studies in sociology and other disciplines.

Sociology and Other Approaches

Sociologists have been subject to the same pressures to conform to the methods, theories and professional interests of their subject as have the proponents of the disciplines reviewed above. Like scholars in any field, and like the people of borderlands, sociologists feel the centripetal and centrifugal forces which make border studies so difficult. On the one hand, researchers want to test theories and hypotheses that reflect the mainstream concerns of their chosen academic subject. In some cases, this makes the comparative study of borders almost an impossibility (see, for example, Stoddard's indictment of the sociology of the US–Mexico borderlands [1975: 34, 52]). On the other hand, academic disciplines provide arbitrary or artificial boundaries to their adherents. International borders provide physical manifestations of the need to cross boundaries in order to appreciate the complexity of the whole border social system. They are the embodiment of what is demanded of border scholars, who must often transcend the limits of their academic discipline in order to contribute to it. Border scholars need to embrace more holistic methodologies and theories, as well as to conduct research in more than one 'national' domain, both to do as complete a study of the borderlands as possible and to add to multidisciplinary and interdisciplinary models of nations and states today. As a result of this effort, much that is good in any one discipline's focus on borders adds to the scholarship of all other disciplines. This also leads to important overlap of scholarly style, subject and structure. It is not surprising, then, that the sociology of borders has evolved in ways similar to geography, history and political science, to arrive in the 1990s at research interests in the relationships between territory, sovereignty and identity.

The study of social groups, institutions and movements has been the hallmark of international boundary studies in sociology. These studies are often framed as analyses of minority groups at and across state and sub-national borderlines. 'Traditionally, and with few exceptions, the study of boundaries has coincided for sociologists with the study of minorities (national, ethnic, linguistic, etc.), often dwelling in border areas' (DeMarchi and Boileau 1982a: 9). This attention to minorities was due in part to the resurgence in ethnic identities in the 1960s and 1970s, and continues today as one of the major themes in the sociology of borders, although the ways in which minorities have been contextualised have changed. Earlier studies of assimilation, nation-building, ethnic conflict and accommodation, and migration have given way to studies of ethnic and national identity, the politics of identity, regionalism, the role of local social groups and institutions in cross-border cooperation, and border communities which straddle borderlines (see, for example, Delli Zotti 1982; DeMarchi and Boileau 1982b; Gross 1978; Strassoldo 1973; Strassoldo and Delli Zotti 1982; for reviews of the range of perspectives in the sociology of international borders, see Strassoldo 1982a, 1989). Central to many of these studies is a focus on how communities, workers and local institutions in border areas are caught between two often competing national societies and polities. This liminal state results in an ambivalent role for border societies in national and international relations.

Raimondo Strassoldo, perhaps the leading theorist in the sociology of borders, concludes that the ambivalence of border life is a defining feature of border societies in several respects (1982a: 152; see also Martínez 1994a: 18–25). Border people may demonstrate ambiguous identities because economic, cultural and linguistic factors pull them in two directions. They are also pulled two ways politically, and may display only a weak identification with the nation-state in which they reside.

This ambivalent border identity affects the role which border communities play in international cooperation and conflict (Strassoldo 1982b). Sociologists have thus sought to understand how the actions of border people and their political and civic institutions reflect their perceptions of sovereignty, territory and identity (in, for example, supranational or regional bodies [Delli Zotti 1996] or at the borders of new states [Mlinar 1996]). How, for example, do border people adapt to the losses and gains in state power, government competencies, economic competitiveness, and personal and state sovereignty? While the globalisation of politics, economics and social relations may have made some borders more porous, it has had the opposite affect elsewhere and at other times. So, at least, O'Dowd and his colleagues conclude with regard to the Irish–British border, which after years of EU initiatives, including the push for a 'Europe without frontiers', has become more militarised, politicised and symbolic of the power of the British state, precisely because of the importance of national territorial sovereignty to it (O'Dowd and Corrigan 1995, 1996; O'Dowd et al. 1995). States are not alone in their desire to strengthen their sovereign international borders. As Mlinar observes, many Slovenians, whose history has been one of ethnic and national conflict, including violent interference from outsiders, desire the protection that strong borders offer. This is a critical issue for Slovenia, whose possible future entry to the EU will depend on what the electorate thinks about the progressive weakening of the Union's internal boundaries.

The idea of abolishing borders has the general connotation of an emancipation from different forms of territorial confines upon social life and thinking. A border is often considered to be a limitation imposed upon people by the state, 'from above'. Thus it comes as a surprise to find out who actually needs such borders: it is we rather than them! At present in Slovenia uncompetitive enterprises, farmers, wine-growers and others are demanding protection, and higher tariffs on imported goods (Mlinar 1996: 148–9).

Thus, sociological studies of borders have had to include spatial and temporal dimensions, of local political, economic, social and cultural institutions and processes, in terms of stability and change, within the context of transformations in the national and international arenas. Like other social scientists, sociologists have had to accommodate the fact that old definitions of sovereignty, which were dependent on the twin bases of state and territory, have given way to new ones of culture and identity.

The evolution of border studies in other disciplines besides those we have reviewed in this chapter follows a similar pattern. Approaches to the study of international borders in legal studies (see, for example, Dupuy 1982; Gessner and Schade 1990), economics (Boos 1982; N. Hansen 1981; Sayer 1982; Taylor 1976), and folklore (Limón 1994; Paredes 1993) have also evolved from disparate methodological and theoretical interests into a set of concerns with nation, state, sovereignty, culture and identity. One thing is clear. Each discipline considered here has shifted its focus. Culture and identity now occupy a new prominence in the latest wave of border studies, reflecting their centrality in contemporary social research more generally.

Culture and the Comparative Study of Borders

Perhaps the evolution of border studies in the academic fields we have been reviewing is akin to that evolution of frontiers themselves which Lord Curzon concluded was an art and not a science. The image of borders in each of our disciplines is a reflection of the discipline itself. The convergence in method and theory which the comparative study of international borders demands, along with the interdisciplinarity necessitated by such an effort, will create a corpus of scholarly work difficult to pin down to any individual academic field. If border studies *in toto* do not adequately reflect one discipline, then it must reflect them all. Perhaps the borderlines between scholarly fields will go the way of state borders; that is, they may get stronger or weaker in the effort. At this juncture, the borders between academic disciplines seem to be in as much flux as those between many states. Some common themes have emerged.

The disciplines discussed in this chapter have all advocated the comparative study of borders (alternatively referred to as frontiers, borderlands, border areas and border regions, depending on the disciplinary focus), a reorientation away from centrist and statist perspectives in order to view borders as international economic, political, social and cultural systems, and a focus on border people, and their related ethnic and national identities, in terms of their roles in networks and institutions of politics and power. This means marrying the study of territory and the state with the investigation of process and agency in and beyond borders.

Through the works of such key thinkers as Anderson, Asiwaju, Martínez, Minghi, Prescott, Sahlins, Stoddard and Strassoldo among others, the comparative study of borders and borderlands may not have created a set of theories for and unto itself, but in our view this is not wholly a bad or surprising thing. What has occurred is that border studies in many academic fields have converged in terms of research problems, questions and hypotheses, and have begun arriving at similar answers, most of which point to the important role which borders have played and continue to play in their related nations and states. In this shared view, borders are important forces in the institutions and processes which have been the subjects of study, such as the state, political parties, regions, civil society and the nation, that have helped define many academic disciplines. Also common to many approaches in border studies is the perception that borders are simultaneously structures and processes, things and relationships, histories and events. Of particular importance to anthropology in these common positions is the role of culture as a marker and agent of tradition and change at borders. In fact, culture has become a pre-eminent aspect of border studies in most disciplines, and has certainly begun to play a more prominent role in all fields.

Anthropology has long researched culture at and across state boundaries, and has much to offer the interdisciplinary study of the evolution of borders, nations and states. Borderlands have always been areas of support and subversion of states. This is no less true in this era of internationalisation and globalisation. In the chapters that follow, we examine how culture inscribes state territory, national sovereignty, and ethnic, national and other identities at borders, through a review of anthropological analyses of such things as rituals, symbols, informal economies, sexual and body politics, and the negotiation of meanings and values both within and across state borders.

—4—

The Symbols and Rituals of Power

The symbolic is not a residual dimension of purportedly real politics; still less is it an insubstantial screen upon which real issues are cast in pale and passive form. The symbolic is real politics, articulated in a special and often most powerful way.

Kessler, *Islam and Politics in a Malay State*

So far we have suggested that the anthropology of borders should be concerned with the interplay of nations and states, and the ways both are experienced in the everyday lives of the people who live at and cross their spatial and political limits. Border peoples perhaps can be seen most usefully in terms of their ethnic and national identities, the subject of this chapter. These identities cannot be studied in a political vacuum, however, no matter how hard some anthropologists try to portray them as local isolates, largely divorced from the ideas and actions of state politics.

The anthropology of borders is thus also the anthropology of state power and practice. But it is not just about how nations and states have a policy impact at local levels, although this has been one of anthropology's principal contributions to the study of borders. Rather, anthropology also has much to contribute to our understanding of how power is embodied, encoded, represented and manifested in the organs and institutions of the state at a variety of levels and in a variety of guises in the borderlands and in the lives of those affected, in however small a way, by their experience of or relationship to their nation's or their state's borders. The anthropological study of power is not only about understanding the actions of those people who possess it (in fact, there has been a long and still vital debate in anthropology about the need to do this, see Nader 1974 and Wolf 1974), but is just as much about how those without the political or economic power to influence the material course of their lives can adapt to that fact, and yet still enter into the social relations of state and society. The powerless, among others, have a variety of behavioural options at their disposal, including violence, avoidance, resistance, inclusion and exclusion, many forms of which have been called by James Scott (1985) the 'weapons of the weak'. Many anthropologists have recognised the ritualised forms of behaviour in and between relatively powerless populations which mark the limits of membership. So too are relations between states ritualised, in sometimes complex and sometimes simple ways, and these help to define the borderlands in which they occur. This chapter explores a number of cases of how the rituals and symbols of national and ethnic identity encode the borders between states, making these borders more or less discernible to resident and traveller, depending on their knowledge of the cultural codes on display.

Border Symbols and Rituals

All social and political identities are now shaped by the state in some way. Some identities emerge from state attempts to define borders, while others result from state efforts to define and control people. Borders are liminal zones in which residents, wayfarers and the state are continually contesting their roles and their natures. As a result, borders and border people have identities which are shifting and multiple, in ways which are 'multivocal and multilocal' (Rodman 1992), but which are none the less fashioned to some degree by the structures of the state.

Borders are zones of cultural production, spaces of meaning-making and meaning-breaking. Experiences of borders, as in all liminal experiences, simultaneously reinforce and disintegrate social and political status and role, and structure and meaning, by putting into sharp relief the full range of our identities. This is especially true of national and ethnic identities, which are configured at borders in ways that often differ from how these same identities are constructed in less peripheral areas of the state. As we mentioned in chapter two (see also Wilson and Donnan 1998a), the anthropological interest in ethnic groups and their boundaries which began with Barth may have led anthropologists to under-emphasise the interplay of ethnic and national identity at the boundaries of nation-states. But we reiterate our view that nations are politicised ethnic groups pursuing goals of political independence or autonomy that are linked to a particular territory, if not a homeland. Thus every national identity involves singular and often unshakeable views of the nation's relationship to territory, regardless of how deterritorialised we may perceive the ethnic or national group in question to be.

But if ethnic and national identities are shifting and multiple at borders, areas in which the territory so important to some of these identities is fixed and delimited, how do ethnic groups arrange themselves at and across the borderlines which provide various degrees of protection, oppression, bifurcation and provocation? And what of local border communities, which after all are the chief focus of most anthropological research on borders?

Although all border communities share many structural and functional features, each has particular characteristics which make them more or less similar to smaller sub-sets of border communities and cultures. For example, ethnic populations at borders seem to be arranged in three basic ways. There are those which share ethnicity across the border, as well as with those in core areas of the state. There are those which share ethnic ties across the border, but whose ethnicity makes them different from other populations in the state. And there are those few ethnic groups which share ethnicity only with members of their state, and are ethnically differentiated from peoples across their borders. This last type would constitute a classic homogeneous nation, in the ideal nation-state, and is the most difficult to find world-wide.

Anthropologists have studied ethnicity and ethnic groups throughout the globe in every conceivable way: as an ideology, as social and political movements, as mythic charters for action, as a minority identity, and in terms of their relationship to religion, politics, economics and social structure and organisation. Because of the methodological, theoretical and intellectual difficulties of immersing oneself in ethnic studies, it is not surprising that anthropologists have shied away from examining national identities. There are, of course, notable anthropological studies of nations and national identities. For example, Fox (1990), Handler (1988), Kapferer (1988), Spencer (1990) and Verdery (1991) have analysed nations as political and cultural entities that have particular relationships with the state in which they reside and which they help to construct. Geertz (1963, 1973) and Wolf (1982) have examined the origin and development of old and new national cultures in Europe and in the post-imperial world, and have done so from significantly different theoretical perspectives. But such studies are few, and are dwarfed by the number of studies which seek to remove ethnicity from its political framework of nation and state (for an overview of ethnic studies in anthropology, see Banks 1996; Eriksen 1993; Jenkins 1997). This is no doubt due to the mercurial nature of studying identity and social action, and ethnicity and national identity within the structures of nations and states. It is easy to ask people about their identities, but more difficult to discern how their actions and identities are related. Nevertheless, anthropologists have enjoyed some success. One of the most important means used by anthropologists to explore ethnic and national identities, at borders and elsewhere, has been through the study of symbols and rituals.

All culture is based on shared symbols, and all social and political systems are structured and expressed through complex relations of symbols and rituals. In the study of nations and states, steeped in rationalist and materialist models, these points are often missed. But to understand politics in any society 'it is necessary to understand how the symbolic enters into politics, how political actors consciously and unconsciously manipulate symbols, and how this symbolic dimension relates to the material bases of political power' (Kertzer 1988: 2–3). Symbols give people a cognitive map of the world. They provide order and meaning to those who recognise them, and are bewildering, if not invisible, to those who cannot decode them. As Kertzer points out (1988: 7), however, there has been a lack of systematic study of the role of symbols in modern states, due in part to the difficulty of studying one's own symbol systems, which are often unreflectively perceived and understood.

Because symbols are among the most important elements of politics which tie people to other people whom they will never meet, and to institutions of which they will not have direct experience, they must form the basis for any anthropological study of contemporary nations and states. To some anthropologists this task is imperative, because 'the central theoretical problem in social anthropology has been the analysis of the dialectical relations between two major variables: symbolic action and power relationships' (A. Cohen 1974: 13).

Anthropologists recognise that one of the most important interfaces between symbols and politics occurs in ritual. This is why political anthropologists are so interested in rituals, and why they conclude that rituals are as important in modern nation-states as they are in any less complex society. As Kertzer succinctly puts it, ritual is 'symbolic behavior that is socially standardized and repetitive' and which can be seen as 'action wrapped in a web of symbolism' (1988: 9). Rituals are perhaps the most formal behavioural patterns in any society, and are certainly amongst the most meaningful of prescribed behaviours. They are clearly significant acts to their participants, who as a result are often proud and willing to demonstrate them to anthropologists and other observers.

But as clear and concrete as the ritualistic behaviour may appear in form and structure, it also has a timeless, abstract and multidimensional quality. Simultaneously dramatic and tedious, profound and often profane, rituals are many things to their participants. Each of the symbols of a ritual may serve to condense many meanings into one object, such as a nation's flag, or one symbol can be multivocal, in that many different messages are received by the ritual's participants (Kertzer 1988: 11). Because a symbol has no single meaning, it can be seen to be ambiguous, yet few if any ritualistic symbols are ambiguous to everyone. Thus, no matter how clear a symbol is to some people, it will be obscure or unintelligible to others.

Mystification, then, is a part of many rituals. Some rites may even have as a principal aim the disorientation of their participants. Such rituals entail participants entering a liminal state, a transitional condition which is confusing, sometimes polluting and almost always transformative. Rites of passage do this by placing people in conditions of marginality, where they often experience isolation or pain, before they are allowed to re-enter society with a new status (see, for example, La Fontaine 1985; Turner 1974). During these rituals the participants, and their relationships within their culture, are ambiguous and in flux. Liminality is an interstitial condition, a journey from one state of social being to another, and as such is a suitable metaphor for life at international borders, and for the role of borders in the social systems of which they are a part.

It should be apparent from our discussion so far that rituals are not confined to religious or sacred matters, although most rituals can be described through use of religious metaphor. This fusing of ritual and religion is predictable and understandable, but it does injustice to the range of other, secular rituals which structure life in modern states. All organisations of power utilise rituals to bind people together, to the hierarchy, and to others in the past and the future. Businesses, governments, universities and sports teams use ritual to socialise people into the corporate ethos. Nor are rituals confined to power holders. Many oppressed and victimised people turn first to religious and secular rituals in order to sustain the will to persevere or overcome. In some cases the rituals of the powerful and the powerless link them together, in what each believes to be for the common good. Such linkages certainly inspire many in a nation-state, wherein the state attempts to build a nation out of disparate cultures through its programmes of political socialisation, education and mass arts and media (see Rabinowitz 1998). For example, there is a heady mix of symbols invoked when Americans 'pledge allegiance to the flag of the United States of America', hand over heart, eyes on the stars and stripes. Regardless of their meanings, this ritual and its symbols function as a levelling and integrating device for the American 'nation', which is constructed as a civic entity and is not defined ethnically. At the same time, there are other Americans who look to other flags, such as the flag of the Confederacy, the 'stars and bars', which while not necessarily replacing the national icon serve the identities of some Americans just as meaningfully.

The point here is that there are many symbols and rituals which transcend differences among people in a society, serving to integrate disparate classes, occupations, ethnic groups, regions and religions. Other symbols and rituals serve other purposes, differentiating these same groups, thereby creating overlapping and competing expectations of loyalty, compliance, assimilation and conformity. International borders are places of extremely complicated and contesting political forces, which might be perceived to be simultaneously centrifugal and centripetal. Careful examination of border rituals and symbols, however, is one way to puncture the façade of the border, to gaze behind the surface in order to see how identity and culture function in support or opposition to the state.

Powerful Rites

Melilla, one of the last strongholds of Spanish imperialism in Africa, is a small city on the Mediterranean shore of Morocco which has been held by Spain since the fifteenth century (see map 4.1). Covering an area of only twelve square kilometres, it is surrounded by sea and barbed wire. Claimed by the state of Morocco since 1961, Spain continues to defend the 'Spanishness' of the city on historical, ethnic, and strategic grounds. Nevertheless, over one-third of the 64,000 population are Muslims from the Rif, the region of Morocco of which Melilla is a hinterland (which is ironically seen obversely by the Spanish of Melilla, who see the Rif as their hinterland), and which, because of its mineral riches, provided the economic incentive for Spain's imperial initiative. Only a very small minority of this Muslim population are Spanish citizens; it has been extremely difficult for Muslims to attain

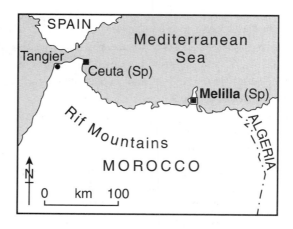

Map 4.1 Melilla on the Spanish–Moroccan frontier

Spanish nationality or to acquire legal working papers. They remain anyway, because Melilla is their home. But other groups call Melilla home, and some are not so sure that the Muslims belong there too. The city is controlled by the Spanish, who comprise almost two-thirds of Melilla's population and who dominate the positions of power and influence.

These Spanish, the *melillenses*, most of whom have been resident in the city for generations, are stalwart defenders of the Spanish way of life, and of Spain's historical and contemporary right to hold onto this African enclave, which they see as sovereign Spanish territory. Although in most ways Melilla is their city, they feel caught between many worlds. They are literally on the border between Spain and Morocco, but are also squarely placed in the frontier between Europe and Africa, between the Christian and the Muslim worlds, between, in their eyes, civilisation and barbarism, and between order and chaos. And they, like many frontier people around the globe, feel alone, abandoned by their fellow nationals who are safely ensconced in metropolitan centres far from the 'front line' of ethnic and national conflict. In this case, the Spanish of Africa feel that *los peninsulares*, the Spanish of Iberia, have turned their backs on them. 'They feel threatened by sporadic problems at the border and by what they call the "March of the Tortoise", the slow yet persistent invasion of Rifians who lack documents of all kinds and who are thought to upset the delicate economic and demographic balance of the enclave' (Driessen 1992: 15). Because Melilla is a poor city, these Spanish, whose prosperity depends on Spanish capital, policy and military, have much to be anxious about.

Melilla is a multi-ethnic city. Besides the Spanish and Muslims, most of whom are ethnically Rifs or Berbers, there are groups of Jews, Hindus and gypsies, as well as a host of the denizens of a port city at the frontier between continents, many of whom are hangers-on and parasites of the Spanish military garrison. In Melilla, ethnicity is principally defined in religious terms, but religious affiliation is seen to constitute much more than simple adherence to beliefs and rituals. Religion is the symbol if not the basis of a person's role in local society. Driessen reviews a wide range of religious and secular rituals, such as mortuary rites, military ceremonies, feasting, forms of hospitality, and religious holidays, to demonstrate that intra- and inter-ethnic relations are ritualised, providing boundaries between the communities and barriers between classes. He concludes that the frontiers between Spain and Morocco, between the Spanish and 'other' ways of life, have been ritualised in order to establish modes of inclusion and exclusion, seen to be necessary in this zone of historical and cultural contest.

Melilla may be surrounded by barbed wire, symbolically patrolled by the Spanish Foreign Legion, but it is in fact an open border economically and socially. Each day people stream into its streets from Morocco and Spain, for business and pleasure in a city famous for both. A free port, Melilla has a large floating population.

> Most soldiers serve a sixteen-month term before returning home. Peninsulars come to buy tax-free cigarettes, liquor, watches, tape and video-recorders, and visit their relatives in the city and army. Foreign tourists and Moroccan migrant workers use the city as a port of transit. Each day, thousands of border people, who have a permanent residence in the hinterland, pour into the enclave . . . They bring eggs, vegetables, grain, meat, fish, fruit, milk, and water into the city and return home with purchases of blankets, shoes, batteries, gasoline and electronic luxuries. They do not come only to trade, but . . . they drink beer and liquor, go to the cinema, bingo, doctors, and prostitutes (Driessen 1992: 14).

This description of Melilla is remarkably similar to descriptions of border cities elsewhere in the world as we will see later. Mechanisms of closure and exclusion are evident in all. In the case of Melilla, the rituals which Driessen documents among the Spanish residents are symbols of hierarchy and power, while rites among the Melillan Jews and Muslims reflect their ambivalence as residents of a European city, on the African continent, which is sovereign territory of a Spanish and largely Christian state.

Death and the Flag

The Spanish of Melilla form the city's elite, and their power and influence are clear to all. At the same time, their political and social positions are ambiguous. Their power derives from Spain, relatively recently democratised, now a member of the EU, and slowly distancing itself from an imperial past. Melilla is a territory in what for all intents and purposes is Morocco, or at least that is what Morocco argues, and it is the Moroccan people who are as responsible for the city's economic well-being as is Spain.

The Melilla Spanish are aware of the fate of other European colonials in Africa and fearful of the future. Muslims in Melilla, on the other hand, are rarely Spanish or Moroccan by citizenship, although many are legal residents of the city. They are in inferior positions to the Spanish, a product of hundreds of years of Spanish imperialism, Christian domination, and internal Moroccan disputes. Although they are the ethnic majority outside of Melilla, they are the minority within. Suspended between two ways of life, two often competing cultural systems, they are none the less committed to the city, even if treated as inferior by the city elite. Caught between these two groups is the thousand-strong Jewish community. Like the dominant Spanish and the dissatisfied Muslims, they too deal with the ambivalence and inequities through rituals that demonstrate power held, power lost and conflict avoided.

The Spanish of Melilla valorise a number of rites which publicly demonstrate the power and glory of the Spanish state and culture. Driessen examines the many elements of death which figure in these rituals, a feature common in Christian and Iberian rituals elsewhere but which here assumes particular significance in the context of the Spanish Melillans' dependence on the maintenance of the border for their power. One of the most dramatic ceremonies Driessen witnessed (1992: 111–21, 135–6) during his fieldwork in 1984 was that of *Sabado Legionario* (Legionnaires' Saturday), which draws on the Spanish cult of the dead.

Melilla is permanent home to a unit of the Spanish Foreign Legion (*Tercio de Extranjeros* or *La Legion*), the only unit in the Spanish army that glorifies death. Its official motto is 'To die is the major honour. A man only dies once. Death comes quickly and it is painless. The most horrible thing for a man is to live as a coward' (Driessen 1992: 135). The Legion's battle cry is 'Long live Death!', and the death's head is one of the legionnaire's favourite tattoos, as is the crucifix. The Legion's anthem is 'The Betrothed of Death', which scarcely veils the conjugal and erotic imagery which the soldiers link to death. 'The message is that the betrothal on the battlefield of the legionnaire with Death, represented as female, contributes to the reproduction of the Nation' (Driessen 1992: 136).

Legionnaires' Saturday is a weekly rite held at the Legion's garrison in Melilla to honour those who have fallen in combat.

> The ceremony is brief and simple. The entire regiment stands in line at the back of the plaza. Six legionnaires, flanked by four guards of honour, come forward holding up a large crucifix in a horizontal position. Marching brusquely, the soldiers carry the statue to a platform on which it is put in an upright position between the Legion's banner and the national flag. This ceremonial act is accompanied by the beating of drums and bugle calls. Then the highest ranking officers salute before the statue. After a minute of silence

the soldiers sing their anthem at the top of their voices; this is followed by a short parade (Driessen 1992: 136).

The symbolism seems clear. Death on the battlefield is akin to Christ's sacrifice. Such a death is an honour and should hold no fear, since those so chosen not only join their fallen comrades in glory, but perform an 'act of self-immolation for "God and the Nation", the greatest honour a legionnaire can achieve' (Driessen 1992: 136). The blood of the Legion's sacrifices gives life to Spain, but in Melilla, among the local Spanish, this sacrifice is also about life for 'this Spanish corner of Morocco' (1992: 136). This is why the *melillenses* incorporate the Legionnaires' ritual into their own civic ceremonies.

One such ceremony was the Melilla city government's response to what it perceived was an insult to Spain, perpetrated by the disloyal and ungrateful of Melilla. The summer of 1983 was a difficult one for the Spanish of Melilla, as it was for the entire city, because it was a time of serious labour and ethnic unrest. Strikes against municipal utilities were crippling daily operations. Muslims sallied forth from their ghetto to protest the terrible conditions in which they lived, which were far inferior to the other neighbourhoods in the city, and for which many politicians expected thanks. One of these protests turned into a riot, and a Spanish flag was torn down and burnt in front of the town hall. The police reacted violently and the Catholic Spanish population was outraged by the desecration of the national symbol.

A few days later the mayor announced that these anti-constitutional acts against the flag, 'the symbol representing the unity of all Spaniards', had forced the town council to plan 'a ceremony of redress', because 'Melilla cannot, and must not remain silent in the face of the insults to the flag of all Spaniards. . . . Long live Melilla, long live the Constitution, long live the King, long live Spain!' (cited in Driessen 1992: 113). Thus on the following Saturday more than a thousand people gathered in the main plaza to witness the ceremony of 'indemnification' of the national flag. They were addressed by the mayor with an inspirational paean to Spanish 'manliness, honour and pride': 'He who contemplates this flag and does not feel pride, if he is a man he is not a Spaniard, and if he is a Spaniard he is not a man' (cited in Driessen 1992: 113). The challenge to the minority populations of Melilla was clear, as was the mayor's attack on the machismo of the non-Spanish and non-Catholic males.

The confluence of gender, sexual, religious and national imagery continued into the next year, when a long-planned ceremony took place, which Driessen calls the 'ceremony of the national flag' (1992: 111–21). On 19 March 1984 a national flag with the new constitutional emblem was presented to the Foreign Legion unit based in Melilla. The date of the ceremony had been decided by the mayor, the Legion commander, and the army commander-in-chief, and was doubly significant as the

Feast of St Joseph and the commemoration of the Spanish army's raising of the Moroccan sultan's siege of Melilla in 1775, a decisive historical defeat of the Rifian Muslims.

The government clearly saw this ceremony as a statement of loyalty to the city, to Spain, and to Spanish civilisation, as well as a demonstration of unity in the face of divisive elements, whom the Catholics, i.e. the ethnic Spanish, recognised to be the Muslim minority. Before the ceremony numerous newspaper articles appeared lauding the role of the army in the maintenance of order and praising the special relationships between Spain and Melilla and between city and garrison. The ceremonial flag was displayed in a glass case for five days before the event so that it might be venerated, in a way similar to Christian rites. This was but one aspect of the exclusionary nature of the event, in which national iconography required appropriate Spanish and Catholic responses. Other groups could be awe-inspired or seething observers, but the ceremony was a display of dominance and power rather than of unity in diversity. As 19 March approached, the press and the government made it clear that this was to be a day to celebrate Spanish history and culture.

On the day of the ceremony all Catholics took a holiday, but most Muslims worked. The mass which opened the proceedings and the wreath-laying at the cenotaph were sparsely attended. The town leaders were unhappy with this lack of support, but their attitude changed on entering the main square, which was thronged with over 20,000 spectators. Speeches recounting the brave deeds of the Legion, and a review of the troops preceded the main event: the exchange of flags. The old regimental banner was escorted to the dais in a mix of military and religious solemnity, accompanied by the national anthem. When the new flag was presented, it was followed by the mayor's wife and the commander of the Legion, who, in Driessen's words, acted as its 'godparents', escorting the flag and the people of Melilla to a new status, a sacred relationship between city, garrison and nation. After the priest had consecrated the flag with holy water, the mayor's wife presented it to the commander, proclaiming that she was proud that this symbol 'to which our fathers, the fathers of our sons . . . and . . . sons will swear their allegiance' had been placed in his custody. The commander then kissed the flag and thanked her as the representative of the 'ideal Spanish mother'. Turning to his troops, he announced: 'My fellow legionnaires, this flag is the sacred symbol of our immortal nation. We hereby pledge our obligation to defend it with our lives' (cited in Driessen 1992: 117). The day ended with the legionnaires performing their ceremony of *Sabado Legionario*, followed by a massed military parade.

Although there were some dissenters in the crowd, which was overwhelmingly Catholic and Spanish, most seemed to approve the ceremony and its messages, which were a clear juxtaposition of national and religious symbols, going so far as to use the words and symbols of marriage and baptism in an overt attempt to wed the city of Melilla to the Spanish nation and state, and all to the Legion. 'The new flag, therefore, is a metaphor of rebirth, in the image of the family, of Spain as a democratic nation and of Melilla as a Spanish city. It is an action through which the bond of Melilla with the motherland is renewed' (Driessen 1992: 119).

It is important to note, however, that all of the imagery is based on what the local elite perceive to be Spanish. In this open port, at this porous national border, on the edge of a variety of competing economic, political, religious and ideological entities, Catholic Spanish rituals serve to establish and sustain social and political dominance and hierarchy, economic inequity and nationalist superiority. The border may be relatively open, but the relations between ethnic groups are not, which is clear in many other rituals in Melilla, including those in the Muslim, Jewish and Hindu communities.

Exclusionary practices sustain ethnic boundaries even after death. Muslims have been promised their own cemetery within Melilla, where a principal symbol of power has been municipal support for ethnically segregated burial. In fact, Muslims have never had their own cemetery in Melilla, and the removal for burial of Muslim corpses from Spanish sovereign territory was for long a central symbol of the ethnic divide in this border port. Cults of the dead also serve as defenders of the nation and the state when they expel the visible remains of their ethnic 'others' to the symbolic netherworld across the borderline.

The Liminal Irish Border

The Irish border separates the twenty-six counties of the Republic of Ireland from the six counties of Northern Ireland (see map 4.2), a political entity since the 1920s and a region of the United Kingdom. Like many borders, this one is clearly delineated by markers of state sovereignty which are difficult to miss, and almost as hard to misinterpret. The visibility of state markers such as guard towers, road signs and national flags, however, are shadowed by other signs and symbols whose significance may be less obvious to the uninformed. Yet these too mark ethnic and national territories, in ways which may or may not coincide with the established and formal demarcation of the state.

The Irish border is marginal and interstitial in a number of ways. In existence as an international border for over seventy years, it may be on the verge of official change in these heady days of ceasefire in the war between the outlawed, terrorist Irish Republican Army (IRA, also seen as patriots and freedom fighters by a minority population in Ireland) and the people and the state in Northern Ireland. The border is also an area of ambiguous and contested ownership and loyalties, where ethnic ties and difference depend not on ritual, although that plays an important part too, but on the politics of national identity and religion, and where, unlike the Melilla case, most of the border population (at least on its northern edge) are not members

Map 4.2 The Irish border

of the ethnic majority. In fact, because of their national identity and religion, they are a minority in both the region and the state in which they live. The Irish border is thus also in a liminal 'state', because it is the gateway to a province which may be viewed, in its entirety, as a borderland, a frontier zone of disputing nations and ethnic groups, out of touch and out of synch with both states to which each of the two Northern Irish communities profess allegiance and cultural affinity. This liminality is an integral part of the Irish border, and is both expressed and confronted symbolically all along its 360 kilometres.

Depending on the cultural codes one has at one's disposal, the symbolic dimensions to borders may be either visible or invisible. Like other forms of 'imagined' communities, the boundaries of the nations and ethnic groups who inhabit borders are symbolic constructions that are often obscure to those who do not share their meanings. Moreover, 'the symbolic character of the boundary – its location in the mind – often accounts for its invisibility to outsiders. It may be a useful invisibility, for if outsiders are unaware of it they cannot attack or subvert it' (A. P. Cohen 1987: 16). At borders, national, ethnic and state boundaries are always being subverted. Sometimes the boundaries between communities on either side of a border, or between nations and ethnic groups on both sides of a border, are particularly difficult for outsiders to discern, because the forms of cross-border culture are converging, to include many of the symbols, such as dress, language, and technology, that once marked difference. But in other instances the meanings which local communities attach to those forms may diverge. 'This is because, whilst the *form* of symbols may be common to those who bear the same culture, the *meanings* of the symbols, their contexts, may differ' (A. P. Cohen 1987: 13, emphases in original). In fact, the symbols that are the most important are those which carry the most meanings; it is their ambiguity and imprecision which make them so important to those who can read them. 'It is this very pliability of symbolic form which makes it so useful, so effective a means of marking boundary and identity' (A. P. Cohen 1987: 14). The visibility or invisibility of the Irish border, like borders everywhere, is as much a matter of local communities' national and ethnic identities as it is a result of the structures of the state.

The people of the Irish border have their own means of marking their local, regional and national boundaries (see Wilson 1993a, 1994, 1996). The border is celebrated by a great diversity of graffiti of political resistance and sectarianism. Perhaps the clearest of these are the slogans of 'Éire Núa', 'Provos' and 'PIRA' (references to the new Ireland which the Provisional IRA, largest and most powerful wing of the armed Republican movement, seeks to create after its achievement of a united Ireland), which can be found both scrawled and neatly painted in conspicuous locations wherever there are nationalist communities along the border, which is just about everywhere. Thus visitors and locals, civilian and soldier, are surrounded by the labels of resistance, found on railway tunnels, bridges, government buildings, road signs, banners and streamers hoisted across roads, and displayed along with other symbols and icons at major crossroads. Even the walls of housing estates in border towns and villages display such graffiti, alongside other famous examples of Northern Irish political symbolism, such as murals. These murals depict the scenes and symbols important to the community (Jarman 1997), whether it be men in black berets, camouflage uniforms, and carrying Armalite rifles (popular IRA imagery), King William astride his white charger (symbol of 'Protestant' victory over Catholics in the Battle of the Boyne in 1690), or images of goddesses and warriors from Celtic/Gaelic mythology (used by both sides to validate their historical right to control Ulster, the traditional name of Northern Ireland, along with some contiguous territory in the Republic). These symbols are not overtly religious, however, because unlike the Moroccan case examined above, ethnicity and national identities, while they have strong roots in religion and ritual, have pronounced political expression in Northern Ireland. Nevertheless, some religious imagery, reminiscent of the Spanish cult of death, is used to territorialise the border. At one crossroads in South Armagh, not far from the borderline, ten white crosses still stand in a field, memorial to the dead hunger strikers of 1981.

Colour is used to delineate competing versions of the Irish border. Kerbstones are painted red, white and blue or green, white and orange to signal loyalist and nationalist allegiance respectively. Flags and banners also litter the landscape. The Irish Republic's tricolour flies defiantly over many a crossroad and village, while elsewhere the red, white and blue of the British 'Union Jack' indicates Protestant areas. Banners in English or Irish stretch across roads in support of political prisoners, to ridicule the opposition (for example, by hanging a picture of a pig in a policeman's uniform), and to encourage electoral support for nationalist candidates and parties. Some nationalist slogans have been produced in the form of road signs, meticulously designed to resemble actual road signs, but with a message subversive of the state and its personnel. Two examples stand out: the silhouette of a man with a rifle held aloft, in the style of a man with a pick, with the inscription underneath of 'Sniper At Work', and a red circle with a red diagonal line through it, superimposed on the letters 'RUC', signalling an area off-limits for the police, the Royal Ulster Constabulary.

The myriad permutations of national, ethnic and religious identities in Northern Ireland are too complex to review here, and even though to speak of two communities risks gross over-simplification, it is sufficient for our purposes (for an overview of Northern Irish political and cultural identities, see Ruane and Todd 1996). On the one hand, there is the majority population of Protestants (made up mostly of Presbyterians and members of the Church of Ireland), whose politico-cultural ideologies mark them as Unionists, supporters of the present United Kingdom and of Northern Ireland's continuing place within it. A more vocal, often more militant, and sometimes violent sub-group of Protestants are Northern Ireland's Loyalists, who see themselves as defenders of both the Union and the Protestant way of life. Few of these people would identify themselves as having an Irish national identity; most claim a British national identity, though increasing numbers see their 'Ulster', 'Ulster Protestant' or 'Northern Irish' identity as gaining in importance. In one sense they are ethnically Ulster Protestant or Northern Irish in a multinational British state. They have British citizenship and thus answer questions about national identity in terms of being British.

On the other hand, there is the minority Catholic community who constitute approximately 40 per cent of the population, and who live mainly in the south and west of the province. Catholics are mostly seen to have an Irish national identity, i.e. they are ethnically Irish, and may prefer to travel under an Irish passport. Many favour increased ties between their community and the people and government of the Irish Republic, with some arguing for the island's reunification. A powerful minority of nationalists are Republicans, who in large part support the use of force to achieve their nationalist aims. Very few Catholics would identify themselves as 'Ulster' people, a title that is symbolically held by Protestants. Many would call themselves Northern Irish Catholics, or Northern Catholics, in order to distinguish themselves from their southern counterparts, from whom they have diverged considerably since the partition of the island in 1921. Regardless of this divergence, however, many Northern Catholics subscribe to the 'great fiction' of nationalist politics which we considered in chapter one, i.e. the goal of self-determination and the achievement of the homogeneity of nation and state.

Thus, all political culture on the northern side of the Irish border establishes the boundaries between the ethnic enclaves of Catholic and Protestant, Nationalist and Unionist, Republican and Loyalist. The symbols which make these boundaries significant are not just those of nation, culture and community which encode the landscape. Rituals also play a role here. The most important of these are the 'Orange' marches which take place throughout the province during the summer. The biggest and previously most significant Orange marches take place in Belfast, capital of the province and historically a symbol of Protestant dominance. Orange marches are parades organised by a Protestant fraternal society, the Orange Order, which has its roots in Presbyterian and Scottish settler resistance to persecution by Catholics and other Protestants (see Bryan and Jarman 1997). Orange is the colour of Protestantism and Loyalism in Ireland (just as green is linked in popular culture with Irishness and Republicanism) because of its historical referent, King William, formerly Prince of Orange of the Netherlands, and hero of the Protestant victory over James, the Jacobite leader and Catholic, which decided the course of British history. This victory, popularly perceived by Protestants to have occurred at the Battle of the Boyne (and thus also a favourite subject for Loyalist iconography, especially in wall murals), is celebrated on the Twelfth of July, on what has become in Northern Ireland a 'national' holiday that can last anything up to a fortnight. The parades themselves are an almost exclusively male affair, involving highly ritualised patterns of speech-making, marching, band-playing (primarily using what are perceived to be the 'Protestant' musical instruments of flute, fife and lambeg drum), and the display of banners. Marchers dress in ritual garb, with men wearing their black, 'Sunday' suits, black bowler hats and an orange collarette known as a sash. Their actions are seen by some as celebration, by others as provocation. The march routes often take them through or near Catholic areas, where the banners, music and volume of the drums are seen by the Catholics as a triumphant revelling in the historical power and domination of Orangemen in the Protestant 'state' of Northern Ireland. This is clearly one of the functions of such parades, to express strength, righteousness and defiance, not only to Catholics and nationalists, but to the British state as well.

Since 1996, the most explosive marches have taken place in Portadown, a town southwest of Belfast, and close to the border. These marches, in the parish of Drumcree, have become an important symbolic battleground for what Loyalists and Unionists want for the future of Northern Ireland, and for what they perceive the British state wants for them, which they think is a concession to terrorism, a climb-down to the IRA, and a capitulation to the Nationalists and Republicans, all epitomised by the British and Irish government-led peace talks taking place in Belfast. The summer of 1996 was especially violent, because the government tried to prevent the Drumcree Orange march from proceeding through a nationalist area, a route which the Orangemen contend is their sacred, traditional path. As a result, loyalists rioted throughout the province, closing down most business and government activities. Due to the efforts of people on all sides, these events have not been repeated on the same scale, although the stand-off which followed the 1998 march continues to threaten the future of the planned Northern Ireland Assembly. Orange marches in Drumcree, Belfast and elsewhere in Northern Ireland, including those by the few but extremely resolute Protestant border communities, persist as a ritualised political warning to the minority population of the province, and the British and Irish states, that Northern Ireland is the homeland of the Ulster Protestants, who may destroy it rather than see it become Irish and Catholic.

Given this history of violence and distrust, and the ethnic memories of death and atrocity, it is remarkable how normal and peaceful the border region often looks and is. Both communities pursue their lives in ways that bracket off their ethnic hatred and mistrust, because in most everyday contexts each side must interact with the other (see Donnan and McFarlane 1983, 1986). Other activities also entail a modicum of integration, though, as indicated above, looks can often be deceiving. Sport is sometimes said to be an integrative device in Northern Ireland. The Irish national rugby team includes players from both the Republic and from Northern Ireland, from both major religious traditions. On the other hand, the Republic and Northern Ireland have separate national soccer teams. Each of the Northern Irish counties is integrated in the all-island Gaelic Athletic Association (GAA), but in the North Gaelic sports are played and watched almost exclusively by Catholics.

This complicated nationalist pattern of sport is reflected in the sports symbols which also mark the border. Flying the county GAA colours from farmstead, housing estate walls and road signs functions in part to establish the Irishness of the border counties. These sports colours are symbols of what the Protestant population most fears, integration within a united, Gaelic Ireland. In fact, sport is so important in the popular culture of Irish nationalism that local sports figures have sometimes been the targets of terrorist assassination, which adds to the environment of liminality at the border, when the people involved in sport, that area of life which is supposed to be about the celebration of health and sociability, are thrust into the arena of ethnic conflict.

Such actions and symbols suggest that the games entailed in sports might reveal something about other 'games' played between ethnic and national groups at international borders, with or without the approval of the state. International 'gamesmanship' of this sort often entails the complicity of agents of the state, as for instance when customs officials ignore certain infractions in the interests of maintaining local popular support, or when border guards enter into complicated cat-and-mouse games with local smugglers, who are known to the authorities, but who are not apprehended until they are caught red-handed with their illicit goods. Describing what often amounts to dangerous activities as a 'game', or as an 'adventure' (as, for example, in the Basque lands at the Spanish–French border [Douglass 1977: 138]), may be stretching the metaphor a bit far for some, but for others such behaviours constitute only a small part of the games of states and statesmanship. As Heyman (1994: 51) has remarked, 'states are aggregations of rules for social and economic action and the bureaucratic organizations required to implement these rules; for short, states are the rules of the game' (see also Mann 1993: 44–91). In the next chapter, we examine how smuggling across international borders has historically functioned to subvert the economic and political order of states which share a border, while at the same time often building solidarity between co-ethnics who are minorities in each of the states. We conclude this chapter by examining how cross-cultural and transnational 'games', symbolised and ritualised in sport, help to encode the border between two friendly states, the United States and Mexico, which is not always a border between friendly people.

The 'National' Pastime in the Border Corridor

Culture is a system of shared institutions, behaviours and ideas, but it is also a system in which there is variation in perception, participation, and performance. If culture binds people together, it also simultaneously separates and divides. Border cultures are potentially places and spaces of hybridity, characterised by, if not dependent on, the two or more 'national' cultures which frame state borders. Border people may share a sense of belonging, and thus have much in common with each other that distinguishes them from the residents of other places in their national societies. But borders also shape relations between borderlanders and people and institutions beyond border regions, and these relations form the basis for differential access to wealth, status and power.

Anthropologists are interested in the study of border cultures not only for what they mean to local lives, but also for what they mean to the wider structures of state polity, economy and society, and to the larger construction of the nation. Border people and the representatives of public and private institutions know that their border regions are relatively disadvantaged in comparison to wealthier and more influential core areas of the state. Such comparisons are accentuated when there are marked ethnic divisions between these regions. As a result, it is not surprising that government leaders, multinational corporations, and others, not least border people themselves, look to a variety of cultural forms to help alleviate the problems of inequality, and to dissipate the tensions inherent in border and cross-border ethnic and economic conflict.

In this chapter we have already discussed some of the ways in which political and social rituals and symbols are used to express either sameness or difference, often in the defence of power or in attempts to stave off peripheralisation. Sport is perhaps one of the least offensive ritual and symbolic structures in border cultures, yet it generates some of the most emotional forms of cultural integration and disintegration at local and national levels. This is especially apparent when a sport deemed to be one of the essential symbols of a nation takes root on both sides of an international border, as for example when baseball, the so-called American 'national pastime', is played in twin border towns which are separated both by the Rio Grande River and by a century and a half of divergent 'national' development, but are also joined by centuries of shared culture.

Along the US–Mexico border there is only one baseball team which has two hometowns, two home fields and two host nations. The Tecos (nickname of the *Tecolotes de los dos Laredos,* or the Owls of the two Laredos) are the minor league team of both Laredo, Texas, and Nuevo Laredo, Tamaulipas, Mexico, and have been since 1985 (see map 4.3). For over a decade the team's owners have attempted to forge a variety of institutional and informal forms of border cultural integration through the actions, rituals and symbols of baseball, as represented by their team. The anthropologist who has chronicled the rise and decline of these efforts, Allan Klein, has framed these actions within the general categories of *autonationalism, binationalism* and *transnationalism,* in order to examine the forms of cultural accommodation and disjuncture which occur at this border (Klein 1997: 6–14).

Autonationalism approximates state or civic nationalism, that type of nationalism fostered by the state through its institutions and symbols in an attempt to create a unified 'nation' to correspond to itself. This sort of nationalism views the border as fixed and impenetrable (Klein 1997: 257), a dividing line between national cultures. Binationalism refers to those state and non-governmental structures that recognise the equality and benefits of 'national' cultures and international coopera-tion. In this view of nationalism, in which each side is equal but separate, the borderline is fixed but open (Klein 1997: 257). Transnationalism corresponds closely to what we have been calling border cultures and communities, i.e. border structures and organisations, immersed in the same or similar ways of acting, thinking and perceiving, which transcend the borderline between states, precisely because the people who share these cultural forms have more in common with each other than they do with the majority populations in their states. However, transnationalism is much more than the sharing of culture which takes place through the institutional cooperation that characterises binationalism, because transnational-ism depends on the recognition of shared, not divergent, histories and traditions, which reflect the importance of local and regional identities as well as national ones. In transnationalist thought and deed, the border is fluid and open (Klein 1997: 257).

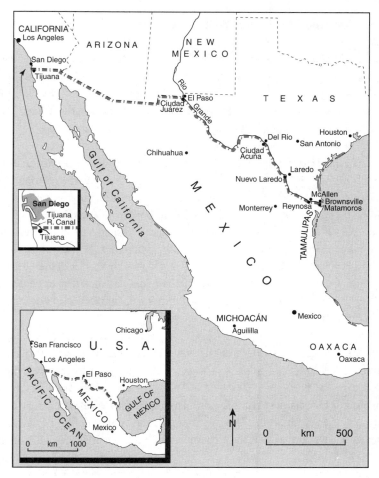

Map 4.3 The US–Mexico border

Over the last decade, the owners of the Tecos designed the team both to appeal to and reflect the binational and transnational aspects of sports in the border region. This was thought to be imperative because of the multiplicity of shared identities between the two Laredos, separated by a few hundred yards of muddy river, but connected by hundreds of years of mutual cultural development. In fact, the two towns were one until the imposition of the international border in 1846, at which time residents had to elect which side of the river, and which national territory, would be theirs. The team owners set out in 1985, when they ventured to take the Nuevo Laredo minor league team into the sports market of Laredo, to establish, with the help of government and business interests in both cities, the first binational sports franchise. They also reckoned that if the team was to succeed, they had to reconstruct its identity by inventing symbols and traditions of team transnationalism, along with appropriating a number of suitable national rituals and symbols. Their message was clear. The Owls would stand as an institution of fraternity and equality, a symbol of balanced need and trust between the two communities. Thus the team would not only play for both towns, but in both towns. It would have both Mexican and American players and, in keeping with the traditions of the Mexican League of which it was a part, would keep to the American cycle of scheduling, i.e. from spring to autumn, unlike most Latin American baseball teams who play 'winter ball'.

If the border between these two countries can be seen less as a barrier and more as a path between two homes, or perhaps a corridor between two rooms of the same home, then the Tecos would be regular travellers along that passageway. This would be one more symbol of what is a fact to border people of the two Laredos, but one which often eludes people further inland, especially the Americans, to whom 'the idea that the international boundary is complex, porous, and consists of a cultural corridor some three hundred miles wide on both sides of the boundary is somewhat novel' (Klein 1997: 7). The Tecos team was meant to appeal to those who lived in that corridor, and to provide enjoyment, camaraderie and pride to the fans on both sides of the river.

However, it must also be remembered that the two Laredos are placed squarely in a quickly changing zone of cultural contest and accommodation, aptly reflected in the river which runs between the two sides. As Herzog has suggested, there is a downside to the particular character of the US–Mexico border, wherein many international, national and local factors 'have transformed the boundary corridor into a field of confrontation of social, political, and economic forces native to the two nations. The border zone has become a place unto itself' (1990: 136; see also Klein 1997: 246).

As a consequence of these often contradictory tendencies, the integration of the roles of a binational and transnational sports team was in many ways a difficult task for the Tecos and their owners, a job made more difficult by the presence of nationalism throughout the border region, among Americans and Mexicans. This is because nationalists often believe that transnationalism undermines the irreducible character of national, in this case, US and Mexican, cultures. Moreover, the Laredo border region has a long history of cultural tensions generated by the meeting of competing nationalist agendas there. This was especially apparent in the history of the 'Washington's Birthday' celebrations, wherein the Anglo minority of Laredo has attempted, since 1898, to inject American nationalist culture into the border milieu, in what has become 'the granddaddy of binational events on this stretch of the border' (Klein 1997: 18). Their attempts have had mixed success, however, because of the dominance of shared national traditions at the border. Klein notes the incongruity of periwigged Washington wannabes speaking Spanish, or people sporting eighteenth-century costumes embellished by Mexican brocades. In fact, the birthday celebrations have evolved from re-enactments of the Boston Tea Party to its present day full-blown *fiesta mexicana*.

As a result of the owners' intention of identifying the team with both towns and both ways of life, as well as their appeal to the shared border culture which might serve as the principal focus of local identity, the Tecos became a mixture of national symbols and rituals, complicated by the addition of baseball symbols and rituals to be found everywhere the game is played. The Tecos played one-third of their home games in their 132-game season in a stadium in Laredo, the rest in a stadium in Nuevo Laredo. Following Mexican tradition, no anthems began games in Nuevo Laredo, but both national anthems were played before games in Laredo. At such times, players respectfully stood to attention. The Tecos' uniforms were changed to reflect their team's binational arrangements. Their hats had 'Laredos' in the front and '2' in the back, with away uniforms identifying them as 'Laredos' rather than 'Tecos' or 'Tecolotes'. The media were enlisted in the attempts to construct the Tecos as home team to both cities.

For the first ten years these efforts bore some fruit, aided by the team's overall winning record. By the time of Klein's fieldwork, however, things were going wrong, and in 1994 the team was sold and Laredo withdrew from the venture. Given the initial support, what had brought this experiment to this sad stage?

The biggest problem facing the Owls was internal dissension caused by nationalist bickering between the American and Mexican players, fuelled by differences in status, class, wealth and day-to-day behaviour, which were the result of forces stretching far beyond the bounds of the border region. This problem was exacerbated by the owners' attitudes towards their players, fans and the media. All of these internal matters seemed to result in the remarkable turnaround in the team's fortunes on the field. In 1993 the Tecos played for the league championship, but by 1994 their dismal record kept them out of post-season play.

Of the team's twenty-five players, five could be 'importados' (the 'Imports' or imported players), who were most often Americans because of an arrangement between the Tecos and a major league American team. Many of these American players had already played in the major leagues, and entertained hopes of playing there again, despite their relegation to the minor league. As a result, there were always tensions between these players and their Mexican teammates, tensions exacerbated by the Imports' disdain for all things Mexican, and by the fact that they lived in Laredo and did not mix socially with the Mexicans, who resided in Nuevo Laredo. For their part, the Mexican players resented the Imports' high salaries, their better homes, and the fact that they travelled to games by plane while they themselves had to travel by bus. When a dispute arose in 1993 over the privileged treatment of the imported players, the team's management backed them, further adding to the disgruntlement of the Mexican players.

The symbolism of the bifurcated role of Imported and Mexican players was not lost on the Mexicans, although Klein believed that it was 'imperfectly understood and/or disregarded' by some of the Anglo players (1997: 194). All the players were hired to win ball games, but the career trajectories were markedly different between the two groups, and to the Mexican players this was a reflection of the differences in wealth, power and status between Mexicans and Americans. This did not always result in overt hostility, and there were examples of some Imports developing good relationships with Mexican players. But these Anglos were the exception. For the most part, the Mexican players were resigned to cooperating on the field, and to responding to the Imports' rare off-field offers of friendship. 'What the Mexican players hope is that some of the Imports will get over their initial contempt [of] the league or the country (as in comments such as, "Baseball-wise, this is the land of the lost," or "I can't believe I'm in this horseshit country,") and develop a limited sense of camaraderie' (Klein 1997: 207).

One of the barriers to closer ties was ironically divergent understandings of masculinity. Both groups displayed similar behaviour, especially in regard to women, drink and competition. But the machismo of the Mexican players was more subtle than the stereotypes led the Imports to expect. Mexican players were kind and gentle with their fans and children, much like the American players themselves, but feelings of affection were often expressed in ways which Klein (1997: 158–65) claims reveal a deep-seated cultural divide between the two groups. According to Klein, the Mexican players expressed their emotions more easily than Imports, and this clearly set them apart from each other. This was particularly obvious when team mates expressed support and affection for one another. Mexican players held each other round the waist, stroked each other's hair, or leaned against each other while watching the game (1997: 165–9), behaviour which some of the Imports found disturbing. As one related, 'I can't get behind that kinda thing. I mean I can bear hug a guy or "five" him or "mosh" [mutual chest bump] a guy, but these [Mexican] guys. I don't know it's different. They put their arms around each other and leave 'em there, man' (Klein 1997: 167).

National divergence over the cultural construction of power also affected the team through the actions of the owners, who treated their players, fans and host communities with haughty disdain. They seemed to favour deals with American major league clubs and Anglo players over local, home-grown talent. As a result, the crowds on both sides of the river stayed away in the 1994 season, making it all but impossible for this binational experiment to continue. It had become an uncomfortable mixture of two national traditions, uneasily set down in the border region. By its failure to integrate American and Mexican ways of playing baseball, it could not adequately represent the Laredoan border culture, which for hundreds of years had evolved into a true transnational arrangement.

In the case of the Tecos, the binational arrangement between two towns and countries could not succeed because of the forces of nationalism, class, status and power which set Mexico off from the US. This can be clearly seen by comparing both cities to their respective 'national' hinterlands. Nuevo Laredo is a wealthy industrial zone compared to its neighbouring regions of Mexico to the south, while Laredo compares poorly to the cities and counties of Texas further north. But when compared to each other, Laredo is better developed and more prosperous than its twin across the river (Klein 1997: 229–30). Their relationship to each other is mediated by a multitude of regional and national economic and political forces in each of their respective countries. The pressures to build binational structures, to bring the two countries closer together, also functions to sustain nationalist (in Klein's terms, autonationalist) behaviours and beliefs, thus putting more pressure on the various transnationalist border cultures all along the 2000-mile Mexican–American divide. The Mexican players on the Tecos team do not seem to perceive baseball as a solely American (i.e. US) sport, regardless of its claim to be the 'national pastime'. But the sport itself could not transcend the national divisions which still seek to separate nations and states at their borders. In the case of baseball and the two Laredos, this experiment in equality could not extend the border corridor between the US and Mexico any farther into either state.

Rituals of Hierarchy

Many international borders are characterised by hierarchical social and political relations, which are often discussed in terms of minority and majority rights, wants and needs. But such terms as minority and majority are always situational and relative. All states have majority nations. In fact, the preponderance of states proffer a self-image of national homogeneity, part of the 'great fiction' of nation-statehood. People who are members of a national majority in one state are often members of minority nations in some other majority's nation-state. Nationalist Irish in Northern Ireland may be outnumbered in the United Kingdom, but they have only to look across the border to 'their' nation's state. Similarly, the Muslims of Melilla, regardless of their allegiances and citizenship, either are, or are seen by the Spanish to be, allies to their co-religionists and co-ethnics in Morocco. The Catholics of Melilla, on the other hand, utilise rituals as a bulwark against the encroachments of the Moroccan nation and state, which they see as symbols of Africa and barbarism, thereby sustaining the port as an island of Spanish imperial territory and a haven of Spanishness.

The rituals of hierarchy are not always symbols of power, however. They may act as rituals of self-deception. In this regard, the Spanish Catholics of Melilla have much in common with many other frontier populations throughout the world. In their case, they are the majority in their city, but a Spanish minority increasingly alienated from their Spanish homeland (in ways reminiscent of the developing relationship between Northern Irish Loyalists and the British 'mainland'). The Rif is no longer the periphery of Melilla. On the contrary, this vestige of the Spanish empire has become the periphery of two states, a liminal marketplace for the consumption of goods and images caught between Morocco and Spain, and between their respective historical constructions.

Rituals and symbols do more than stake claims to power, or hide the position of powerlessness which some ethnic minorities experience. Symbols of cooperation and integration are often used to disguise hierarchies of power. In the two Laredos, the attempt of a sports franchise to transcend nationalist barriers through its appeal to the spirit of binationalism and transnationalism failed because of the underlying differentials between the players, between the players and the owners, and between the border towns and their respective countries.

This chapter has reviewed a number of cases in which symbols and rituals encode relations within and between ethnic groups and nations at international borders. These ritualised and symbolic actions are by no means the only way in which ethnic entities interact, nor are they always the principal means by which ethnic and national groups establish meaningful relationships. But political symbols and rituals are always part of the hierarchical relations between ethnic groups and their states, and between ethnic groups across state borders. Anthropologists have been at the forefront of the analysis of the symbols which construct the cultures of the world, and the ethnographies discussed above highlight ways in which such studies can aid our general understanding of how culture transcends borders, and how certain border communities sustain a variety of relationships with other people and institutions further afield, in their own and in neighbouring states. In these case studies it is clear that border populations have great difficulty influencing let alone transforming their nations and states. But they do try, and some succeed. One way has been through the economic subversion of the state and its policies at international borders.

–5–

The Subversive Economy

A frontier dweller's political loyalty to his own country may . . . be emphatically modified by his economic self-interest in illegal dealings with the foreigners across the border. Moreover while the motive is economic the activities cannot be limited to the economic. They inevitably set up their own nexus of social contact and joint interest. Men of both border populations, working together in this way, become a 'we' group to whom others of their own nationality, and especially the authorities, are 'they'.

Lattimore, 'The Frontier in History'

It is something of a truism to claim that borders unite as well as divide, and that their existence as barriers to movement can simultaneously create reasons to cross them. Though the rigour with which different borders are policed can make them more or less difficult to cross, the imbalance between the opportunities which may exist on either side can create compelling reasons to try. Indeed, the realities of everyday life for those who live at the border often pay scant regard to the fact that borders principally exist to demarcate political space in and out of which the flow of people and goods is controlled. Barriers they may be, but as anyone returning from abroad and claiming their duty-free allowance of alcohol and tobacco knows, borders create their own special opportunities. In this chapter we examine some ways in which those who live at borders attempt to exploit this unique locational ambiguity by building their lives and livelihoods around the particular resource which borders offer. Specifically, we focus on activities which are generally defined by the state as 'illegal', though they are not always so regarded by those directly involved. We defer consideration of legal economic activity, such as consumer shopping, and its role in the construction and negotiation of the border until chapter six.

Anthropologists are no strangers to the study of illegal and semi-legal economic activity, which they have usually researched under the heading of the 'informal', 'black', 'hidden' or 'shadow' economy (see, for instance, Henry 1978; Mars 1983). Such 'second' economies are generally held to thrive on the margins of mainstream economic life, though should not be seen as separate from it, sometimes preying parasitically on the official economy and other times contributing to its effective operation by ensuring that the jobs which no one else wants are effectively carried out. MacGaffey's definition perhaps best encompasses the kinds of activity we consider in this chapter: 'a highly organized system of income-generating activities that deprive the state of taxation and foreign exchange . . . Some of these activities are illegal, others are legitimate in themselves but carried out in a manner that avoids taxation' (1988: 168, cited in Flynn 1997: 324; see also Evers 1991).

Three main types of activity occupy our attention: prostitution, the passage of undocumented migrant labour, and smuggling. By referring to these activities as a 'subversive economy', however, we do not mean merely to suggest that by being illegal they fail to contribute to, or wish somehow to 'cheat', the national economy. As politicians and others are often quick to point out in relation to such activities, revenue may be lost through tax evasion, by the siphoning of income outside the state, and by occupying state resources in costly surveillance operations. Though this is often true, such activities can also make a recognisable and valued contribution to the wider economy, and, like other aspects of the 'informal' and 'black' economies located elsewhere in the state, may smooth the workings of the system by offering employment where otherwise there may be very little (see, for instance, Birkbeck 1979; Okely 1983: chapt. 4).

Rather, and at the risk of exaggeration, we will suggest that such activities threaten to subvert state institutions by compromising the ability of these institutions to control their self-defined domain. Such activities do not play by state rules. They ignore, contest and subvert state power. They challenge state attempts to control the behaviour of its citizens and subjects, to impose a morality, to regulate the movement of people and flow of commodities, and to define what are and what are not marketable goods. They sometimes force the state to rethink and change its policies. Though doubly peripheralised by being on the margins of the economy as well as on the edges of the state, border prostitution, undocumented migration and smuggling strike at the centre of political power, flouting state authority and even threatening to undermine it. At the same time, however, they are rarely revolutionary. Smugglers, prostitutes and migrants do not seek to overthrow the state, since in some sense their existence depends upon it and, in particular, on the borders which the state seeks to establish and uphold. Without these borders they could not sustain viable and profitable enterprises. These activities at the edges of the nation-state, like those already examined in chapter four, offer a fruitful perspective from which to view the shaping of the state itself. Furthermore, illicit activities at the furthermost reaches of the domain of the state also give shape to the meanings and symbols of national culture, both in the lives of borderlanders and among others in their respective nations.

Border Livelihoods in Wider Context

Obviously the state and its borders are continually being shaped by many forces, and any consideration of border livelihoods must be understood within this wider context. Many of the world's borders are today in the process of being transformed in response to the globalisation of culture and economics, a theme to which we return in the next chapter. Some of these global forces have been set in motion as a result of a deliberate and conscious restructuring of the political economy of states and regions, as in the setting up of supranational bodies like the European Union and continental free-trade zones such as the North American Free Trade Area, or have emerged as a consequence of the pursuit of profit, as in the growth of transnational corporations. Other forces too have been set in chain by these developments, such as international labour migration, where the outcome of global economic restructuring is economic dislocation and a flight across borders in search of a better life (see chapter six).[1]

Of course, the boundaries of nation-states have always been partly shaped by the dynamics of global economic integration. It would be historically naive to ignore the role played in the developing world economy by the early voyages of 'discovery', and later, in the eighteenth and nineteenth centuries, by the imperial powers. The world was quickly carved up into discrete geographical units whose boundaries were guaranteed by, and whose resources 'belonged' to, whichever European colonial power could enforce its claim to them. The result was a number of imperial economies, like that of the British Empire, within which goods and personnel moved around the globe with less regard for the empire's internal national boundaries than for where the next pound could be made. Today's economy may be characterised by vast differences in scale, by a global, round-the-clock money market, and by the speed with which commodities can be transacted and transported, but the essential features which permitted these contemporary developments to occur were established well over a century ago.

But if the boundaries of the nation-state have been shaped by the forces of global economic integration, they have also been shaped, less obviously perhaps, by the illicit activities which at once exist because of the state border and give borders their raison d'être. In this chapter, we consider the three illicit activities already mentioned, namely cross-border prostitution, illicit trade and the undocumented cross-border passage of labour, in order to show how a variety of border cultures gain their lifeblood from borders, while ironically providing sustenance to those state structures, like the police, army and immigration authorities, whose task it is to make their borders less penetrable in the political and economic interests of the state.

1. These forces clearly do not affect all parts of the globe in equal measure. Free trade, for instance, while nominally reducing the role of borders as barriers to commerce, is arguably managed to favour the richer countries, and though offered as the solution to the economic problems of less developed countries has often had an economically devastating impact on them (O'Hearn 1994). Moreover, the unevenness of migrant population flows is most acutely evident at the borders separating the West from the Third World, as we consider in chapter six in relation to the US–Mexico border.

Smuggling, prostitution and undocumented cross-border labour have been largely written out of scholarly views of the state, perhaps because of their perceived small scale or the difficulties of studying something which the state labels 'illegal', or because of their relative and inherent 'invisibility'. Yet such activities are of historical and contemporary significance in shaping borders and in structuring relationships between citizens and state. The perspective of those involved in these activities, which might be characterised as a 'view from below', has too often been obscured in accounts which privilege the influence of corporate capitalism in defining the state and its limits. Free trade agreements may have opened up borders for the corporate bodies in whose interests such agreements have been fashioned, but many outside this mercantile elite pursue livelihoods which have long depended on finding other ways to transcend the limits of the state. Analyses of border economics which focus on statistics and development curves, imports and exports, planned development, the injection of capital, and the 'creation' of jobs rarely have room for such bottom-up perspectives. It has been left largely to anthropologists to fill this gap, even if they too have sometimes done less than they might.

Border Economies

Anthropologists have seldom had much to say about economic life at international borders. Paradoxically, despite their long-standing fascination with the liminal, anthropologists have been historically most comfortable when dealing with cultural and social 'wholes', and were often only too ready to let the political borders of the state bound their community study for them. Where anthropologists did trace ties beyond the local community, they rarely pursued them much beyond ties to regional or national elites. At least until the 1960s, anthropologists were consequently little interested in economic relationships beyond those of the locality they were studying.

Those who carried out research alongside state borders were obviously less able than their colleagues who worked in the interior to ignore the fact that economic relationships did not always conveniently stop at state borders. Increasing interest in international labour migration and the realisation that this required study of both ends of the migratory chain similarly made it more difficult to ignore economic ties which stretched far beyond a particular locality. Likewise, those who worked with nomadic populations whose livelihoods depended upon crossing state lines and exploiting differential economic opportunities on either side similarly realised the inadequacy of bounding the economy according to lines drawn on a map (see, for instance, Tapper 1997). Nevertheless, despite the mention of some cross-border economic connections, the border itself was more rarely problematised or made the focus in these analyses.

This is not to say that anthropologists have been unaware of the fact that borders create their own special kinds of opportunities for informal commerce and illicit economic dealing. Indeed, their methods of working uniquely equip anthropologists for the study of such activities, which are often accessible only to researchers willing to stick around and win the confidence of those engaged in such pursuits. Anthropological methods of participatory involvement – which in this context can obviously raise ethical dilemmas of a sort – and long-term residential field research are ideal for exploring those elements of the border economy to which other disciplines have no ready or appropriate methodological access or which their theoretical models fail to encompass. As we now consider, anthropologists have thus been rather better than most at exposing the border's economic underworld and at insinuating themselves into those cracks and crevices where economic pursuits of an informal and unofficial kind are likely to flourish.

Sex for Sale South of the Border

For hundreds of German men who drive across the border each week, the E55 motorway, between Dresden and the Czech town of Teplice, is a glorious gateway to cheap, anonymous sex. Dozens of women line the road on the Czech side of the border, dressed in cleavage-hugging t-shirts and the tiniest of hotpants. They scurry across to every car that stops, peering in the window, flashing a knowing smile and flirting in faltering German. At £15 a time, sex south of the border is less than half the price charged by German prostitutes. Besides, the Czech, Slovak, Bulgarian and Romanian girls, many of whom are still in their mid-teens, are much more biddable than their professional colleagues to the north. For an extra £5, most will agree to risk HIV infection by having sex without a condom. Many are happy to indulge customers' bizarre fantasies for a similar supplement (*The Irish Times*, 27 July 1996).

Border zones have been widely reported as providing opportunities for illicit sex. Indeed, fiction and film have made the image of seeking sexual licence across state lines something of a stereotype. From the lyrical innocence of 'South of the border, down Mexico way', which invites us to find true love by crossing state lines, to Thelma and Louise's fatal leap in pursuit of another kind of boundary-crossing, 'the border' as metaphor is variously massaged by popular culture to invoke a range of potentially transformative (often sexual) experiences and life-cycle transitions. Thus the state border has been used as a dramatic device to underwrite the passage from childhood to puberty, from youth to adulthood (usually from boyhood to manhood), and from 'conventional' to 'liberating' sexual practices (including adultery and prostitution). In each of these cases, crossing state borders stands as an image for, and holds out the promise of, border crossings of a sexually emancipatory kind. Once across the border and safe from whatever regulatory controls normally constrain us, such popular narratives seem to suggest, we open ourselves to the possibility of sexual discovery. It would be unfortunate, however, if in the over-fanciful metaphorical tangle which sometimes can characterise fictional accounts, the border became merely a convenient idiom in which to talk about sexual freedom, for we would risk losing sight of something which as ethnographers we would like to highlight, namely, the relationship between the state and those elements of a localised border economy – in this case marketing sex – which seek to operate outside and beyond the state.

Although some scholars have argued that prostitution 'thrives in places like border cities where language and cultural differences foster impersonality and contempt between the adjacent societies' (Price 1973: 94), and that 'vice is usually found in large doses in border areas and ports throughout the world' (Martínez 1988: 11), the reality is inevitably more complex than such generalisations imply. Prostitution is not found at all borders, nor, of course, is it found only at borders. Many factors can contribute to its presence or absence, among them its legality or illegality in the states concerned, the ability or willingness to enforce legislation, and the moral voice of the wider society. Labour market conditions obviously play a major part, with prostitution ubiquitous along those borders which separate states where the economic imbalance and differential standards of living are particularly marked. Where scarcity or non-existence of jobs, poorly paid employment, and limited openings for the unskilled are juxtaposed with easily accessible and comparatively prosperous potential clients, prostitution seems to flourish.

There are many such examples in the ethnographic and popular record. In some cases the disjuncture is between a comparatively stable economy and one characterised by collapse or transformation. The borders between former Western- and Eastern-bloc countries in Europe are a case in point here, as the E55 motorway, or 'Street of Shame', at the German-Czech border illustrates, and as Hann and Bellér-Hann's (1998) account of prostitution on the border between north-eastern Turkey and the former Soviet socialist republic of Georgia also testifies (see also Hann and Hann 1992). Taking advantage of the opening up of this corner of Turkey, 'some highly conspicuous foreign women, often exaggerating their distinctiveness through their clothes, hair styles and the use of make-up . . . cash in on opportunities to provide services for which men previously had to travel as far afield as Ankara' (Hann and Bellér-Hann 1998: 250). Such women hang around in the *gazinos*, small bars selling alcohol and offering entertainment, and when propositioned might open the bidding at one million Turkish *lira* before settling for much less in a bargaining process that recalls the new marketplace that has similarly sprung up with the opening of the border.

In other cases the disjuncture may be between a developing economy and one in the process of recovery from the ravages of war, a disjuncture which, as French (1996) describes, the Cambodian prostitutes who solicit Thai clients have had no choice but to exploit. Thai men cross the border in groups, wading through lanes ankle-deep in mud, to reach a Cambodian market renowned for its prostitutes, and whose presence there is locally advertised by a checkpoint sign warning of the risk of contracting AIDS. And in yet other cases, prostitutes may exploit the economic disparities in the frontier between developing and developed economies, as is the case between Morocco and Spain (Driessen 1992: 182–8), at the town of Maputo between Mozambique and South Africa (Gordimer 1990: 73–4), and, most notoriously and widely known, between Mexico and its powerful neighbour to the north.

The US–Mexico border (see map 4.3), like many in the world today, has been made infamous for its decadence and vice. At least this is the way it has been depicted by many purveyors of popular culture, who represent the area as a zone of seedy bars, available women and degenerate men. Somewhat sensationally described as a 'sixteen-hundred-mile pleasure strip measurably oriented to gringos with low libidinal thresholds' (Demaris 1970: 4)[2], the US–Mexico border throughout the twentieth century has been widely presented as a source of sexual thrills. A number of authors have made their reputations by writing lurid and deliberately exaggerated accounts which have stimulated voyeuristic titillation in some and provoked indignant and outraged offence in others. Among the best known of such tabloid-style accounts is that by Ovid Demaris, and though his account of border night life, ironically titled *Poso del Mundo* ('The Sink of the World'), perhaps tells us more about the wild imaginings of the author than it does about the border, it nevertheless reveals the almost mythical status that border sexuality has acquired in popular culture (see also Frost 1983).

Not surprisingly, the work of social scientists largely avoids such unrestrained fantasies, though it too has documented the well-organised and widespread availability of prostitution and 'adult entertainment' in the Mexican towns and cities which border on the US. What their accounts reveal is a highly structured and profitable business, one in which to varying degrees the state itself and its agents have been implicated. Two main kinds of prostitute are usually identified: the 'freelancers' or *clandestinas* who work solely for themselves and the *ficheras* who work for a particular bar and who are entitled to a percentage of the income from the drinks patrons are encouraged to purchase. Bars which provide prostitution are themselves of a number of types and may be variously classified according to the arrangement which they have with the prostitutes who work for them (see Roebuck and McNamara 1973), as well as by their clientele and geographical location. Historically, the first *zonas de tolerancia*, as the areas given over to prostitution are known, developed in or near the commercial centres of the border towns themselves, often in close proximity to, or on the margins of, the major traditional tourist haunts, as with the Zona Norte in Tijuana. As efforts to attract a different

---

2. Elsewhere the length of the US–Mexico border is variously given as 'over 2,500 miles long' (Price 1971: 36), as 'approximately two-thousand-mile[s]' (Stoddard 1983b: 211), and as '1951.36 miles' (Arreola and Curtis 1993: 192).

kind of tourist grew, many of these *zonas* were allowed to decay, or were removed altogether. In many cases the action simply shifted elsewhere, often to the edge of town, to the kind of site known to geographers as 'disamenity areas', areas difficult to reach and flanked by industrial estates, railways or low-income housing. Frequently referred to as 'boys' towns', or in one instance as the 'bull pen', these *zonas* are purpose-built with a range of bars and other facilities within a walled enclosure, access to which is controlled by strict policing of a single entrance. Within the enclosure itself, prostitutes and establishments are hierarchically ranked, largely on the basis of cost and perceived desirability to potential clients, with the least attractive women consigned to the rear of the compound where business is transacted in tiny cabins or 'cribs' that open directly on to the street. *Zonas* can be ethnically segregated, catering mainly either for Mexican or American clientele, or for black Americans and white Americans, and may also be segregated depending on the type of sex on offer .

From the very start the US and Mexican governments played a part in the development of border prostitution, both indirectly by facilitating the conditions under which it was able to flourish, and more directly by the interest which they eventually took or failed to take in its regulation. The American military is some-times credited with introducing the idea of out-of-town *zonas* in the first place, when, during the occupation of Chihuahua in 1916, General Pershing set up restricted areas for prostitution in an effort to control the spread of veneral disease among his troops, an innovation which provoked surprisingly little public outcry given the moral reform then sweeping the US (see Sandos 1980). Indeed, it was this spirit of moral reform and the resulting introduction of Prohibition in 1918 that forced most of the south-west's 'merchants of sin' (Martínez 1988: 114) to relocate across the border to Mexico where, in the wake of widespread economic depression and the border cities' loss of free-zone status, they found a willing welcome for any enterprise that might attract American dollars (Curtis and Arreola 1991: 340–1; Price 1973: 50–1). Switching jurisdictions – which often involved only a short bus ride – could thus render the illegal legal, and even when it did not, as one Mexican wryly observed, the visitors from the north 'would rather break our laws than their own' (cited in Demaris 1970: 5). Thus began those early border city boom years under American management which persisted until the end of Prohibition in 1933, and which were continually castigated by fundamentalist opinion for, in the words of one Episcopalian pastor in California, 'casting a foul stench' across the border to the north (cited in Machado 1982: 350).

The 1940s and 1950s saw another cycle of prosperity for those involved in organised prostitution, now chiefly in Mexican hands, with a new and ready market in the thousands of American servicemen from the massive military bases just to the north. Once again the economy was booming, with prostitutes among the highest paid women in border areas, and prostitution being used by some as a means of supplementing income from other more recent sources of employment such as factory (*maquiladora*) work (Fernández-Kelly 1983: 142–4; McNamara 1971: 7; Price 1973: 94). With large sums of money changing hands, the state and municipality sought to extract their cut by maintaining various ways of 'tracking' prostitutes in order to tax them; by imposing a levy on the bars from which they worked and by requiring registration with the Sanidad or Health Department, to which each registered prostitute or 'clean girl' (*penicillino*) had to pay a fee (McNamara 1971: 14; Roebuck and McNamara 1973: 242).[3]

By the late 1950s prostitution topped 'the list of income-producing services' in the border region and generated almost a million dollars annually for one municipality, nearly half the city's income (Christian 1961: 60–1, cited in Roebuck and McNamara 1973: 232). Moreover, untold sums were pocketed as *mordida* or bribes by members of the police and municipal bureaucracy who, paradoxically, harassed the only prostitutes operating within the law – the *clandestinas* who worked the streets rather than the bars. Complicity between illegal organised prostitution and the state thus operated at individual as well as institutional level in a lucrative economy whose pay-offs were so great that, in the words of one official in Tijuana, 'we must keep one eye closed' (cited in Arreola and Curtis 1993: 105). While who gets how much from whom – 'from bartender to bar owner to police to municipal authorities' (McNamara 1971: 18) – is one of the most difficult questions to answer in this context, it is clear that the illicit trade in sex has been and remains central to the border economy.

It is in this sense that prostitution could be said to be part of a subversive economy. In addition to the uncounted millions lost to the state by laundering through unofficial and unregulated channels, attempts to 'clean up' the area and eliminate corruption are persistently compromised by a dependency on the income from the very activities which the Mexican government's Programa Nacional Fronterizo has sought to eradicate since the early 1960s. State attempts to shut down the *zonas* are frequently short-lived, as in Reynosa where the *zona* was closed as a result of anti-prostitution electioneering, but subsequently reopened to become one of the largest in the region (Curtis and Arreola 1991: 334). In short, ridding the border cities of prostitution is highly problematic 'because of the considerable financial returns that such activities provide both legally through taxes, official fees, and personal income as well as illicitly through various forms of corruption' (Arreola and Curtis 1993: 106).

We have seen that the involvement and connivance of the state in organised prostitution has a historical basis at the US–Mexico border. Ethnographic and historical accounts allow us to glimpse the relationship between the state and this

---

3. Prostitution itself is not illegal, but federal law prohibits pimping, i.e. the procurement of prostitutes for others (see Price 1973: 92).

aspect of the border economy; specifically, they enable us to identify how the regulatory power of the state can be both compromised and evaded in a border region, not only in the state within whose territory the illegal activities occur, but also in the neighbouring state. Similar contradictory and potentially subversive processes can be discerned in the cross-border movement of people and in the attempts to constrain them, as we examine in the following section.

Undocumented Workers and 'Illegal Aliens'

Julian Samora (1971) begins his classic account of undocumented migration from Mexico to the US with a detailed description of forty-six Mexicans who in 1968 attempted to reach Chicago by way of San Antonio. Concealed in the back of a locked U-Haul truck having crossed the Rio Grande on foot, they reached San Antonio dazed and gasping for air, only to be apprehended by the police within hours of arrival. Thirteen of them were taken to hospital where three died. Of the remainder, twenty-three were immediately returned to Mexico and twenty held as witnesses in the case, which ultimately resulted in the indictment of the three smugglers involved.

Much of the 'illegal' human traffic enters the US by similar means and often with similar results. Some come concealed in trucks as in the case above, others hidden in tankers with false bottoms, in refrigerated lorries, or in the boot or even under the bonnet of private cars. Estimates inevitably vary as to the volume of this traffic. One estimate suggests that between 1939 and 1973 the nine million undocumented Mexicans caught and deported constituted only 30 per cent of those who had crossed and escaped detection (Ross 1978: 12). Indeed, much of the large literature on the topic adopts an economic or political perspective devoted precisely to determining just what numbers are involved and to considering the potential public-policy implications and legislative reform which are required by way of response (for a useful overview see Stoddard 1983a). Anthropologists too have been involved in debating these issues, extending the discussion to a consideration of the human rights violations and exploitation which such undocumented and 'hidden' populations frequently experience by virtue of the fact that they must live outside and thus beyond the protection of the law (see, for instance, Weaver 1988; see also chapter six).

However, as one might expect, anthropologists have been more generally concerned to document the social organisational aspects of this migration, as well as the patterns of adjustment and cultural strategies pursued when these workers reach the north. Drawing on life history material in addition to ethnographic field research, this work has emphasised the complex character of this population flow and has helped scholars to move beyond over-mechanical push–pull models of migration with their tendency to reify the border and flatten out the many differences among those Mexicans who seek work by crossing to the US. Ellwyn Stoddard (1983a: 204), for example, points out that however distinct the categories of legal and illegal immigration may appear on paper, in reality they are not always so easy to separate. Consequently, he suggests, it makes much more sense to think in terms of 'degrees of legality'. He therefore distinguishes between four different types of illegal entrant which he refers to as the 'thrill-seeker', the 'criminal', the 'pre-citizen' and the 'economic refugee' (Stoddard 1976: 188–92). The latter are the most numerous in the US and can again be usefully sub-divided, Stoddard argues, into those who seek agricultural work along the border and those who find employment further north.

Many of those who cross the border without documentation find work in the large agri-businesses along the border itself. This both facilitates relatively easy movement back and forth across the border for those who possess forged documents and can take advantage of seasonal fluctuations in demand, as well as providing an intermediary staging post and zone of socialisation for those unfamiliar with life in the US. Stoddard suggests that the process of learning to be an 'American' begins almost immediately, with the shedding of traditional Mexican garb for the blue jeans and straw hat of the agricultural labourer in the southwest, the apprenticeship continuing with the acquisition of a few phrases in English and the ability to offer false personal details or adopt other strategies of concealment if challenged by the US Immigration authorities.

Ethnographic research has also shown the inadequacies of viewing undocumented migration from a single-sided approach, one which denies or plays down the many similarities and interdependencies which characterise those who live and work on opposite sides of the 'Tortilla Curtain'. Basing her conclusions on fieldwork carried out in the borderlands between San Antonio and Houston to the north and Monterrey and Matamoros to the south, Whiteford (1979) argues that illegal (and legal) migration is best understood as functioning within an 'extended community' which transcends the border itself, and within which people occupy differential roles as if the US and Mexico formed a single regional economic system. People's economic strategies and the resources on which they draw would differ markedly, she claims, if the border were *not* there. By viewing the border as a 'semi-permeable membrane which provides differential access to certain categories of goods, services, and people, we move away from stereotyping the border and begin to appreciate the diversity and complexity of strategies employed by different groups of residents' (Whiteford 1979: 134), a perspective which clearly echoes and builds upon the position argued by Stoddard.

It has been largely left to anthropologists, therefore, to document at local level what has long been recognised in a general sense: the mutual interdependency of economic actors on either side of the border and the contradictions to which this can give rise. Critics have often identified an ambivalence in US policy towards undocumented labour, pointing out that political pressure from contradictory interest groups such as farmers seeking cheap labour on the one hand and employment unions striving to protect jobs for locals on the other has forced an uneasy course between ignoring illegal migration and taking action to prevent it (see, for instance, Ross 1978: 14). Despite public policies which proclaim the contrary, the practice of immigration control along the border to some extent strategically and cyclically permits undocumented entry in response to the political and economic realities of the American south-west. In short, continuing budgetary support for the service immigration control offers depends in part on a publicly acceptable head-count of arrests, while at the same time maintaining local political and electoral approval requires meeting the needs of those powerful agriculturalists whose profits rely on extracting cheap labour from those whose reproductive costs are met elsewhere.

Anthropologists have perhaps done more than most to demonstrate how this tension is played out in everyday life at the border. Stoddard (1976: 195–203) has argued that legislative reform is unlikely to make a substantial difference to illegal migration, given that the latter is so deeply embedded in the wider economic and social structures of the region, and given the protective and supportive role that legitimate institutions on the US side, such as family and friends, farm owners, local communities and churches, offer the undocumented worker. More surprising, perhaps, is the implicit support of border control agencies. In order to avoid alienating local good will, the operations of the Immigration and Naturalization Service's Border Patrol are directed 'against the unemployed, transient ["illegal Mexican alien"] in systematic deliberate campaigns while an *implicit code* . . . gives adequate warning and means of concealment' for those undocumented labourers who constitute agribusiness's permanent workforce (Stoddard 1976: 200, emphasis added). Other government services, like the social security office, also informally support the use of undocumented labour for similar reasons.

The tension is also evident within the US Immigration and Naturalization Service itself, which in its public pronouncements clearly regards illegal migrants as a drain on the national economy:

> They are occupying jobs that are needed by unemployed citizens. They are not paying their share of taxes, and often pay none at all. At the same time they are using public services, educating their children in our schools, and often collecting welfare and even unemployment payments. Unless adequate resources and legislation are forthcoming immediately, the flood of illegal entries we are now experiencing will become a torrent (former Immigration and Naturalization Commissioner, cited in Ross 1978: 13).

This view is shared by many in the US (see Martínez 1988: 135) but for members of the Border Patrol such calls to halt the 'alien invasion' sit uneasily with 'verbal restraints from upstairs' (Stoddard 1976: 200). Though existing to prevent illegal entry to the US, the immigration authorities' public goal is routinely subverted in the daily practice of those officials employed to implement it, as Stoddard's (1976) study suggests. In a richly documented account which greatly extends this line of argument, Heyman (1995: 261) shows how the worldview and praxis of agents of the immigration service give 'cohesion to a contradictory policy that balances publicly visible arrests and invisible but effective perpetuation of undocumented labour migration'. According to Heyman, a tacit policy (like Stoddard's 'implicit code') of encouraging illegal entrants to return voluntarily to Mexico offers a cheap alternative to expensive detention, trial and deportation. In 1989, 87 per cent of those apprehended were allowed to depart voluntarily by being released into Mexico at the US border, in the knowledge that many of them would subsequently and perhaps successfully attempt to re-enter in a self-perpetuating cycle of voluntary departure and return. The trick, or 'thought-work' in Heyman's terms, which Border Patrol agents must master in order successfully and reliably to select illegal migrants for this treatment involves distinguishing 'illegal but honest workers' from 'immoral drug and alien smugglers' (a bureaucratic procedure which recalls the distinction between 'deserving' and 'undeserving' welfare claimants in British social security offices; see Howe 1985). By this policy, the US government 'at once arrests many persons, thereby enforcing the state idea of bounded citizenship . . . for media sale and consumption . . . and negates the effectiveness of these arrests' (Heyman 1995: 267).

Once again, then, we see the paradoxes confronted by the state in dealing with an aspect of economic life at its borders. In the case of illegal migrants, publicly declared policy towards them is regularly subverted by the requirements of managing everyday political and economic realities and of addressing the disparity between how they are perceived in the local and national consciousness. As Kearney (1998a) has argued, the consequences are contradictory for both states involved, whose inability to define the legal and cultural identities of their border populations is revealed by the passage of these migrants. In short, the effect of undocumented migration across the US–Mexico border is to confront the state with the limits of its power.

The US–Mexico border may seem like a special case, and in some respects it is. But it is, of course, far from being the only border where such illegal activities are evident. The member states of the European Union have become increasingly forbidding doormen, jealously monitoring the Union's external borders against an alleged flood of would-be entrants from a range of politically turbulent and economically less developed countries as far flung as Romania, Nigeria and Morocco. A broadly similar situation to that at the US–Mexico border characterises the Mediterranean shores of Spain, where once again undocumented workers seek to cross a frontier at which the West and the Third World could be said to meet. According to Driessen (1998), Spain's historical record of the non-assimilation of minorities has made especially problematic the lives of the North African workers who clandestinely make the hazardous passage across the Strait of Gibraltar, only to encounter imprisonment, exclusion or the denial of citizenship when they reach the other side. This 'new immigration', as Driessen refers to it, has become a hotly contested local and national political issue, with fears expressed about threats to Spanish standards of living and xenophobic graffiti proclaiming 'Spanish people first' and 'Moors out' daubed on buildings in the Algeciras district (Driessen 1998: 105–6). These new immigrants tie up the resources of the state, evading arrest and remaining invisible to wider society. By definition, they must remain beyond the reaches of the law, thus forever testing the limits of the power of the state to monitor and control.

Driessen also draws attention to how different kinds of border crossings generate competing and contested images of this frontier. Viewed from Europe, southern Spain has long been seen as a gateway to the Orient, to the exotic and the primitive, and has been sold as such to the many day-trippers and shoppers who regularly make their way across the Strait, and whose encounters with the 'other' there confirm their own identity as Europeans. Viewed in the opposite direction, from the beaches of Morocco, the vision of an imaginary European paradise soon gives way to the realities of a life of squalid boarding houses, menial jobs and harassment from members of the public and the state authorities alike. This example clearly suggests that efforts to control borders operate not only at the politico-jural level of regulating population flows but also at the level of meaning construction, where the relatively benign interpretations of the border promulgated by the state are continually subverted by the experiences and understandings of subaltern groups who seek entry, understandings which, in turn, confront, if not yet transform, localised and historically sedimented conceptions of what it means to be part of the Spanish nation. Yet again, then, the limits of state power are exposed.

Smuggling and Illicit Trade

One can barely open a book about borders without finding at least passing reference to smuggling and the clandestine movement of people and goods from one side of the national boundary to the other. This is because smuggling and the border are to some extent defined in terms of each other. Whether at land borders, sea ports or other places of entry such as airports, borders exist at least partially to control the passage of goods from one political entity to another. Indeed, their effectiveness may be measured in terms of their ability to do just this. State institutions such as customs and excise agencies are established precisely to regulate and monitor this flow. Where they fail to do so, or where such control is weakened or removed, the practical and even symbolic significance of the border is correspondingly diminished, as has been the conscious policy of the European Union in its efforts to develop trade through the creation of an internally borderless Europe. This may have a knock-on effect on the state, as we consider later.

While borders are only partly defined by their function of regulating the flow of goods, the existence of a border is the very basis of smuggling. By definition smuggling depends on the presence of a border, and on what the state declares can be legally imported or exported. Imports and exports are rarely given equal weight in the practice of border control. The regulatory mechanisms at borders are directed mainly towards what can be brought into a country rather than to what can be taken out, though breaches in the latter may cause sporadic concern, as with leakages of 'intelligence' or the illegal export of arms. Scholars too have tended to pay more attention to the smuggling of goods into a country rather than out, particularly the smuggling of consumer goods and drugs, and this is reflected in the discussion which follows. What obviously makes such items attractive to the smuggler is their unavailability or illegality in the country into which they are smuggled, as well as opportunities for evading the trade tariffs on imports which borders are partially erected to extract. Without the imposition of tariffs on the free movement of goods, the smuggling of legally marketable commodities at least would cease to exist, since its chief purpose is the generation of profit by evading such barriers. The level and intensity of smuggling is thus highly susceptible to historical fluctuations in state-imposed tariff controls (on such fluctuations in the Basque Country, see Douglass 1977: 137–8; Leizaola 1996: 98–9).

Price (1973) has pointed out that smuggling is a crime against the state rather than a crime against individuals or their personal property. It arises not out of common law but from statute laws enacted by a legislative body. It is therefore unique, he suggests, to societies with state structures, and is not found in 'simpler forms of societies [which] lack the corporate and legal expression of societal self interest to build legal barriers against the flow of goods' (Price 1971: 29). Indeed, to refer to clandestine transborder trade as 'smuggling' risks adopting a statist perspective which may be at odds with the self-perceptions of those most closely involved, who often see their own activities as entirely legitimate (see Driessen n.d.: 10; Flynn 1997: 324). But if the advent of the state creates the crime of 'smuggling', it does so in ways which it is instructive to explore empirically in relation to the wider political context, as a window on 'the inner workings of states and their relations with neighbouring states' (van Schendel 1993: 189). Depending on how smuggling is managed locally, it may have differential impacts on the viability and stability of the state itself.

This can be clearly illustrated by a comparison of smuggling along Ghana's eastern frontier in the colonial and post-colonial periods (Nugent 1996: 55–60; n.d.). Like many of West Africa's colonially created boundaries, the Ghanaian border was remarkably porous (cf. Collins 1976 and 1984: 196 on the Niger–Nigeria border). Under the British colonial state, the increased opportunities for smuggling brought about by the transformation of the regional economy through the penetration of merchant capital were managed largely through a series of what Nugent refers to as ultimately pragmatic measures. Recognising from experience in other parts of the globe that stringent restrictions and the introduction of a prohibition on liquor would be likely merely to encourage smuggling and illicit distillation, the colonial administration sought instead to control its border populations by two related methods. First, by establishing a visible presence in the form of customs posts staffed by uniformed guards whose ostensible task was to monitor movement and collect revenue on the major routes from French Togoland into British territory, a task which, given the terrain, was always likely to meet with limited success. And secondly, through the imposition of fines of up to three times the value of any contraband seized. Since culprits were likely to go to court only if such fines remained unpaid, the objective here was the pragmatic one of discouraging smugglers by a financial disincentive rather than by criminalising them (Nugent n.d.: 7). The aim of having highly visible uniformed guards and the threat of financial penalties was therefore as much to convince smugglers that smuggling was simply not worth the risk as it was to convict them for having offended. Nugent tells us that customs officers themselves were never under any illusion about the effectiveness of these measures and recognised that they were much less in control of the situation than their officers sometimes liked to pretend. There was thus a pragmatic acceptance by the colonial authorities that a certain level of cross-border leakage was simply the price to be paid for bringing this region under colonial control (Nugent n.d.: 11). In fact, Nugent concludes, it was the continuing permeability of the eastern border under the colonial state which, paradoxically, 'helped to make it acceptable to the border communities themselves'.

Independence and the emergence of the post-colonial state saw a dramatic increase in opportunities for smuggling. Substantially higher prices for cocoa across the border in Togo were only one aspect of a deteriorating economy which made smuggling almost irresistable for Ghanaians, for many of whom it became the only means of acquiring even the most basic of consumer goods such as sugar and tinned fish. The state reacted to what it saw as a direct threat to the national economy and even to the very basis of its being by militarising the border and introducing ever tighter controls and penalties, the most draconian of which was the introduction in 1972 of the death sentence for anyone found guilty of smuggling timber, gold and diamonds. The smuggling of other goods was similarly subject to increasingly severe penalties with convicted cocoa smugglers liable to receive prison sentences of anything between fifteen and thirty years. Despite these measures, as Nugent shows, the overall level of smuggling continued to rise at every level, from what one border guard colourfully described as the 'armpit smuggling' of small items for personal use to the organised and professional smuggling of huge quantities of goods, a trade in which many border guards themselves, some allegedly at the highest level of the service, became implicated in an effort to supplement their incomes. The authorities now recognised that smuggling was no longer just a personal economic act, but had become a kind of secessionist activity which jeopardised the nation's integrity: 'smuggling activities along the borders of Ghana, and into and from Ghana is [sic] centrally organised, planned, co-ordinated, directed and financed by the Togo Government against Ghana. This is a fact. It is sad and unfortunate that some Ghanaians are being used as front men' (head of border guards in 1977, cited in Nugent n.d.: 15). These anxieties proved well-founded. The visible failure of draconian border policies and the growing allegations of corruption among the military and state officials did indeed ultimately contribute to the complete collapse of the Ghanaian state in 1979 and the outbreak of revolution in 1982, events which led the succeeding regime to realise that its only practical alternative was a return to the *modus vivendi* with border communities of the kind pursued in the colonial period.

This example of how illicit cross-border trade can undermine and even overturn the workings of the state is not an isolated case. Elsewhere in Africa, residents at the Bénin–Nigeria border have forged a new identity for themselves as border-landers, an identity based on shared economic interests in mediating cross-border commerce and one which cross-cuts local ethnic and national allegiances (Flynn 1997). In response to wider economic changes and increasing encroachment by the Nigerian and Béninois governments, these border residents have emphasised their common interest in transborder trade as one means of expressing the boundary between themselves and the state. 'By exacting their own controls on goods and people who cross the border within their transnational territory, border residents defiantly assert their independence from state structures' in a manner that clearly brings them into conflict with those structures (Flynn 1997: 320). As a consequence, relations with the local agents of the state, the border guards and customs officials, are necessarily ambivalent. While the presence of these officials is resented, their goodwill must be nurtured if the cross-border traffic is to continue, a contradiction which can only be managed by enlisting their complicity (through bribes and other favours) or by the clandestine movement of goods. Either course results in the subversion of state structures, and a sense among borderlanders of increasing detachment from the central government. This in itself is not unusual. On the Caribbean island of Grenada, for instance, smuggling is no longer just the only way to 'beat the system', but has become an explicitly political act, and a means of expressing opposition to what is seen as an elitist and malignant regime (Tobias 1982: 393–4). What is particularly striking about the Bénin–Nigeria case, however, is the potency of the binational border identity which has emerged, and which is expressed in the claim that 'we are the border' (something in marked contrast to the Tecos described in the last chapter). Anyone who breaks rank by passing information to customs officials is vigorously denounced as a 'traitor', further strengthening the boundaries between border and state (Flynn 1997: 325).

Similar ambivalences and subversions are also evident among the smugglers who ply their small craft across the River Ganges between Bangladesh and West Bengal. While there were differences in the relations between smugglers and border guards on each side of the river, mainly to do with whether or not the border guards were recruited locally, the relationship was generally 'based on protection: the border guards guaranteed the uninterrupted operation of cross-border trading in exchange for a fixed share of the proceeds . . . and were also instrumental in creating and legitimising [smuggler] leaders' (van Schendel 1993: 194-5). Although this relationship was fragile and full of circumspection, there was a recognition by both parties that each could not exist without the other. Significantly, however, the border guards were the more dependent party, not least because they relied on pay-offs from smugglers to supplement their income, a fact not lost on the smugglers who perceived 'border security personnel as motivated more by personal gain than by national interest' (van Schendel 1993: 204). As elsewhere, smuggling on the Ganges thus also exposes the limited grip of the state in border areas, testifying to its 'inability to inspire sufficient loyalty in many of its servants, even among those . . . entrusted with its very security' (van Schendel 1993: 205; see also, Tobias 1982: 393).

However, it is not only at former colonial boundaries that the economic activities of borderlanders can compromise and challenge the state. In some respects the examples considered above recall attempts by the US government to clamp down on illegal practices along the US–Mexico border. On at least two occasions major initiatives by the US government to hamper drug smuggling from Mexico have resulted in widespread disturbances and criticism of official handling of the issue (see Martínez 1988: 138–9). In 1969 Operation Intercept, which introduced rigorous inspections all along the border, inflamed the anger of many border residents who felt that the disruption caused by the policy far out-weighed the quantity of drugs seized. A similar operation in 1985 resulted in similar objections, with a coalition of businessmen and politicians in Juárez on the Mexican side launching a retaliatory campaign which recommended the boycotting of all trips to the US. In both instances, as in the Ghanaian case, the government was forced to rethink its border management procedures, and was compelled to return to less restrictive and more pragmatic policies. Prostitutes have responded in similar vein with similar consequences when the state has threatened their livelihood. In 1989 prostitutes in Chihuahua protested closure of their *zona* by threatening to strip in front of the government palace (Curtis and Arreola 1991: 344). Such cases suggest that smuggling and other illicit practices may structure relationships between border people and the state in ways which impose practical limits on the exercise of power.[4]

4. Examples can be multiplied from elsewhere in the globe. Anti-smuggling measures inspired by the International Monetary Fund and introduced into northern Morocco in 1983 sparked off widespread civil disturbance which resulted in the measures being withdrawn (Driessen n.d.: 20), and the Shabe region along the Bénin–Nigeria border has a history of local interference in state attempts to erect border markers and customs checkpoints (Flynn 1997).

Smuggling thus both recognises and marks the legal and territorial limits of the state (Price 1971) and, at the same time, undermines its power.

Anthropology's Uncomfortable Gaze

A subversive economy as we have described it here, then, is one which exposes the weaknesses of the state and reveals the complicity of state agents in many illegal cross-border activities. In any particular locality state policy towards the activities we have outlined varies historically. At times the state may simply ignore them, or minimise its intervention, or, in the case of prostitution, view them as an outlet for behaviours it decries at home. Only when the moral tide threatens eviction from office, or when revenue losses through unpaid import tariffs become so great, do policies change. To this extent, the subversive economy is susceptible to fluctuations in the wider market economy and to wider social and political events. But try as it might, the state is unable quite to bring the subversive economy under control and, at best, can only engage it on its own terms, regulating its activities through spatial relocation as in the case of prostitution in Mexico (see Curtis and Arreola 1991: 345), by adopting policies on the ground which are at variance with those proclaimed publicly as in the case of undocumented immigration to the US, or by a pragmatic recognition that a certain amount of border leakage is inevitable as with smuggling in Ghana. Through these activities the state is exposed as at once too big to manage such local affairs effectively, and too small in having no jurisdiction beyond its own boundaries.

For their part, the actions of those involved in the subversive economy remain profitable only as long as they evade the state and ignore its rules. It is in this sense that those 'living along the edge of a nation's territorial domain may function outside the established political and economic systems', entertaining only a very ambivalent loyalty to the state to which they officially belong (Martínez 1994a: 23; see also Baud 1992, 1994). In so doing, they both test and redefine the limits of state power, keeping the state at bay and serving as a reminder that its influence is less pervasive than sometimes supposed. This is not to romanticise those who thus defy the state, but to recognise instances of 'outwitting the state as original strategies of constructive coping with the imposition of state power' (Skalník 1989: 3).

At the same time, paradoxically, these activities reaffirm the very borders which they seek to subvert, for without borders these activities would simply cease to exist. To see them only as 'subversive', therefore, is to risk minimising their complex, multiform and contradictory relationships with the state. Not only do these activities attest at one level to the significance of the border and thereby confirm its existence, but state officials may themselves become involved. Agents of the state, individually or in groups, while officially charged with regulating illegal border activity, may collude in its perpetuation for the financial or other benefits they receive, in actions which swing between 'resistance' and 'complicity' (cf. Moore 1994: 49). State policy itself may lend tacit support to some of these activities, not as a matter of official and publicly declared goals, but in its practice and uncodified *modus operandi* by, for example, permitting the flow of undocumented seasonal labour. This raises questions about where the state ends and anti-state resistance begins, questions which can only be answered by inquiring into how the state is variously constructed by historically-situated and differently positioned actors (cf. Gupta 1995: 392). The activities considered in this chapter are thus the subversive but integral underbelly of the state, undermining it at the same time as they constitute it.

In this context, anthropology clearly remains the 'uncomfortable discipline' by exposing the many ways in which state efforts to control its internal and external markets are routinely subverted and challenged by the actions of ordinary people. The anthropology of these border practices enables us to see the power and policies of the state in practice, rather than as the outcome of some distant and manipulative entity, and allows us to study power with a microscope in an attempt, as Heyman (1995: 277) puts it, to connect 'the magnified grains with the overall lines'.

−6−

Border Crossings and the
Transformation of Value and Valuers

> Constantly guarded, reinforced, destroyed, set up, and reclaimed, boundaries . . . expose
> the extent to which cultures are products of the continuing struggle between official
> and unofficial narratives: those largely circulated in favour of the State and its policies
> of inclusion, incorporation and validation, as well as of exclusion, appropriation and
> dispossession.
>
> Minh-ha, 'An Acoustic Journey'

In this chapter we look more closely at what it means to cross borders, and at how
border crossing can lead to a radical transformation of value and meaning for those
involved. When people cross borders, they move from one economic, social and
political space to another. Just as borders may be both bridge and barrier between
these spaces, so their crossing can be both enabling and disabling, can create
opportunities or close them off. Since borders are used to mark difference, those
who cross potentially threaten to undermine and subvert the distinction between
'us' and 'them'. One question this raises is about what happens if those classed as
'them' seek to become 'us', a transformation over which most states endeavour to
maintain a monopoly. In Minh-ha's terms, cited above, border crossings implicate
the twin narratives of inclusion and incorporation on the one hand, and of exclusion
and dispossession on the other. In this chapter we examine these processes in
relation to four main categories of border-crosser: migrants, refugees, tourists and
shoppers.

When people cross state borders, whether it be as political or economic refugees,
or as tourists, or to purchase or trade goods, they become part of new systems of
value. These new value systems are simultaneously materialist and idealist. Migrant
workers, cultural tourists, borderland entrepreneurs and shoppers are adding or
diminishing economic value, in a class sense, because they are taking part in
relations of production and exchange which allow capitalists, in the economic
systems of which the borderlands are a part (within the state, the region and the
world), to accumulate wealth and to exchange money for the labour of others.

In reference to migrants and other transnationals, Michael Kearney has referred
to this change in class position and relations – a change which is a product of

crossing international borders established by states to regulate the flows of people, technology and capital – as 'reclassification' (Kearney 1996, 1998b). In this pun he captures the dual nature of such a transition, because whether by design or by force, these migrants, such as the Mixtec people of Oaxaca in southern Mexico who seek jobs in south-west United States (Kearney 1998a), leave one set of class relations to become part of new fields of unequal power and economic value, in which they are also classified anew in terms of the receiving state's definitions of citizen, visitor and migrant.

This latter type of classification is one of political and legal status and identity. Migrants are not the only ones affected by this type of transformation. All people who cross international borders must negotiate not only the structures of state power that they encounter, and new relations and conditions of work, exchange and consumption, but also new frameworks of social status and organisation, with their concomitant cultural ideals and values. This may mean nothing more than adapting to new local conceptions of social class, though this will also entail the negotiation of new value systems, structures of meaning that will sometimes require that the migrant, day worker and shopper, among others who cross international borders, re-evaluate many of their own notions of culture and identity.

The state is a key ingredient in these transformations in economic value and in the value systems by which people are judged and by which they judge themselves. At an obvious and commonsensical level, the official crossing of state lines clearly involves a recognition of the regulations of at least two states as well as possession of the appropriate and requisite documentation: a passport or visa, a work permit, or a bill of lading and import–export licence. Where all is in order, the crossing may be straightforward and unhindered. In other cases, permission may be granted to leave but not to enter, or vice-versa. State policy at some borders may specify openness, while at others it may dictate the rigorous rejection of all who seek to enter, opposing tendencies which through time can be evident at the same border. Equally obvious is the fact that it is the absence of requisite documentation which may result in a crossing being designated 'illegal'. Here a strategy of subterfuge and evasion is required to cross the border, with its associated risks and dangers. Whether 'legal' or 'illegal', official or unofficial, the would-be crosser must enter into dialogue with the agents of the state and engage in practices ultimately deter-mined by the state: either directly through compliance with and acceptance of state regulation, or indirectly, through avoidance, dissimulation and concealment. Though both modalities may be tinged with a sense of precariousness, vulnerability and exposure, they rarely are to the same extent. Moreover, both kinds of border crossing involve a transition and transformation of value, as we examine below, where we explore the social and cultural changes accompanying the passage from one state (in the sense of status and of nation-state) to another.

Liminal Migrants

Migration across international borders is not, of course, a new phenomenon. In the nineteenth century shiploads of migrants left Europe to seek a new future in North America, a land of opportunity in which they sought to make new lives. Consequently, most of them got on to the boat never expecting to return. In contrast, many of the twentieth century's transnational populations seem to sustain a hope of one day returning to their 'homeland' and even if they never realise this dream, many of them maintain a steady stream of remittances to kin who stayed behind, or interact with 'home' through television, film and video (see Preis 1997; Shohat and Stam 1996: 164–5). Unlike their earlier counterparts, today's transnational migrants also have at least the possibility of frequent and easy movement from country to country as a result of cheaper and more efficient transport, an opportunity which makes remigration possible even for those who decide to return 'home' permanently, like the Brazilian 'yo-yo' migrants in New York described by Margolis (1994: 263). One consequence of this difference is that migratory lives now frequently span countries and even continents, so that the border is not something to be crossed once and for all, but something to be crossed and re-crossed, in the imagination if not always in reality. As a result, lives are lived in more than one location, generating fragmentary and fugitive biographies that defy fixity in politically delineated space. These are lives for which the border has not only become the central trope, but whose everyday material realities reflect whatever economic and political inequalities the border represents.

We touched briefly on this point in chapter five, where we noted how the productive and reproductive role of Mexican migrant labour in California is dissected by the international divide: while workers shed the sweat of their brow in the strawberry fields of the American south-west, familial and cultural reproduction take place on the Mexican side, in a not so subtle but highly profitable territorial displacement of the costs and benefits of international labour. We return to these workers here, to examine how the migrants' crossings of the border to the north result in a stark transformation of value and bifurcation of identity: from kinsfolk, co-villagers and fellow nationals to workers and non-citizens at the mercy of employer and state, the creation of an internationally mobile underclass. This process, and the core characteristics and experiences of this class, where class is understood as a positionality in the field of power, are especially apparent among those who enter without the required documentation. Seen from the north of the border, these people are 'illegal aliens'; seen from the south they are returning home to the 'historical/mythological Aztlán' (Anzaldúa 1987: 11).

Leo Chavez (1991: 257) has suggested that we view the movement of undocumented migrant labour from Mexico to the United States as a 'territorial passage that marks the transition from one way of life to another way of life'. It is a passage, he argues, which can best be understood by drawing on the theoretical insights of Arnold van Gennep and Victor Turner, who advocated a three-phase model to explain the changes individuals undergo as they move from group to group or from one status to another. In conventional *rites de passage* such as birth, marriage and death, individuals pass through three stages: separation, during which one's existing status is ritually and symbolically erased; transition, during which one's status becomes liminal by being made neither one thing nor another; and finally, incorporation, the culmination of the ritual process following which successful transition to the new status or group is publicly recognised. In broad terms, Chavez suggests, this model can be used to make sense of the experiences of Mexican migrants as they cross to the United States: the period of separation draws attention to their reasons for migrating, the liminal stage to their experience of border crossing, and the final phase to their ultimate absorption into American society, a culmination of effort which, as Chavez notes, may be marked by its own rite of incorporation when the migrant is called to the Immigration and Naturalization Service for confirmation of legal residency. However, for some migrants the passage is never completed. Crossing the border without documentation, these migrants remain trapped in the liminal phase, as unincorporated outsiders in American society for whom even return to Mexico is problematic. It is these migrants who concern Chavez and on whom we concentrate here. Their lives reveal in stark relief how people's identities and daily existence are transformed and re-valued by having crossed the border and how they come to terms with the changes that result.

Chavez carried out his research in San Diego County in southern California (see map 4.3). This is a land of stark contrasts and blunt contradictions where cardboard shacks sit side by side with multi-million dollar condominiums and the 'BMW and Volvo set rubs elbows at the supermarket with the dusty migrants fresh from the fields, where the haves routinely run head-on into the have nots' (Bailey and Reza 1988, cited in Chavez 1991: 261). It is truly a place where, as Anzaldúa (1987: 3) has it, 'the Third World grates against the first and bleeds'. For the undocumented, the passage here is precarious, though no more so than the life which follows. Many prepare for their liminal existence in North America by gathering at the 'Soccer Field', a broad plateau some fifteen miles east of the Pacific Ocean, and itself a liminal space offering a popular and unofficial point of departure for the journey north. Although it is actually in the United States, those standing on the Soccer Field are not regarded as having yet officially entered the country, and the US Border Patrol monitors activities there without attempting to assert control. No fence or marker belies the presence of the border at the Soccer Field, the only clue to its existence being the abrupt halt to buildings on the Mexican side. As befits a liminal space, the usual rules of behaviour appear to be suspended. According to Chavez (1992: 46), Border Patrol officers sometimes approach the waiting migrants and strike up a conversation: 'Good luck. I'll be seeing you', was one of the exchanges he overheard; on another occasion the Border Patrol distributed Christmas presents to the waiting migrants. But they do not attempt to apprehend them. There is mutual recognition that this is neutral ground.

As night falls, the would-be migrants begin to trickle northwards down the gullies towards San Diego, some in the company of the *coyotes* who for a fee will act as guide, others trusting to their own sense of direction. Once the neutrality of the Soccer Field has been left behind, the migrants risk, at best, being apprehended and returned to Mexico. At worst, they risk being robbed, raped or killed by bandits who prey on them from both countries (Chavez 1992: 57). Many others have been killed crossing the freeways which run north from the border, an occurrence now so common that the county authorities have erected road signs to warn motorists of possible pedestrian traffic (see Chambers 1994: 1; Hannerz 1997: 537). Elsewhere on the border, along the Tijuana River canal, a chain-link fence and large floodlights hamper passage northwards, though do not deter the intrepid who have cut holes at convenient locations. Yet others seek entry by trying to blend in with the thousands who cross legally at the official port of entry every day. Though here the danger to life and limb may not be so great, the risks of apprehension are higher.

Crossing the border is only the beginning of the liminal phase for the many undocumented migrants who make it to San Diego. The city itself is a kind of liminal zone; bounded in the south by the Mexican border, it is also bounded in the north by immigration checkpoints intended to deter those who might attempt to move elsewhere in the United States (Chavez 1992: 14). Hemmed in on all sides, San Diego is thus a buffer zone, a borderland with semi-official recognition as one place where the 'problem of illegals' can to some extent be contained. Life here for the undocumented is inevitably truncated, fragmentary and forever overshadowed by the fear of arrest. Many of the men seek employment as farmworkers, supplying the back-breaking work required by the labour intensive production of strawberries and avocados. Many of these labourers are seasonal, temporary farmworkers who ebb and flow across the border as production demands. But many others attempt to set up home more permanently, bring their wives and families to live with them, and now feel themselves to be part of the society. Their children may go to school locally, and their wives seek work as childminders or as domestic cleaners.

The living conditions of these labourers reflect their undocumented and liminal status in American society. Makeshift camps of brushwood and plastic are home to many, concealed as far as possible in the canyons and hillsides on the edge of town but only minutes away from the affluent suburbs of San Diego's prosperous middle class. The continuing marginality and liminality of these undocumented labourers is evident in more than just the fragility of their dwellings. Chavez (1992) outlines at length a number of contexts in which their lives are affected by their ambiguous status, as needed but largely unwelcome workers. For those who find work the hours are long. At best workers can expect a minimum wage, at worst they may be forced by hired thugs to work for no pay at all (Chavez 1992: 64). Such conditions are not uncommon among undocumented workers in the United States. Margolis (1994: 176), for instance, reports how undocumented Brazilians in New York are similarly reluctant to complain if they are not paid for their work, and are frightened to report crimes committed against them for fear of revealing their status to the police. Chavez tells us that seasonal workers see themselves as a particularly vulnerable and 'discardable work-force'. Often given the most physically demanding and dangerous jobs, they are especially susceptible to injury. Some employers will take them to a doctor but the unscrupulous may not, since injured workers can easily be replaced if they have no documentation. As a result, 'many farmworkers either take their health problems back to Mexico with them or simply suffer' (Chavez 1992: 75), in another instance of where the reproductive costs of productive labour are absorbed across the border. Pregnant women workers often similarly go back to Mexico, because of the financial expense and risk of exposure involved in giving birth in a hospital in San Diego, returning north across the border once the baby has been delivered.

Life for undocumented migrants is very circumscribed and forever haunted by worries about being caught by the authorities (cf. Margolis 1994: 175). Farmworkers only rarely leave the confines of farm and camp for fear of local antagonism or apprehension by the Immigration and Naturalization Service. Metaphors of confinement poignantly evoke what this life is like: 'We are trapped in this place, in a very small circle'; 'Right now we're, as they say, in a chicken coop' (quoted in Chavez 1992: 157). Such anxieties give rise to a wide range of coping strategies, from self-imposed incarceration at home to the purchase of forged documents and the expenditure of large amounts of money on legal fees in pursuit of naturalisation.

Chavez argues that once the migrants cross the border, they are by necessity separated from the social structure of their own country, so that the rights and obligations which they could expect of kin and friends there are now suspended. Yet once in San Diego they interact little with the wider society, remaining outside the social structure of the communities in which they work, socially marginal despite playing an integral role in the local economy and doing the menial but necessary tasks shunned by those for whom they work.

The public discourse surrounding undocumented immigration to the United States reveals some of the obstacles to the incorporation of migrants and the exclusionary narratives that seek to keep them at bay. Mexican migrants in particular are viewed as a drain on tax-payers' money, as compromising the value of real estate, and as a shifting and threatening presence which wilfully remains outside the local social system (Chavez 1991: 261–2). At worst they may be seen as criminals or as carriers of disease, a 'medicalization' of public discourse that employs health as an agent of social control (Chavez 1992: 116) in a manner that we will look at more closely in chapter seven, and which suggests a slippage between different justificatory discourses of exclusion. What clearly is at issue here is an 'othering' of this migrant labour which defines them as radically distinct from 'us'.

Being classed as 'us' entails certain rights as defined by the state: rights of citizenship and belonging, rights to the protection of the state and the benefits this brings such as the right to work, to move freely within the confines of the state, and to avail without fear of state welfare and education provision. Being 'undocumented' entails the absence of such rights. As Chavez (1992: 116) makes clear, being undocumented is an identity defined by a constellation of negatives – 'illegal residents, transients, homeless, poor, unemployed or temporarily unemployed, criminals or potential criminals' – identities which contrast markedly not only with the legitimacy of those considered to belong to the category of 'us', but also with the migrant's own status prior to crossing the border. This revaluation is underwritten by the material asymmetries of the border, which drive a wedge through the lives of those who cross without documentation. They may find work, and even buy a home, but they remain liminal outsiders isolated from the rest of society, however much they might imagine themselves to be part of the larger community. Yet it is, in turn, this very pursuit of an elusive legitimacy, this attempt to '*in-state* themselves in the promise of the North' (Chambers 1994: 1, emphasis added), that refutes the official ideology which classifies the migrants as transient outsiders (cf. Chavez 1991: 274). It is this 'continuing struggle between official and unofficial narratives', to recall Minh-ha's words, that helps to make border cultures what they are.

Refugees and Displaced Persons

Much of the world's contemporary refugee population is to be found clustered along international borders, which are often the first places to bear the brunt of massive and sudden population movements (A. Hansen 1993, 1994). The passage of refugees and displaced persons across state borders is conventionally understood as a forced or involuntary movement of people, one which can result from an extremely wide range of historical and political reasons. The status of refugee or displaced person, however, is a classification which is ultimately in the power of the state to withhold or to grant, and one strikingly open to manipulation by the settled nations involved:

> the historical and official adaptation of such terms as 'displaced person', 'illegal immigrant' or 'voluntary immigrant' – rather than 'refugee' – proved to be a useful device through which the host society could either endorse arguments by those at home who opposed giving entry to the influx of unwanted aliens, or deny the problem of

refugees by hastily declaring them 'resettled', and hence equivalent to voluntary migrants (Minh-ha 1996: 4).

While there may indeed be many similarities between migrants and refugees, an important difference is the role which the state plays in deciding 'refugee' status, which can depend as much on the state's foreign policy interests as on the people's own motives for moving (cf. Hein 1993). Subaltern voices claiming asylum are thus all too likely to be challenged, as hundreds of hopeful entrants to Britain awaiting a hearing in Heathrow airport's holding camp confirm, in a world where official and unofficial narratives once again would seem to collide.

In anthropology, the growth of 'refugee studies' has been closely linked to the field of development (see, for instance, Allen 1996; A. Hansen 1994). Malkki (1995a) has argued that, although it is sometimes criticised for its failure to engage with issues of wider theoretical concern, the study of refugees in anthropology has, in fact, implicitly drawn upon theoretical assumptions from 'development anthropology' and the psychology of displacement, often without critical scrutiny or empirical testing. Of particular interest here is the implicit functionalism that Malkki identifies in much of the writing on refugees. This implicit functionalism is especially clear, she suggests, when researchers tackle questions of identity, culture, ethnicity and 'tradition', and when displacement is constructed 'as an anomaly in the life of an otherwise "whole", stable, sedentary society', as in the work of those who suggest that the 'experience' of being a refugee involves passing through a number of characteristic stages (Malkki 1995a: 508).[1] In such literature assumptions are repeatedly made, Malkki argues, about how territorial displacement from a national community automatically results in a loss of culture and identity: '[t]he bare fact of movement or displacement across nation-state borders is often assumed a priori to entail not a *transformation* but a *loss* of culture and/or identity' (1995a: 508, emphases added).

Yet, like Malkki, at least some ethnographic research on refugees has stressed how territorial displacement can effect a transformation rather than a loss of identity and culture, even while it recognises the disjunctures and upheavals involved. Culture and identity, like class-consciousness and class relations, do not disappear among the people who make the crossing. They simply change: they change within their home communities because of the loss entailed in their going as well as within the new political and economic context in which they find themselves, and they

---

1. In illustration, Malkki cites the work of Stein who, following Keller (1975), suggests that refugees pass through several stages which begin with perception of threat and decision to flee, proceed to repatriation or resettlement and end with adjustment and acculturation, an overall 'experience' which confronts refugees with 'the loss of their culture – their identity, their habits' (B. N. Stein 1981: 325, cited in Malkki 1995a: 508).

change in the communities who are now host to the border crossers. Cultural reworkings among refugees can take many forms. Among Kosovo-Albanian refugees in Sweden, for example, the reciprocal sharing of clothes by young women is both a means of coping with exile and one way of 'refashioning' social relations remembered as typical of home (Norman 1997). Such exchanges loosen the boundaries of ownership, symbolically merging the bodies of the women who participate and incorporating them as if they were 'family'. Indeed, the reconstruction of 'home' has, for some refugees, proved easier to achieve by remaining in the country to which they have fled than by returning to their own country (see James 1996).

Wendy James's account of the Uduk in the Sudanese–Ethiopian borderlands argues that historical memory has provided a critical 'cultural archive' for the reconstitution of Uduk life following a wave of successive territorial displacements which span more than a century and which, most recently, has culminated in their seeking asylum across the border in south-western Ethiopia. The shared experience and knowledge of the grim events of the past provide surviving Uduk with a cohesion and reconstituted sense of community through which they can still see themselves, despite their cruel experiences, 'as whole men and women' (James 1979: 19). This past, as a collective cultural resource in the Uduk historical imagination, is now central to every aspect of Uduk life: it is both what has enabled them to survive as a people and what shapes their contemporary social and symbolic worlds. Indeed, 'their historical position as a weak and politically unsuccessful people colours their thinking and action in many fields . . . from their everyday working activities to the intimacy of their marriage and family relations' (James 1979: 18–19). Experiences of displacement have thus been absorbed into Uduk identity through a process of remembering that has reconstituted the Uduk in a way that no unilinear 'loss of identity' model can hope to encompass. Although the Uduk have undergone so much 'upheaval and demographic, political and cultural change that it is difficult to say in what sense they have remained "the same people"' (James 1997: 117), they remain bound by their shared and collective images of history; it is these which have proved to be enduring, as James (1979: 47) herself had predicted. Thus when those Uduk refugees fleeing across the border into Ethiopia from the current civil war in Sudan express fear, 'they speak, still, in the same responsively articulated vernacular idiom of political, experiential and psychological concepts which served earlier remembered, and without doubt also unremembered, predicaments' (James 1997: 117).

In her analysis of displaced Hutu in the refugee camp of Mishamo in Tanzania (see map 6.1), Malkki (1997) makes a similar point but takes it a stage further by showing how these refugees are caught in the gap between the way they see themselves and how they are seen by the state and by the local and international humanitarian organisations with which they must deal. Malkki argues that the elaboration of legal refugee status into a moral identity does not follow an automatic or predictable course, but is something the meaning of which can be differently articulated depending on one's particular political and cultural position. For the Hutu, refugeeness is seen as a matter of 'becoming', an identity cumulatively acquired through experience and knowledge of life in the camp and one transmissable from generation to generation as long as they are in exile. Their historical narratives of their previous life in Burundi, and particularly of their experiences of violence at the hands of the Tutsi in 1972, in their eyes situate them as a 'nation in exile', one whose collective experience as refugees is ultimately deserving of return to their rightful homeland. As with the Uduk, for these Hutu, being a refugee is thus a 'positive, productive status and . . . a profoundly meaningful historical identity' (Malkki 1997: 227; see also, Preis 1997). This contrasts markedly with how these refugees are viewed by those who administer the camp as well as by those who deliver them aid, such as the United Nations High Commission for Refugees and the Tanganyika Christian Refugee Service. However well meaning these organisations may be, and however much their aid and assistance are critical for the physical well-being of the refugees in Mishamo, their international humanitarianism tends to construct the refugee as universal 'victim' (cf. Allen and Turton 1996: 9); a conception of refugeeness in which visible signs of impoverishment and bodily injury figure more prominently than the refugees' own particular and individualised narratives of their past. For these organisations, then, as Malkki (1997: 233) puts it, 'history tended to get leached out of the figure of the refugee', a process which strips the Hutu of their role as historical actors and silences their voice.

Crossing the border from Burundi to Tanzania as a displaced person thus involves a loss, but it is a loss of agency and voice, rather than of culture and identity, one in which Hutu self-conceptions come up against the material consequences of imaginings with more power behind them than their own. To this extent it is a transformation that would seem to bear some resemblance to Chavez's discussion of the experience of the undocumented Mexican labourers in the United States, though unlike that account Malkki takes greater pains to avoid idealising the world that has been left behind. It is unhelpful, she suggests, to conceptualise that world as 'the place where one fits in' and where culture and identity are unproblematic (Malkki 1995a: 509). After all, anthropologists have been arguing for at least a decade that we must rethink the relationship between culture, identity and space in a way that incorporates the paradoxes, incompleteness and contradictions of people's lives wherever they are. It is therefore inadequate to see territorial passage and displacement as a temporally bounded experience which leads 'from uprooting to integration' (Sørensen 1997: 146), for one's culture and identity are no less in a state of becoming in the world one abandons than in the world one joins. 'Belonging', with its sense of identity and community, is just as never-ending and historical a project as is displacement, and should be examined as such. A focus

Map 6.1 Tanzania's border with Burundi

on border crossings opens a window on just such a study, allowing us to examine critically the idea that every population has its own proper 'place' and 'homeland' from which it derives its identity (Malkki 1995a: 516; Turton 1996).

Shopping the Border

Even the most uncomplicated and innocuous behaviour by those who cross borders to work or to consume may have a significance beyond that recognised by its participants, precisely because of the movement into new systems of economic and cultural value. In one sense there is no more innocent activity at international borders than cross-border shopping. To many people shopping is not (just) a duty, requirement or chore, but a pleasurable pastime, a hobby, an avocation, even a 'devotional rite' (Miller 1998: 9). Many consumers, for example, are familiar with such phrases as 'shop 'til you drop', and 'born to shop'. To some people shopping has become a social necessity, on the order of anything else that they might need to do in a day or a week. In this sense, shopping at international borders may encompass more than buying the staples required for physical and social survival. It is also about buying things which are not available on your own side of the border, or not in the quantity or at the lower price for which they can be had across the borderline. Such goods may also add something to one's social standing, as signs and symbols of the wealth, mobility, acumen, political connections, ambition or other social skills which might be associated with the possession of such products. An expanding literature on cross-cultural consumption has confirmed how the value and meaning of goods are transformed by crossing borders (see, for example, the essays in Howes 1996 and Spyer 1998a). Comaroff (1996: 19), for instance, has argued that the importation of foreign dress by the Southern Tswana during the colonial era acted as 'a privileged means for constructing new forms of value, personhood, and history on the colonial frontier'. Referring to these goods as 'social hieroglyphics' (Marx 1967, 1: 74), which encode the structure of a newly emergent world, she suggests that the consumption of foreign dress styles 'played powerfully into the making and marking of new social classes, rupturing existing communities of signs and hastening the conversion of local systems of value to a global currency' (Comaroff 1996: 21; see also, Spyer 1998b).

The possession of consumer durables and luxury items is not only the goal of day-trippers, but is also the aim of international migrants, whose new wages and locations of work and residence often enable them to accumulate enough money and consumer goods to make the effort of migration worthwhile, or at least to seem so. In some cases they may even accumulate enough to send back to their home communities, sometimes in preparation for their own eventual return but also to alleviate pressures on loved ones left behind, as well as to sustain or improve their own place in the home community's status hierarchy.

Thus both casual cross-border shoppers and migrants consuming the 'good life', which ironically may be among the worst lives of the new country in which they find themselves, as we saw earlier, share a belief in the power of goods to mould their social lives and make them more meaningful. Russell Belk has analysed the role of possessions in the structure and meanings of the 'extended self', i.e., one's body, ideas, experiences, and those persons, places and things to which one feels attached (1988: 141). This concept of extended self refers not only to the possessions which one finds meaningful, but also to the role which control plays in that relation-ship. People often define themselves in terms of what they can possess, and the more difficult it is to attain these items the more they want them, and the more important they are to their sense of self (Belk 1988: 141). An individual has multiple levels of attachment to possessions, sometimes to the degree that they speak of the possessions owning them, or of acquiring an identity which they would not have had without ownership of a particular object. It may seem like a chicken and egg question, but does a Harley-Davidson bike give its owner an identity, or does it take a certain type of person to buy one, ride one and wear the jacket with the logo prominently displayed?

But the extended self is not just attributable to individuals, for groups of people identify with things which give them meaning and identity, and without which they would be impoverished in important ways. One need only consider the importance of national territory and national icons to see how the extended self might apply as a concept of identity and possessions among large groups of people.

The point here is that cross-border shopping, i.e. the movement of people across an international border with the expressed intention of buying goods and then returning home, is part of many webs of significance that stretch, like the border itself, in many indeterminate ways. Shopping is not just a personal relationship between consumer and seller, and between owner and possession. It is also part of group economic, political and social relations, between consumers and entrepreneurs, between workers and capitalists, between citizens and the state, and between nations.

Most readers of this book, at least those who have some knowledge of international borders beyond those of airline terminals, are likely to have experience of borderland shopping. Almost every major road and railway crossing between states has some type of market as close to the border as allowed or practicable. This is because there is almost always some form of economic differential at play between two nation-states, and some product, service, price or quality that is in more demand on one side of the border than on the other. The item or service in question often changes over time, in some cases to the exact opposite, so that it is then in demand on the other side of the border, where its former sellers must go to get it. This has certainly been the case for petrol along the Irish border, where petrol stations rise, make small fortunes, then disappear, to be replaced by identical stations on the other side of the border. This see-saw trait of border life in Ireland is the product of the differentials in state tax, consumer prices, and the currency exchange rate.

Because all borderlands are frontiers of economic negotiation, wherein there are many opportunities for legal and illegal enterprise, even the innocence of shopping draws the attention of the state and its agents. For example, customs and excise agents patrol the Irish border today to regulate the use, sale and resale of commercial diesel fuels, sometimes laying enticement traps for unwitting consumers who attempt to fill up their car from a lorry parked at the side of the road. On some occasions shopping can even threaten to become an international incident. In the summer of 1996 Bulgarian border policemen had to use rubber batons to control a 300-strong crowd of Macedonians who were attempting to break through fencing and cross the border. They were bound for a nearby town on a shopping tour, and they were fed up with the delay in handling their documents at the border post, a delay which they claimed was an attempt to elicit bribes to speed the process along. Bulgarian authorities replied that Macedonian authorities were doing the same thing to Bulgarians, and they warned that the stricter security measures on the Bulgarian side that would result from this incident might end up in people being shot on sight in the case of any more such border violations (BTA News Agency, Sofia, 20 August 1996).

Shooting shoppers on sight may seem to be the cure-all for those of us who remember the pre-mall days when shopping was an activity and not an identity, but it is definitely an extreme alternative in international relations. At least it would appear to be a drastic measure, until cross-border shopping is placed within wider negotiations of economics and politics between nations. Since the changes of 1989, the countries of central and eastern Europe have been beset by many of the problems associated with the legal and illegal trade of consumer goods across state borders, making such trading a state concern of economic and political sovereignty, a subject to which we shall return below. But even long-established borders between allies can be the scene of economic differentials which make shopping there a national and international concern.

In 1979, the Republic of Ireland joined the European Monetary System while the United Kingdom remained outside. This resulted in a split between their currencies, as Ireland went off the sterling standard which, in turn, made prices on each side of the Irish border diverge considerably. In the 1980s local cross-border economic relations, with shopping for lower-priced goods at their core, became a national phenomenon among the people of the Republic of Ireland. Because of lower sales (value added) tax on a variety of products – most notably spirits, beer, wine, cigarettes, toys, electrical appliances and petrol – thousands of consumers from the Irish Republic flocked to Northern Ireland border communities each year. Busloads of shoppers arrived in Northern Irish border towns, sometimes after many hours on the road, and dispersed for a hectic round of spending. After a few hours of such activity, they returned to their hired coaches with full shopping bags.

The reasons for this massive influx of shoppers were clear. Prices were up to a third cheaper on the northern side of the border, Irish customs agents were over-worked, there were many unpatrolled border crossings, and, for many people on the southern side of the border, there was easy access to Northern Irish villages and towns, their natural centres of commerce which were denied them when Ireland was partitioned in the 1920s (see map 4.2). In fact, at the height of cross-border shopping in the mid-1980s, small markets literally sprang up overnight on the northern side to service consumers from the south (Wilson 1995).

By the mid-1980s the Irish government was experiencing such a severe loss of revenue that it began to plan measures to limit cross-border shopping. Not only were shopkeepers on the Irish side of the border losing customers, which made them a vocal and irate constituency, but by 1986 the Irish state was losing up to IR£300 million a year to the North, in the value of consumer purchases, and was suffering IR£20 million a year in lost taxes (Fitzgerald et al. 1988). In fact, the issue of cross-border shopping was considered so critical for the Republic's finances that it was prepared to challenge European Community law because of it.

In 1987, the Irish Minister for Finance made virtually all items taxable on one-day shopping trips to the North. Anyone leaving the Republic of Ireland for less than forty-eight hours would no longer be able to claim tax-free allowances for goods bought duty-free or in shops. This severely affected many shopkeepers on the northern side of the border, who in fact depended on being able to offer lower prices in order to maintain cross-border consumer interest. In 1986, for example, there was a 30 per cent difference in the price of alcohol. Such price differentials were enticements to break the new law. Throughout the 1980s and into the 1990s, more shoppers continued to travel north rather than the reverse. They shopped for alcohol, tobacco, petrol and household appliances, such as televisions, video recorders, and washing machines. These appliances were priced at levels which placed almost all of them over the import tax-free limit, so that the 1987 restriction did not modify the illegal nature of their importation into the south, which usually occurred on one of the many unapproved roads which criss-cross the border. But the savings to individual consumers or to organised smugglers might be worth the risk. For example, in 1986 a large television set which retailed at IR£540 in the Republic cost the equivalent of IR£356 in Northern Ireland (Fitzgerald et al. 1988: 80).

These economic enticements to brave the agents of the state notwithstanding, the overall effects of the Republic's forty-eight-hour rule were devastating for many Northern Ireland border communities. As the Republic enforced its ruling, stopping cars and hired buses at border checkpoints, large-scale cross-border shopping dwindled rapidly. People from the Republic still came north for petrol, alcohol and tobacco, but their visits were less frequent, shorter and more purposeful. Even the sale of spirits, beer and wine began to drop as these became the new targets of customs officers once the cross-border trade in electrical appliances all but ceased in 1989.

Eventually the European Union forced the Republic to modify its forty-eight-hour rule, and now the volume and types of cross-border shopping are much more modest than before. Without the lure of shopping, fewer shoppers from the Republic visit Northern Ireland towns, especially over the last few years when the Irish pound has been weak against sterling. The peace process has encouraged tourism, but the on-and-off IRA cease-fires, coupled with the continuation of the war by splinter republican and loyalist groups, remain as barriers to many types of cross-border cultural integration.

This link between the Northern Irish peace process and cross-border shopping may seem fanciful, but it is less fanciful than might at first appear when one considers that commerce has been one of the principal factors encouraging people from the Republic to travel across the Northern Irish border during the present conflict. While there are many aspects of border culture that have bound people together across the borderline, the further one travels from that line, the fewer these ties. Religion and church membership, sports, and kinship have sustained many people's connections with the 'others' across the border, but for many southerners the main attraction of crossing the border was the promise of goods not readily available at home, and at lower prices (Wilson 1993b, 1995). This was true despite a widespread perception among southerners of Northern Ireland as a military camp, a region under siege, which required the presence of some 20,000

British Army troops to support the 7,000-strong Royal Ulster Constabulary in their attempt to police armed Irish republicans, who represent that minority of the Northern Irish population seeking a united Ireland.

Thus shopping across the Northern Irish border has maintained ethnic and national ties between people who would attest to having an Irish national identity, but it has also allowed communication and adaptation between Irish and British people in Northern Ireland as well, and should not be overlooked when assessing the changes in values and beliefs over the last thirty years of sectarian conflict. The peace process is clearly a result of many forces. But cultural change on the order of one people altering their nationalist aspirations as enshrined in their constitution, as the people of the Republic so voted in the referendum of May 1998, and others sitting down across the table from their longstanding enemies, which has happened in the peace negotiations and which may continue in some form in the proposed Northern Ireland Assembly, is also a product of gradual recognition that the 'others', whether they be Catholic or Protestant, Irish or British, Republican, Nationalist, Loyalist or Unionist, have some things in common which can be built upon for the good of all.

Shopping at international borders reflects not only the cultures of borderland life, but also the economic and political conditions of the states which meet at that border. Because the border, all borders, play important roles in production, trade and consumption, borders become marketable items themselves, commodities to be packaged or portrayed in ways which will sustain other economic processes, and support the image if not the facts of life in the country to which they act as gateways. Borders are economic resources, to be consumed like other resources in a variety of ways. This is especially apparent to those who use the border as one way to add value to their own products, or who market themselves as masters of the border in order to entice people to use their services. In this sense, shopping at the border is part of the process of shopping the border itself. In the next section we consider some examples of trader tourism, in order to return to the point that borders are not only zones where values are renegotiated, and areas where the inequities of economic value and political power are played out, but are also places where states establish the rules for all of this to occur.

Trader Tourism and the Rules of the Game

In post-independence Zimbabwe women traders, linked in networks with each other and with traders in neighbouring states, have acted as sales agents and brokers of consumer goods, in ways that allow them some freedom of movement and capital, as well as relative freedom from male-dominated international smuggling. As in other African states (see, for instance, Hannerz [1996: 103] on Nigerian women who illegally import dried fish from Lagos to London by strapping them to their thighs), these women play an important role in Zimbabwe's formal and informal economies (Cheater 1998). Working class, peasant and middle-class women approach potential buyers in Zimbabwe, take their orders for clothing, electrical appliances, software and household goods, and agree a delivery date when they will return with the goods, no strings attached. If the customer still wants the products, payment can be made in Zimbabwean currency. None of these goods are illegal or restricted, but they are offered at attractive prices, and are delivered to one's doorstep.

The sources of these goods are in nearby states, especially in Botswana and South Africa. All travellers who leave Zimbabwe are allowed a holiday allowance from the state, and certain duty-free import limits. These women traders travel to these countries, use allotted hard currency to buy the goods needed, often at much cheaper prices than are found at home, then import them within their limits at selected crossing points. Other women do not leave Zimbabwe at all, but run relatives and friends, some of whom work in South Africa, as buying agents, who carry or ship the goods home, to satisfy the demand of Zimbabwean consumers. These trader networks, which seem to have few ties to organised crime (which begs the question, of course, about the organisation of 'non-organised' crime), sometimes charter buses to take the women to warehouses across the border, where they can collect the 'ordered' products from similar networks there. Many of these women bring traditional craft-goods from Zimbabwe to sell for hard currency, which they use to purchase consumer goods to import into Zimbabwe for resale to their customers.

Cheater suggests that these activities threaten the state, much like the smugglers and others discussed in chapter five. Cheater's women too are often seen as subversive of state order and policies, which target them as anomalous and dangerous citizens (1998: 207–9). In an apparent attempt to control these women, the government and its agents began a campaign to brand them as a disgrace to the nation and as unpatriotic. The state has even gone so far as to redefine citizenship, in ways which seem to disenfranchise, socially if not literally, black women of the urban and rural working class. It has done so in order 'to strengthen the state against its citizens, collectively and with respect to specific subcategories, rather than to ensure the individual rights, freedoms and entitlements conferred by citizenship in older-established nation-states' (Cheater 1998: 199). Part of the reason for this – and Cheater gives evidence that when middle-class, white men and women buy goods in much the same way and for the same reasons they are not denounced by the state (1998: 204–5) – lies in the government's attempt to subordinate Zimbabwean women in what still amounts to a patriarchal state. Women traders, largely free of male domination, are seen by the state to be a threat not just to its policy and practice, but to the very value structure which gives it, and the males who run it, meaning. Efforts to use selectively debates over citizenship and patriotism to denigrate these women entrepreneurs are attempts to bring these 'dangerous' citizens under symbolic control, along with other measures such as those which until 1996 forbade women citizens from passing on citizenship rights to offspring under the same conditions that applied to men (Cheater 1998: 207).

This gendered construction of citizenship and the state is also the gendering of the border, and is indicative of the differential values that can exist on either side of a borderline, particularly as they relate to differences in the production of economic value within class relations. Central and eastern Europe's new state borders, many of which have existed for much of the century if not longer, but which have been revitalised after the demise of communism and the Soviet bloc, provide remarkable opportunities for the testing and negotiation of competing value systems and the values inherent in certain economic relations. Trader tourism also operates there, to supply the many informal open-air markets which have become essential features of the economies of all the post-Soviet states. Trond Thuen's study (1998) of the city of Varna on the Bulgaria–Turkey border demonstrates how that border acts as both an impediment and a stimulus to cross-border trade, especially at the level of the individual and local communities who need certain consumer goods, in small quantities, and at cheap prices.

Trader tourism, a concept which Thuen ascribes to Hann and Hann (1992; see also, Hann and Bellér-Hann 1998), involves the movement of buyers into neighbouring countries, under the guise of tourism, to purchase goods such as food, clothes, household items, tools, car parts, plumbing materials and all the other things that are necessary for the orderly functioning of daily life but which are in short supply in the region due to decades of totalitarian government, corruption and the failure of state economies. The trader-tourist goes to markets in other countries, buys the goods, then returns home to sell them in a local market for hard currency, or in some cases to barter for other scarce goods. Thuen (1998: 215) reminds us that trader tourism is not new in central and eastern Europe, but since the collapse of the Soviet system it has spread, for at least three reasons: there is more opportunity to travel across state borders and within states; high levels of unemployment and inflation require new and more adaptive techniques; and home industries have collapsed, increasing the demand for what used to be produced locally. To these three reasons must be added the incentive to have consumer goods on the model of western society, which is present on their televisions nightly, and given reality by the western tourists who visit the region, demonstrating the values of consumerism.

Varna is a tourist destination on the Black Sea which attracts visitors from throughout Europe, East and West. But this injection of capital is not enough to sustain the local economy, so traders go singly and in groups to the markets of Turkey to purchase goods necessary to local Varna life. While there is an ethnic dimension to such trading, in that many traders are either Bulgarian Turks or Roma, all ethnic and national groups participate in the Varna market. Thuen did discern some division of labour and some division of morality and values, however. The Roma have traditionally been agents in the informal economy and, as such, dealers in money and currency. The Bulgarians long eschewed such tasks as beneath their dignity and social standing, but can no longer afford to do so. They insist, however, that such activities are temporary, and a stepping-stone to a better life, whereas the Roma seem to involve all members of their families in ways which suggest a desire to strengthen their niche in this informal economy. Thuen's review of these class and social distinctions has less to do with such constructions and more to do with the attributes each group of traders brings to the act of trader tourism, because each group had different abilities and expectations when trying to articulate the border as an economic resource. To some the border is ultimately an impediment to a better life, while to others it is an opportunity taken and a challenge met.

Although trader tourism operates in a number of ways, one of the most significant is through the chartering of buses, in which a travel agent arranges transport and the easy movement of the traders and their goods across the international border. Travel agents depend on their reputation to get the Varna traders safely to and from Istanbul, their preferred destination (map 6.2). Each of the traders must pay the travel agent a fee, as well as a sum, based on the size of the illegal load, to be paid to the border guards as a bribe. Buying and selling in Istanbul is done through hard currencies, such as the American dollar, which is legally available in Bulgarian banks, and which is also the currency of bribery. Trader-tourists' own reputations depend on their bargaining and haggling skills in Istanbul, as well as on their ability to pick a reliable travel agent. That agent, in turn, deals with border and customs guards in secret, leaving traders in some doubt as to the exact bribe which is handed over (estimated at $2–5 per luggage bag). But they must trust the travel agents, for no one wants to anger the customs agents to the degree that they query customs declarations, passports and the contents of each bag. These bus trips last hours, with most buses crossing the frontier late at night on both legs of the journey.

This system of trader tourism, in which the goods from Istanbul end up first on the stalls of the Varna market and then in people's homes and businesses, is like a game, in which sets of rules have evolved to allow each of the players, such as the Roma, the Bulgarian traders, the travel agents, and the customs guards on both sides of the border, a part to play that gives them both some economic reward and some sense of justification and satisfaction (Thuen 1998: 217–26). The rules also allow people some critical distance from the harsher realities of what they are doing and with whom. Thuen was surprised to note that the Roma, long villified in local society, sit alongside Bulgarians and Bulgarian Turks in these long bus trips. They are also left alone by border guards, who perhaps in another era would have singled them out for rough treatment. All of these people allow each other a role, so that the whole system does not fail. Even the border guards rely on Roma tips. But the façade of cooperation may be thin indeed. As the bus rolls through the night,

Map 6.2 Turkey's borders

Bulgarians do not talk to Roma, preferring silence as one way of marking the invisible boundary of status and morality that exists between them, at least in their own eyes.

This merging of morality, class, status, ethnicity, profession and occupation among trader-tourists, customs agents and soldiers also signals divergence of attitudes and values. Economic relations, between classes and ethnic groups, within states and across their borders, make strange bedfellows, and are dependent on regular if not regularised activity as such. But the meanings which one imputes to this activity are embedded in culture in ways which have many effects beyond the strict confines of the economy. In culture we see the mix of labour value and value systems, and at borders we see the confluence of culture, power and the state. As we noted in chapter four, states act as aggregations of the rules for social and economic action, and 'areas of disparity and of transition between rules offer unusual advantages for the creation of capitalist value' (Heyman 1994: 52). This creation of value, whether it be in the *maquiladora* programme in Mexico, on the road between Varna and Istanbul, or in the shops and factories of Ireland, develops in those spaces and places between areas of long-term capitalist investment and state control, and in those areas where there has been disruption of one or the other. Both class and cultural values have been touted in functionalist social science as methods of smoothing out the perturbations of state and economy, and making one's role in the system both meaningful and palatable. In the border cultures reviewed in this chapter, found among migrants, refugees, shoppers and trader-tourists, as in those discussed in the chapters above, disjuncture is the fact of life, and is an essential part of the 'system'. In the lives of border peoples the border is a resource, an opportunity and a barrier, but it is also a symbol of their role in cultural value systems and in systems of economic value, which are important to the daily functioning of the states in which they live.

—7—

Body Politics

Fantasies about the body and the family are transmuted into descriptions of one's own group, other groups, shapes and features of the world. Projected outward, the fate of the body becomes the fate of the world.

H. F. Stein, ' The Scope of Psycho-Geography'

In this chapter we suggest that the bodily experiences of those who inhabit or traverse border regions are often shaped by the forces of power and domination that give form to the territorial borders themselves. Those forces that demarcate geographical and political space as lines on a map simultaneously inscribe the body's topography, and from each can be read the history of the struggle to define and delimit individual and personal identities, both on the part of the state and of those who oppose it. In certain critical senses which we elaborate here, border maps are thus also body maps. This is hardly a novel or controversial claim. For some time anthropologists have documented how the body is socially constructed, marked by the wider relationships in which it is embedded. As Synnott (1993) has noted, the body and its component parts are layered with meanings, associations and ideas which vary across history and culture. The body is not so much a biological given as a

> creation of immense complexity, and almost limitless variability, richness and power
> . . . [it is] . . . the prime symbol of the self, but also of the society; it is something we
> have, yet also what we are; it is both subject and object at the same time . . . both an
> individual creation, physically and phenomenologically, and a cultural product; it is
> personal, and also state property (Synnott 1993: 4).

As we shall see, the relationship between state borders and the body is both symbolic and metaphorical, as well as one which can mark the body in quite physical and visible ways.

Interest has often focused specifically on the subjectification of the body, under regimes which explicitly endeavour to control and restrain. These might be penal institutions (Foucault 1979), institutions for the mentally infirm (Saris 1996) or refugee camps (Malkki 1995b), though attention has also focused on the 'panoptic power' of cities and the practices which evade it (de Certeau 1988 [1974]). From such studies anthropologists have increasingly realised that even the most intimate aspect of our being, the manner in which our bodies are 'felt', is subject to – and may in some sense constitute – the wider social orders in which our bodies dwell. 'The body is directly involved in a political field; power relations have an immediate hold upon it; they invest it, mark it, train it, torture it, force it to carry out tasks, to perform ceremonies, to emit signs' (Rabinow 1987: 173). Nowhere is this more evident than at the edges of the state, where claims to sovereignty and aspirations to nationhood may be written on the body by practices designed to subject it to the authority that the state tries to enforce, and those who challenge the state try to subvert. In this chapter we explore some of the ways in which this can be the case, focusing on the dual process by which the body is both subjected by, and can stand as a metaphor for, the wider political fields of nationalism, minority and majority politics, ethnic and other social and political movements, and international and inter-state relations.

Foreign Bodies

We have already considered how borders act as screens to regulate the flow of goods and people. Policing this flow obviously involves the physical search of vehicles and baggage, as well as the use of x-ray and metal-detecting technology of the kind familiar to air travellers. But it may also involve searches of a more personal and intimate kind, from the emptying of pockets and opening of wallets and handbags to the body frisking now common at many European airports, techniques requiring such close physical contact that the most innocent traveller is likely to feel vulnerable, embarrassed and exposed by this intrusion on their person, a view apparently corroborated by an airport security official who half-jokingly confided to one of the authors: 'I've seen some things in my time! I've *felt* some things too!' At their most extreme, such searches of the person may involve a 'strip-search'. This requires the removal of clothing for detailed examination and even a probing of the body itself. Such bodily investigations are not uncommon in the search for drugs, as one customs official on the US–Mexico border graphically described:

> If we have good information on a suspect and can't find anything, we'll take him to the hospital for a flush job. This is perfectly legal; lots of case law gives us the right to search a person's body cavities . . . Frankly, the visual examination is not too valuable. I've had lots of people spread their cheeks and never saw a thing, then a doctor comes along and pulls out two ounces of junk tied up in a contraceptive. Sometimes it can be quite a job getting it out if it's in there far enough, and it's dangerous. But not as dangerous as the characters who swallow it. Here's the way it works. The first thing the buyer will do is get a room on both sides of the border. He buys an ounce of heroin from a peddler, takes it to his room over there, pulls out a bunch of small balloons, about the size of your small finger, and spoons in about two grams per balloon, ties off the neck of the

balloon, clips the excess rubber, and ends up with fourteen round little balls, which he swallows with water. He hurries to his room over here, sticks his finger down his throat, and regurgitates an ounce of junk. About a ten-minute operation from the time he swallows to when he brings it up. A very common procedure. These guys are out there trying to beat you all the time (Customs Inspector, US–Mexico border, cited in Demaris 1970: 158–9).

At the US–Mexico border searches such as these are not supposed to be carried out unless there is some justifiable, objective suspicion for doing so (Price 1971: 39). However, as the quotation itself suggests, the grounds for undertaking such a search may be slim, with considerable uncertainty about the need for it even after a suspect disrobes. This means that in practice bodily searches are often carried out on the basis of intuition, using knowledge and experience acquired while working as a border official rather than by applying some official criteria learnt through more formal training. Such knowledge is often difficult to articulate, but becomes a part of the habitus of the long-serving border guard who comes to believe in his or her ability to recognise the tell-tale signs (see Heyman 1995). Ironically perhaps, it is the bodies of the border crossers themselves which provide the clues: the furtive eye movements, the sweaty palms, the facial flush when under pressure. As another border guard remarked, 'where he hides the stuff is less important than how he behaves' (cited in Price 1971: 39). Similarly, a customs inspector at Kennedy Airport explained to one of the authors how smugglers can be successfully detected: 'It's all in the eyes. I only look at their eyes'. In this regard, the meaning of the body takes on a particular inflection which is read in a manner specific to the 'culture' of the border. Even posing as a dead body may not conceal the clues. In the northern town of Kastoria, near the Albanian border, Greek police set off in hot pursuit of a funeral hearse on suspicion that its occupants were 'living, breathing illegal immigrants' (*The Irish Times*, 29 December 1998). The embodied knowledge of the border guard thus confronts the bodily demeanour of the border crosser in a meeting where the bodily dispositions and performances of the 'protagonists' are structured by the rules of the state and the attempt to evade them.

Such practices reinforce the idea that border checkpoints and customs posts are liminal spaces, ones within which the usual western conventions of bodily contact cease to apply, and where the interactions between those who meet there are as much structured according to a set of rules peculiar to this setting as they are by the rules which apply in the travellers' homeland. They are liminal spaces within which state power is absolute, and can be imposed upon even that most intimate element of our being, our body. Such border stations have 'a neutral or "no man's land" quality, almost a third country where only the official staff are the assured citizens' and where ordinary civil rights are suspended (Price 1971: 27). In the final analysis, even our bodies are no longer our own in such settings, their agency displaced by the raw power of the state which can be revealed there.

Of course, it is not only illegal drugs which the body may carry across the border. Fear of disease has long been a rationale for vetting those from beyond one's own borders, even though the non-voluntaristic nature of carrying disease clearly distinguishes it from the carrying of drugs. Various mechanisms have been deployed nominally to inhibit the spread of disease: health inspections at border crossings, though these are relatively uncommon, spraying the interior of aeroplanes with disinfectant on arrival at a foreign port, or by requiring medical certification to confirm that certain vaccinations and innoculations have been carried out prior to departure. Entrance may be refused to those suspected of 'carrying' infectious disease, or a period of quarantine imposed before entry is granted, practices which become highly charged politically if thought to be directed at a specific category of prospective entrant.

The perception that disease originates from 'outside', beyond the bounds of home, is very common, and parallels the Western notion, described by Helman, that germs constitute an external threat to the human body's own boundaries which are supposedly sealed (Helman 1991, cited in Green 1998a: 260). Here we might recall the words of Victor Turner (1967: 97), who suggested that 'transitional beings are particularly polluting, since they are neither one thing nor another; or may be both; or neither here nor there'. There are many examples of the spread of disease being blamed on foreigners, in an often contradictory round of allegation and counter allegation. One Sudanese anthropologist recently told us that while working in Sudan he consistently heard how AIDS had come from outside, from Europe in particular, while when studying in Britain it was always described to him as a disease of African origin. Among Mexican migrant labour in North America AIDS is believed to be an exclusively North American disease (Bronfman and Moreno 1996: 66).[1] Seremetakis (1996: 490) has similarly noted how the Greek media have provocatively blamed Albanian migrants for carrying AIDS across the border into Greece, as well as other viruses and bugs such as hepatitis B and cholera, while public health officials in Albania attribute the proliferation of new viruses there to movement in the opposite direction. As Desowitz (1997) has quipped, 'People move, and with them move their worms and germs'. Clearly bugs have no respect for borders, so the bodies that carry them must be controlled.

A good example of foreigners being blamed for disease is to be found in an article by Lyons (1996), the title of which we have borrowed for the heading of this section. Lyons describes how in Uganda a wide range of foreigners have been

---

1. Mexican farmworkers in the United States are the focus of a vigorous campaign to prevent the spread of AIDS. One such programme is in the form of a *fotonovela* or comic strip called *Tres Hombres sin Fronteras* ('Three men without borders'), which outlines the benefits of using condoms (Mishra and Conner 1996: 160–3).

accused of spreading AIDS, from Tanzanian soldiers and traders to Kenyan long-distance lorry drivers and western tourists and development workers. As elsewhere, one response in Uganda has been to suggest the construction of another kind of border, the *cordon sanitaire*, which would isolate in some remote area all those who have tested HIV-positive, and who, like the lepers of the past, would constitute their own colony. As Lyons shows, Uganda has a long historical record of attributing disease to outsiders, one which stretches back to its colonial past and beyond.

For much of this century, and following a route already well-trodden by their pre-colonial ancestors, the Banyaruanda sought entry into Uganda from neigh-bouring Rwanda, propelled by repeated famines in their own country and attracted by the prospect of work in the industries and tea and sugar plantations being vigorously developed under colonial rule. They settled mainly in the south of Uganda, many of them permanently, and quickly became one of the largest ethnic groups in the country, constituting almost 20 per cent of its population. Almost from the outset the Banyaruanda were 'pathologised' as 'disseminators of disease' by both the local Ugandans and the colonial authorities. An epidemic of sleeping sickness in 1905 led to widespread speculation as to the cause, and while the precise origin was often in dispute, there was general agreement that it had been introduced from outside. Particular 'tribes' where identified as likely health hazards in the colonial records which, as Lyons (1996: 132, 137) carefully analyses, variously describe the Banyaruanda as 'disease ridden', as a 'source of infection' and as 'a lowly, unintelligent and dirty race'. By 1925 the situation was thought to be so bad that repatriation and closure of the border were considered as ways to stem the influx. In the event, strict medical examinations for the recruitment of labour at the border were introduced instead, resulting in a rejection rate of 70 to 75 per cent, though this did little to prevent individuals from crossing to Uganda independently (Lyons 1996: 137). Other attempted innovations and restrictions followed, including proposals to build special camps where Banyaruanda could be detained and treated, and the introduction of tight controls on cross-border movement, but these too were quickly compromised by lack of funds or by the fact that migrants simply crossed the border elsewhere.

More tellingly, however, it was the contradictory demands of public health and the need for labour which ultimately determined colonial policy. As Lyons points out, concern for public health as reflected in the measures designed or introduced to promote it was greater in years of labour surplus. Once health inspections and other entry restrictions looked like seriously impeding the flow of labour, they were promptly shelved or abandoned. Public health was simply the price to be paid for perpetuating the border's economically desirable porosity. The simple fact was, says Lyons, that Banyaruandan bodies were more highly prized for their labour, however diminished this might be as a result of disease and undernourishment, than they were feared for the disease which they allegedly carried. How individual

Banyaruanda experienced their bodies, and the bearing their bodies had upon their future, were thus directly susceptible to fluctuations in the policies pursued by the colonial state at the limits of its rule. It was not individual Banyaruanda who were perceived as crossing the border but variously 'diseased bodies' or 'working bodies'. The consequence, as Lyons (1996: 141) depressingly concludes, was that state perceptions of economic necessity ensured that 'individual migrants were expendable'. State policy on health in colonial Uganda is thereby revealed for what it was, not an untainted philanthropic or altruistic concern for the needy, but a medicalised rhetoric for the control of labour (much as in the case of the undocumented Mexican immigrants described in chapter six).

Reduced to being 'disseminators of disease' the bodies of the Banyaruanda thus in some sense become merely the viruses and bacteria that they carry in a process that strips them of their humanity and individuality. In this regard they bear obvious similarities to the livestock that is similarly vetted for disease at international borders. In Britain, for instance, fear of rabies and foot-and-mouth disease has long justified the rigorous inspection of imported cattle and sheep, as well as a six-month period of quarantine for domestic pets. Similar restrictions exist throughout Europe where since the early days of the European Economic Community they have been the subject of vigorous and increasingly heated debate, particularly following the BSE crisis and the EU-imposed ban on the export of British beef. In the Republic of Ireland, much to the exasperation of many in Northern Ireland who feel that it is the military supply lines to the conflict there which should be the focus of police efforts, the bodies which the lonely Irish border guard sheltering from the cold in his patrol car seeks to halt are those of potentially BSE-infected cattle being smuggled out of the North.

In circumstances such as these, where both people and animals are labelled as diseased and where, as a result, they may be quarantined or denied entry, there is often a ready elision made between the bodies of the two. Diseased humans are no more or no less than diseased livestock when it comes to crossing borders: to both may be attributed the same bovine passivity, and both may be subject to the same or similar treatment. This 'animalising' of the human body operates in other contexts too. The supposed characteristics of certain kinds of human border crosser are commonly likened to features thought typical of certain types of animal. Thus on the US–Mexico border it is the *coyote* who leads prospective migrants across the Rio Grande, his natural instinct, wile and intimate knowledge of the terrain contributing to the likely success of the venture. Elsewhere, it is the wolf (*les loups*) who offers to secure passage across the Strait of Gibraltar from Morocco to Spain (Driessen 1998), or the 'snakehead' who guides the Chinese who seek to enter Hong Kong (Peter Webster, personal communication). At the same time, it is the very cunning of these figures that constitutes their danger. A characteristically ambiguous figure and the contradictory trickster of indigenous Mexico and North

America, the *coyote* can no more be trusted (Kearney 1998a; Meléndez 1982: 300) than the European wolf whose proclivities are likewise culturally encoded in nursery rhyme and fairy tale. Illegal migrants themselves are often similarly conceptualised in animal categories. In colloquial Mexican Spanish, 'illegal' border crossers are referred to as 'chickens' (*pollos*) or 'little chicks' (*pollitos*), 'defenceless creatures, vulnerable to the predators who prey upon them in the border zone . . . [which] . . . is infested with predators who rob, rape, assault, murder, apprehend, extort and swindle the vulnerable *pollos* whose only advantage is their large numbers' (Kearney 1998a: 129). In Spain too, those who cross the Strait illegally are seen as vulnerable, this time conceptualised as sheep (*les agneaux*) dependent on the shepherding of others. Out of necessity, and with no guarantees, both the *pollos* and *les agneaux* must entrust themselves to *coyote* and *les loups* who in the end, as Kearney remarks, may either deliver them or eat them up. In other contexts illegal entrants to North America have been viewed, for various reasons, as more of a threat, and the metaphors used to refer to them have differed accordingly. Thus exiled Marielitos from Cuba were referred to as 'bullets' (Borneman 1986), while unwelcome arrivals from South America have been referred to as 'killer bees' (Malkki, personal communication).

This reclassification of undocumented entrants as other than human is another aspect of the liminality of the border zone, one which we might reasonably expect given what anthropologists have had to say about liminality in general. Moreover, it is one which potentially opens up these border crossers to other kinds of subjection by the state and its agents. Once stripped of their humanity, they can be hunted down, like the wild animals which some of them are taken to represent. For instance, Albanians crossing illegally into Epirus on the Greek side of the Albanian border, reopened since 1990, are associated with nature, or 'wilderness', rather than with culture, which they are said to lack: 'They're like animals; don't ever imagine that they're like you or me', one local Greek is quoted as saying (in Green 1998b). As such, they are 'searched out in the wilderness of the Epirot borderlands, are collected together and are herded back to Albania, after a head count is made for the [official] statistics' (Green 1998a: 269). Undocumented immigrants can be rounded up like sheep, corralled and domesticated to the will of others, like the Moroccans penned up in the holding centre on Tarifa's outer quay, the town's most peripheral location, literally on the edge of Europe (Driessen 1998). The animal categories used as forms of verbal abuse which Leach (1972 [1964]) famously described become in these circumstances the object of more physical abuse too, particularly so when violence erupts along the border, as we shall see later.

Migrants may see themselves in similar terms, as beasts of burden bound to do the bidding of their masters, even when they have entered legally. This is forcefully borne out by the comments of Mexican migrant labour in the US, who frequently observe that 'here we live and work like beasts'. As one Mixtec farmworker living outdoors in a makeshift camp reportedly remarked, 'the bosses treat their animals better than they treat us. They give their dogs, horses, and chickens houses to sleep in. But us they leave out in the rain. They even have barns for their tractors, but not for us' (cited in Kearney 1998a: 138). Like the farm animals and machines alongside which they toil, it is the labour of these migrants that is critical. This labour is seen in terms of a metaphor of 'sweat', which is what the migrants leave behind in exchange for money, and through which the migrant's labour becomes disembodied. As Kearney (1998a: 130) elaborates, 'sweating for others in the United States contrasts with sweating for oneself in one's own community in Oaxaca'. By falling on one's own land in Oaxaca one's sweat produces for oneself rather than for others. In Oaxaca the toil of one's body, its sweat, and the community are organically linked, so that one's sweat is retained by the collective social body with which one identifies and to which one 'belongs', rather than being 'soaked up' in the US where the migrant is incorporated as 'alien' rather than citizen. To be an 'alien' then, Kearney (1998a: 130) argues, is not only to experience the 'disembodiment of one's labour, but also to be socially disembodied, that is, to be removed from one's community to the degree that one's sweat, one's labour and identity' are absorbed by the United States.

The processes at work in the examples above are hardly surprising to anthropologists, who have long documented the element of danger and risk associated with the outsider and stranger, but they are nevertheless revelatory about the relationship between the body and the border. Spread of disease and the use of animal imagery are transparently metaphors for talking about something else: the undesirability of the alien. By narrating this in terms of disease and animal categories, the antipathy to the alien is naturalised and even racialised as an element of foreign bodies which is immutable and inherent, a justificatory mechanism of exclusion and closure. In such a discourse it is not just the behaviour and habits of immigrants which are the focus of fear, nor just the anxiety that they might 'take' the jobs of 'local' people. More fundamentally, their difference and undesirability are embodied in their very being. In this world view, the boundaries of the body become analogous to the borders of the nation and the nation-state; both are vulnerable to penetration and corruption from the outside, susceptible to disease and alien intrusion respectively.

All of this suggests, as Seremetakis (1996: 490) has argued, that many borders represent 'an infection', leaking not just people but contaminated and contaminating substances. Both the body and the body politic are at risk. While it may indeed be true of Greece that this 'medicalization of the border and of mobile people [points] to *new* forms of violence emanating from this space' (Seremetakis 1996: 490, emphasis added), such has long been the case elsewhere as we saw with Uganda. The leakage is at once both physical and moral, a two-fold violation whose threat is most visibly represented by the bodies of prostitutes charged with the spread of sexually transmitted diseases. There are many such examples where the association between borders, disease and moral corruption is personified and gendered in this form: in Greece, as Seremetakis mentions (see also Green 1998a), at the German border with the Czech Republic (see chapter five), at the US–Mexico border (Mishra et al. 1996), and at Turkey's borders with Syria (Stokes 1998) and the former Soviet Republic of Georgia (Hann and Bellér-Hann 1998). We shall return to some of these examples later in the chapter. For the moment, however, we turn to other forms of violence which characterise the border.

Frontiers of Violence

Frontiers and borders have long been associated with violence and lawlessness, most obviously because of the military and political expansionism which they so often represent and the logistics of enforcing order in areas usually geographically distant from the centres of control. Famous among them is the American frontier, the uncertainty and instability of which are central to Turner's well-known thesis about the shaping of the rugged, individualist character of American society and the substance of so much popular fiction and film ever since. As one revisionist historian recently put it, 'the frontier was the principal arena of single male brutality in American history' (Courtwright 1996: 3).

Physical violence on the American frontier manifested itself in a variety of ways, only some of which we can touch on here, with the kinds of violence perpetrated frequently exceeding what was required to succeed militarily. Courtwright (1996) suggests that frontier violence was rather more than a means to a military end. As has often been remarked, it also involved the dehumanising of the 'savage'. The 'civility' and 'etiquette' of European warfare with its exchanges of letters between opposing generals prior to battle, the following of European norms of diplomacy and truce-making, and the general observance of the *rules* of war contrasted sharply with accounts of native excess and 'barbarism' in the newspapers, popular fiction and captivity narratives of the time: the mutilated bodies and desecrated graves, the killing and torturing of children and babies, the rape and impaling of women (see Courtwright 1996: 114; Colley 1997). Such propaganda not only helped to drum up support for the 'civilising' mission of the settlers, thereby legitimating their westward expansion, but further served as a means of articulating difference, especially in regard to what we would now call national identity and ethnicity. And it was this civilising process, propelled by American notions of manifest destiny, which ultimately led to the establishment of the US–Mexico border, which many Mexicans today still see as bifurcating old Mexico, 'violating' their traditional national territory.

But the situation of frontier violence was more complex than North American and government propaganda would suggest. White Americans too perpetrated atrocities, pulling down the bodies of Indians left in trees and scaffolds and chopping them to pieces for bait or fashioning their bones into curios. Bodily parts were taken as trophies on both sides, as claims to prestige and bravado. Citing Colonel Richard Irving Dodge writing in 1883, Courtwright (1996: 117) has pointed out that scalping was common among soldiers and settlers, who were 'as prompt to take a scalp as any Indian', for reasons of both status and the claiming of bounties. According to Courtwright, many white frontiersmen also

> helped themselves to Indian heads, hearts, fingers, ears, bladders, breasts, and genitals. One soldier in Chivington's Sand Creek command declared his intention to fashion a tobacco pouch from a dead Cheyenne's scrotum. Here again the dead and mutilated bodies are a text in which is written the frontiersmen's sense of Indians as animals from which fleshy souvenirs might be taken (1996: 117).

Moreover, such atrocities were carried out not just on the aboriginal population, but were also frequently a feature of the rivalry between colonial Europeans. The English, for instance, were not averse to taking French scalps. Indeed, as Colley (1997) has recently documented, accusations of 'savagery' were as frequently made by the French of the English as they were by the Europeans of the native American Indians, though it is the construction of the non-European 'other' in this manner which has received the bulk of the attention in post-colonial writings. But the point is that whoever the victim, the same mechanism was at work; through mutilation and dismemberment the body's identity was being actively reconfigured in a frontier setting where new identities were in a process of being formed. It is through violence, as Malkki has argued in another context, that the 'bodies of individual persons become metamorphosed into *specimens* of the ethnic category for which they are supposed to stand' (1995b: 88, emphasis in original). Such specimens distance the perpetrators of violence from those aspects of culture and biology which they share with their victims, thus enabling them to pursue their racist, ethnic and nationalist goals.

Malkki's remark helps us to make sense of much of the apparently 'random' sectarian violence between Catholic and Protestant in Northern Ireland, whether this takes place at the border with the Irish Republic or along the boundaries between Belfast's communal ghettos. In Northern Ireland individuals have often been selected as targets for sectarian assassination on the basis of a range of characteristics which are held to reveal their confessional loyalties. Dress, demeanour, place of residence, education, name, linguistic style and face are all elements of the cultural practice of 'telling', a 'system of signs by which religious ascription is arrived at in practical settings' (Burton 1979: 62). On its own, the body itself is said to give much away: the colour of hair, the space between the eyes, the pallor of skin, the set of the jaw. Bodily mannerisms extend this list of identificatory traits. In one

Northern Irish border town, a history of violence is 'embodied in how people walk, purse their lips and talk, in body postures, clothes and hair styles' (Kelleher 1990: 9), a respository of signs which identify an individual as one of 'us' or 'them' depending on how they are practised. Through such signs people in this border town, as elsewhere in Northern Ireland, position themselves and are positioned by others via a sectarian language written on and read from the body's performance, which may deliver a message of support for the state or antipathy to it.

Although the practice of 'telling' in Northern Ireland is sometimes used to structure behaviour in such a way as to avoid giving offence, by allowing one to avoid controversial topics or offensive opinions in the presence of those identified as members of the other group, it may also be used to provoke violent confrontation by deliberately exposing rival loyalties. As Feldman (1991: 56) remarks, in decoding the other 'telling' also 'encodes the self, a symbiosis that renders "telling" a nexus for the construction of political agency'. Properly coded bodies thus enable the proper (sectarian) ordering of social space, and determine the consequences when this is transgressed.

Feldman (1991: 68–71) argues that the semantics of political violence in Northern Ireland are worked out in part through bodily metaphor, in particular through the notion of the 'stiff' and its associated verb 'to stiff'. These are pivotal metaphors, he suggests, for the body encoded by political violence in this border zone, and have become extended from their previously wholly criminal associations of 'murder' to signify political assassination. 'The corpse and the border are both points of separation and contact between opposing spaces. These thresholds define the space of political exchange. The corpse and the border form a metonymy that permits political codes and values to circulate. Corpses or stiffs become mobile borders or interfaces and thus bearers of political spectacle' (Feldman 1991: 74).

We agree with Feldman that there is much that is suggestive in his paralleling of the body and the border. His claim that violence is 'the physical erasure of individuality as a deviation from an ethnic construct . . . [and that] . . . [t]he ethnicity of the body is built in its dismemberment and disfigurement' (1991: 64) would certainly seem to hold elsewhere. The trainloads of massacred and mutilated bodies of those who had sought refuge on one side or another of the newly created border between Pakistan and India following partition of the Indian subcontinent in 1947 is one example. Here too attention often fixed upon the body, with potential male victims required to lower their trousers to expose a circumcised or uncircumcised penis, revealing them as Muslim or Hindu respectively, and the genitals the subsequent focus for mutilation. So too with the Hutu and the Tutsi among whom, as Malkki describes, bodily signs act as an iconography of the ethnic other and can mark the difference between life and death.

Malkki (1995b) provides a sophisticated analysis of how bodily differences are used among Hutu refugees in Tanzania to express social and political inequality.

Her account focuses on the Hutu refugees who fled the massacres in Burundi following failed attempts by Hutu to displace the ruling Tutsi in the decade or so after independence. She concentrates in particular on those who fled the 1972 massacres, and who left Burundi to establish residence in the Tanzanian border town of Kigoma (linked to Burundi by a regular ferry service across Lake Tanganyika) or in the more isolated refugee camp of Mishamo (see Map 6.1). These Hutu narrate their troubled pasts in a form which Malkki refers to as 'mythico-history', a style of narrative through which they both moralise their world and impose some fundamental, cosmological order upon it, and in which categorical distinctions between self and other, Hutu and Tutsi, good and evil are discursively elaborated and explored. The body occupies a central place in these narratives, with 'the Tutsi' constituted not just as categorical opposite and enemy, 'but also as the embodiment of such abstract moral qualities as evil, laziness, beauty, danger, and "malignity"', and 'the Hutu' as their antithesis (Malkki 1995b: 54).

As with Catholic and Protestant in Northern Ireland, Hutu and Tutsi are believed to be recognisable by putative physical differences whose provenance pre-dates the current conflict. The colonial records present the Tutsi as the 'tall, stately, thin people, and the Hutu [as] the short, stockier plain peasants', stereotypical attributes which are elaborated and transformed in a contemporary cataloguing of physical types whose characteristics bear an eerie resemblance to those mentioned earlier for Northern Ireland: 'nose shape, color of tongue and gums, size of pupils, hair texture, prominence of ankle bones, protrusion of calves, lines on the palm of the hand were all markers of difference' (Malkki 1995b: 79).

These supposed physical differences are closely linked with moral and social difference but in contemporary Hutu usage are understood in ways that do not always converge with the value they were given in the colonial period. As 'stockier' and stronger, the Hutu have the 'habit' of hard work, their history of oppression having ensured that the harder they were made to work, the stronger they became, something which the Hutu now evaluate positively as a consequence of their experience of exile. In contrast, the Tutsi are 'weak of body' and govern by 'malignity' and 'trickery'. Malkki (1995b: 81) suggests that these character-isations are indicative of two forms of power: a physical power which inheres within the body and is augmented by hard work, and a power like that of the Tutsi which is located outside the body and thus more volatile and precarious. Moreover, the hard work of the Hutu organically binds them to the land, the sweat of their brow enriching the soil they cultivate, and justifying their claim, in comments which recall the views of the Mexican migrant labour mentioned above, that 'It is we who feed the Tutsi. We are their granaries. We call them insects; they do not work; they just live, like insects. They eat our sweat' (Malkki 1995b: 80). In Hutu eyes, such parasitism morally precludes the Tutsi from membership of the nation.

This reasoning culminated in the violent conflict and massacres of 1972 when physical difference was used as a clue to determine who would or should be killed. Malkki's analysis of Hutu atrocity accounts reveals that the focus on the mutilation of particular body parts was not accidental but had great symbolic significance when recalled and reconstructed within the mythico-history. Moreover, the animal metaphors mentioned earlier in relation to illegal migrants resurface here, this time with more sinister implications:

> When asked about a Hutu uprising, one old man retorted: 'There *was* no war. We were gathered like sheep, like goats. These are assassinations'. Hutu docility was often described through such analogies to domestic animals. One village Chairman in Mishamo, for example, explained: 'The Tutsi, he is like the shepherd who guards the herds. So, it is easy for him to say, "Today I will slaughter a cow". It is easy. Or else, if one has chickens – one can slaughter them when one wants. We are like herds before the Tutsi' (Malkki 1995b: 100).

The focus of Tutsi violence, as recalled by the Hutu, seems largely to have been determined by the sex of their Hutu victims:

> The mouth, the brain, and the head as a whole, as well as the anus, were the focal areas on the bodies of men in particular. Women's bodies were said to have been destroyed largely through the vagina and the uterus. When the women captured were pregnant, the violence seems invariably to have focussed on the womb and specifically on the link between mother and child. In the case of the school girls, the violence was initiated through the vagina. In the case of both men and women . . . a systematic connection was made between the vagina and the anus and the head through the penetration of bamboo poles . . . The penetration of the head through the anus, as well as other means of crushing the head, were seen as a decapitation of the intellect, and, on a more general level, as an effort to render the Hutu people powerless, politically impotent (Malkki 1995b: 92).

Such violence, according to Malkki, dehumanises victim and perpetrator alike, essentialising both 'Hutu' and 'Tutsi' as categories of identity. The violence and defilement are attributed to the Tutsi as a whole, not just to the specific individuals responsible, and, resonating with their parasitism and trickery mentioned earlier, make them morally unworthy of belonging to or forming a 'natural' element of 'the nation'. In Hutu mythico-history, 'the enemy of the "authentic nation" of Burundi is "the Tutsi"' (Malkki 1995b: 94).

In each of the cases considered so far – the American frontier, Northern Ireland, and Burundi – dehumanising violence perpetrated on the body is a major element of identity formation in contexts where drawing the border round the nation is in dispute. In each case physical violation and defilement, and the particular symbolically meaningful form which these take, are ways in which the ethnic other is imagined and constructed, mapping on to the body itself as a semiotic object the limits of inclusion and exclusion. Littlewood's words (1997: 11), in an essay on military rape, are apposite here:

> [s]exual violence . . . seems less a standardized pattern of conflict enacted against a defining other across some accepted boundary, than a way of clarifying, developing and affirming such boundaries; less playing the accepted war game beyond the rules, than a working out of boundaries on the woman's body, symbolically but also pragmatically (as destruction of the opponent's social institutions).

However, the body is more than just a powerful communicative device for articulating and representing difference. It is at once both object and subject as Synnott reminds us in the quotation cited earlier. In other words, it is experienced and felt by those who suffer.

French (1994) takes up this theme of the lived experience and meaning of the body upon which violence has been inflicted in relation to refugee camps on the Thai–Cambodian border. Following Foucault's suggestion that 'it is largely as a force of production that the body is invested with relations of power and domination' (1979: 25, cited in French 1994: 75), French shows how the experiential world of those who have suffered personal injury can only be grasped by understanding the wider political economy within which these camps are located. Her particular focus is the many amputees, injured in landmine explosions, who are a ubiquitous feature of this border landscape and a major element of the displaced Khmer population now forced to dwell there. She conservatively estimates that an incredible one in every seventy people on this border in 1991 was an amputee (1994: 72), some of them soldiers but many of them civilians caught by a landmine when foraging for vegetables or firewood in nearby forests. Amputees were thus an everyday feature of the streets and markets of the camp in which she worked. Confounding her original assumptions, these amputees were rarely viewed with compassion, or as living reminders of the ravages of war, but were generally looked down upon by other camp residents who feared them for their reputation for violence and theft. To understand the antipathy and sense of abandonment which marked the experiences of these amputees, French suggests, they must be located within the politico-economic contexts from which their disability now greatly reduced and even precluded their effective involvement.

Before their injury many of the amputees had fought for the loosely based military coalition which had sought to oust the Vietnamese from Cambodia, an objective which they had often supported as much out of the practical need to maintain their families as from ideological commitment. The bond they forged with their commanders was, in their eyes, a reciprocal moral relationship with leaders to whom they offered their loyalty and productive labour in prosecuting war in exchange for the protection of a powerful patron in a time of political uncertainty and scarce resources. Their rejection by their commander after their injury was a shocking transformation of the moral into the utilitarian, and an abject denial of this mutual obligation. So too amputation severely diminished the contribution amputees could make to the domestic economy, resulting in feelings of shame and anger at no longer being able to fulfil cultural expectations as male providers and generating a fear that they would lose their place in that most basic of Cambodian institutions of social support, the family (French 1994: 80).

Shame and frustration at these changes gave to amputees a kind of carelessness about their behaviour, which was frequently manifested in violence and bravado, resulting in a further distancing from the other camp inhabitants in a recursively negative downward spiral. Because of the way in which 'radical self-interest had become a virtual prerequisite for survival' (French 1994: 92) in the straitened circumstances of this border camp, compassion had become not just a difficult but imprudent response which could leave one vulnerable to victimisation. The camp economy, as French says, had become one of scarcity and hoarding, in emotional as well as material terms. The wider political, economic and social realities of camp life thus gave form and confirmation to the amputees' subjective experience of their own bodies, creating a localised border culture, or 'unique "local moral world"' in French's terms (1994: 93), within which certain actions and responses were predictable and certain emotions virtually impossible. Like the sexualised bodies of the contested border zones examined in the following section, the 'specific cultural meaning of these [amputee] bodies is not distinct from but deeply embedded in the relations of domination and production that have framed the war for these people' (French 1994: 72).

Sexualising Borders

As we have seen from the examples above, as well as from our earlier discussion of cross-border prostitution, sex is frequently an element in the body politics of border regions (cf. Kelsky 1996). As a commodity purveyed in the local border economy, as a factor held responsible for the spread of disease, or as a focus for violent deeds, sex, and those bodily parts associated with sex, may be used as a means of both enacting as well as representing relationships in the wider society. In many border settings, sex seems to provide a ready analogy for many of the features typical of relationships across state lines and along their edges. In this section we explore this association in greater detail, examining the way in which sex and sexual relationships at borders are often employed as an idiom of power or the lack of it. Though different writers have approached the issue of sex at borders in different ways, underlying much of this work is a common thread which, borrowing Bailey's (1983) resonant phrase for emotion's persuasive force, might be referred to as the 'tactical use of passion'.

The state itself may use its ability to legislate on sexual behaviour as a means of underwriting its position in a manner which recalls Synnott's claim, cited above, that while the body is personal it is also state property. Steedly (1996) describes a case where alleged sexual misconduct was used by the state to legitimate and extend its control in an otherwise administratively unconsolidated and relatively ungovernable border region in Sumatra in 1949. The incident involved a court case brought against a border guard, Majek Bangun, for 'rape by misuse of office', an offence which Steedly (1996: 3) interprets as the border guard having allowed his victim 'to cross the border in exchange for sex'. Majek was found guilty, and made to dig his own grave before being blindfolded and shot in the back of the head, a judgement some considered harsh though in keeping with the rule of law.

Almost fifty years later, Steedly (1996: 5) found that contemporary local memory recalled Majek's death as a 'sacrifice to the national project of "governmentality"'. The execution was, says Steedly, an instance of pre-emptive retaliation, designed to prevent similar incidents in future and, importantly, to ensure governmental continuity. In contrast to other kinds of border crime such as smuggling, the accusation of rape was particularly well-suited to the purpose of enforcing government rule in the area. For unlike the crime of smuggling, which brings 'the interests of the government into conflict with the interests of the governed . . . the charge of rape brings those interests together' (Steedly 1996: 9–10). This was especially so in Majek's case where both victim and accused, as well as others involved in the drama, were of the same ethnic background. There was thus no suggestion that rape was here being used as a brutal tool of ethnic conflict as so commonly reported from elsewhere (for example, see Roussou 1986: 32–4). Instead, Majek was acting from within the social body itself: 'within the state, as a "misuse of office"; within the nation, by "adding to the suffering of the people" on one's own side; within the domestic order by disrupting the protective regime of the father' (Steedly 1996: 6–7). The accusation of rape ensured that these three levels converged. Any possibility that smuggling might also have been involved, or that Majek's accuser was a fellow smuggler, is not mentioned in the published accounts of the court proceedings. The accuser was therefore presented as a passive victim, eligible for the full protection of the state. Majek's crime, on the other hand, was threefold: against the state, the nation and the family. By punishing Majek, the state could thereby enhance and consolidate its local authority by being seen to protect its subjects, in this case the woman involved, as well as the country's major institutions. Where the border is regarded as a 'scene of sexual *and* economic transactions between a state and its population', Steedly suggests (1996: 2, emphasis in original), 'the sexualized (female) body [can thus be seen as] a symbolic site upon which the "protective" impulses of state, communal and familial patriarchal orders converge'.

To some extent this is also borne out by an example from the Middle East, though as a negative case as we shall see in a moment. Bowman (1996) has described how the Palestinian merchants in the tourist markets of pre-*intifada* Jerusalem used sex with foreign visitors as a way of imagining and acting out a power which objectively they did not possess in this Israeli-dominated disputed frontier zone. Business for these traders was precarious: they offered almost identical merchandise to a generally uninterested, transient and frequently hostile clientele. Bowman tells us that in these circumstances selling style was critical, and, that in an effort to bring trade to their shop, merchants vied with each other over the novelty of their street-side displays and ability to switch language and cultural code according to potential customer. After hours, in the bars and cafés of the quarter, stories of successful economic seduction were recounted to fellow merchants, together with graphic accounts of the sexual conquest of foreign customers, often embellished to enhance the status of the teller. Both types of tale formed a central element in the traders' self-image, their value lying as much in the telling as in the successful sale or sexual act themselves.

Bowman relates a typical tale that was told by a merchant called Salim. According to Salim, a rich, beautiful, married American woman had entered his shop and after several hours of sweet-talking persuasion had bought for $400 a Bedouin dress which he said was worth only $200, a bargain in her eyes since she had negotiated a $50 discount from the original $450 price tag. Following on this success, he invited her out that evening, an invitation she declined though evidently taken by his charm and virility. He told her anyway that he would meet her that evening in the lobby of her hotel. Arriving late, he found her exquisitely dressed and anxiously awaiting his appearance. He invited her to a friend's house. She refused at first. But

> [i]n spite of her wealth, her nationality and her often mentioned (by Salim) husband asleep upstairs in the $120 a night hotel room, she could not resist his seductiveness. The upshot was that Salim took her from the [hotel's] opulence to 'a dirty little room' where 'he fucked her till 5am'. She, allegedly, was ecstatic about both the size of his 'Palestinian cock' and his technique, and was carried to heights of sexual fulfilment. He, on the other hand, was dropped into disgust and depression by the whole experience. Looking down on her, supposedly flushed by orgasm, he told her she was 'just a slut' and that he was sure 'she fucked with everyone in all the countries she'd been in'. She was, he said, deeply offended, but he claimed that saying this 'made him feel good afterwards' (Bowman 1996: 93–4).

Salim continued by recounting how he had overcharged for the dress – 'I figure I got a good deal with the profit and the fuck thrown in' – but concluded by noting that should he ever marry a fellow Palestinian, he 'would go out on the street, take out [his] cock and piss on all the foreign women, even if one of them was the Queen of Sheba' (Bowman 1996: 94).

Bowman suggests that what is at issue here is Salim's ability to overcome the woman's power as represented by her wealth and nationality. Despite these advantages, and even when confronted by someone as structurally disadvantaged as Salim, she is incapable of defending either her economic or bodily integrity. As a result, Salim's power is doubly asserted, his ability to take the woman's money reinforced by his ability to take her body in a complete reversal of their structural positions (Bowman 1996: 95). His closing image of 'the merchant's penis as a sign in an agonistic discourse with foreigners rather than as an element connected with the creation of family, community and nation' (Bowman 1996: 99) is indicative of the dislocation and disconnectedness experienced by these particular Palestinians in this border zone.

Bowman and his merchant friends have little to say about more local tourists, such as Palestinian or Israeli women visiting Jerusalem on holiday, although such domestic visitors constituted more than half the market's trade. All we learn is that Israeli women 'didn't count', their seduction reportedly requiring neither skill nor effort. More tellingly, however, Bowman (1996: 96) does speculate that Israeli power may have been 'too imminent to be denied even in a displacing language . . . of sexual politics'. In this sense then, the very absence of these women from the merchants' sexual narratives may provide negative evidence for claiming that the sexualised female body in Jerusalem as in Sumatra may be regarded 'as a symbolic site upon which the "protective" impulses of state, communal and familial patriarchal orders converge'.

For these Palestinian merchants, then, it is the seduction of foreigners – a category which apparently does not therefore seem to include Israelis – that is critical. In Bowman's terms, the structurally 'fucked'[2] become the 'fuckers' in a symbolic inversion which 're-masculinises', through sexual domination of foreigners, those 'feminised' by their economic and political position, at least in the eyes of the merchants themselves if for no one else. This process is clearly illustrated by the one case of sexual failure which Bowman recorded. Ironically it involved a merchant renowned for his body-building and aggressive demeanour towards tourists. While in the course of intimate foreplay with an English woman behind the closed doors of his shop, he ejaculated prematurely when the woman inserted a finger in his anus. He immediately jumped up and forced her, half-naked, on to the street. His anger, Bowman suggests, can only be understood in relation to the pejorative term *manioc*, a term of abuse which refers, among other things, to

---

2. In an earlier version of this article, Bowman (1989: 88) briefly elaborated on what he meant by the 'structurally "fucked"', referring to them as 'the victims of a market and of a map', a phrase dropped from the more recent publication.

'the one who takes his pleasure in the ass', who enjoys sex passively, 'like a woman'. The merchant's dismay was thus about 'being figuratively feminized while he was attempting – literally and in terms of a discourse on social intercourse – to assert his dominant, "masculine" role over a tourist woman' (1996: 97).

These processes of feminisation and demasculinisation, processes which are symbolically counteracted by the relatively powerless through the bodily control of others during the sexual act, while obviously not exclusively found in border regions (see, for instance, Herzfeld 1985), nevertheless seem to have a peculiar resonance there, especially when the border itself is similarly gendered in such terms as we shall see below. Young Turkish men in the Hatay, on Turkey's contested southern border with Syria (see map 6.2), display similar anxieties to those evident among Bowman's Palestinian merchants. Both are confronted by the problem of how to project an image of power in circumstances where the realities of their powerlessness are all too obvious. And both express the problem by displaying a mix of swaggering aggressiveness and passive docility towards local Arabs and visiting tourists respectively, as well as by the sexual domination of those perceived as powerful and threatening. In the Hatay this style of behaviour is associated with the self-proclaimed *kabadayi*, young Turkish 'lads' in their early teens or twenties who strut around the local bars and brothels loudly proclaiming their presence and indicating their readiness for violence. Stokes (1994: 41) describes the obsession of one such individual, Cemal, with a local Arab prostitute, whom Cemal visited regularly. The position for intercourse which Cemal adopted with this 'Arab prostitute (*arkadan* – "from behind", he explained with a contemptuous laugh on the way to the baths) is not one of productive marital coitus, but a psycho-drama of coercive domination, of female by male and Arab by Turk' (Stokes 1994: 48), an interpretation with obvious relevance for the Palestinian example already considered (and perhaps also for the sexual positions adopted by some migrant Mexican labourers with their American partners; see Bronfman and Moreno 1996: 65).

Though found elsewhere, it is their proximity to a border, and the image of that border, that gives to these practices their particular resonance and meaning. This is clearly evident from Stokes's study of the Hatay, whose interpretation of *kabadayi* sexual preferences is borne out by other aspects of sexuality in the region. According to Stokes, another arena in which local relations between Arab and Turk are worked out is through a form of cultural performance known as Arabesk, a popular musical genre which both articulates and helps to explain some of the feelings of ambiguity and submissiveness experienced by the Hatay's Turkish inhabitants. Turkish gendered nationalist historiography constructs the country's borders as an act of paternity on the part of Atatürk, the 'father Turk', whose decisive and effective procreative action conceived the modern Turkish nation-state out of the remnants of the Ottoman empire. The exception is the Hatay, at which border, Stokes argues, Turkey's virile national masculinity is compromised in the popular imagination, because it was left out of Atatürk's scheme and because of the state's continued ineffectual involvement there. This imagery of depleted masculinity is in turn reflected in the sexual ambiguity of many of the best-known Arabesk performers and in a corresponding hyper-machismo on the part of their following, such as the *kabadayi*. Many of the former are openly gay or transsexual, ambivalent and 'unproductive' sexual identities which mirror the anomalous gendered representation of the border as an impotent product of the state. Like the heterosexual male who 'takes a woman from behind', sex here is a penetrative but not a procreative act. It may signify dominance, but at the same time it isolates these men from kin and nation by denying the 'proper' role of sex in reproducing these bodies, in an ambiguous act that parallels the indeterminacy of the political boundaries alongside which it takes place.

The sexual act may thus mark rupture or relationship. It can be a powerful idiom of inclusion or exclusion. As such, it is a versatile rhetorical device for marking boundaries. Moreover, as we have seen, it may be deployed in border zones as both violent act and as symbol. Rape and penetration are both metaphor and physical threat. Sexual violation is simultaneously a way of talking about borders and one way of violently enacting their reality in an arena where political boundaries are readily perceived as the boundaries of the body itself. In the contested politics of border zones, the sexualised body may become the weapon of the disempowered as well as of the state in its effort to consolidate control.

The Birth and Death of the Body Politic

Feldman (1991) suggests that there are good reasons for the body being the endpoint of resistance and control. As the state expands so the room for political agency contracts (cf. Sahlins 1989). The structurally disadvantaged and those who resist the state's advances may increasingly find their geographical and conceptual space for political expression reduced, the forces of the centralising state scattering them to the edges, its centrifugal energies forcing their backs against the wall, pushing them up against the border, literally so in the case of the paramilitary prisoners described in Feldman's *Formations of Violence*. Jenkins succinctly summarises Feldman's position in his review of his book:

> On the one hand, as a consequence or an expression of the expansion of the spheres of domination of the state, the space available for political enactment shrinks (this is a process of subjection). On the other hand, however, and as an integral part of the same process, as available space shrinks, the potency of the acting political subject expands: the more constrained the possibilities for political practice become, the more symbolism and semantic power is condensed within that practice. These condense upon the surfaces of the body, in particular, which can then be treated as a text, laden with meaning (Jenkins 1992a: 233).

The body thus becomes the last resort for 'the redirection and reversal of power . . . The ex-inmates of the H-Blocks [the Maze Prison, near Belfast] as well as veterans of the interrogation centers admit that in negotiating these spaces of domination they deploy their bodies like weapons' (Feldman 1991: 178, 179), as apparent in the 'Blanket' and 'Dirty Protests' when prisoners refused to dress in prison clothing and to 'slop out', and subsequently in the Hunger Strike of 1981 when prisoners used their bodies as a final refuge of defence and retaliation (see Aretxaga 1993: 224). As if echoing the popular adage – 'the only time you know where you are is when you're on the edge' – one prisoner reflected, 'The H-Blocks broke all your inhibitions about your body. It made you more aware of your body', an observation amplified by a fellow internee: 'The H-Blocks changed the whole way you thought about your body . . . From the moment we hit the H-Block we had used our bodies as a protest weapon. It came from the understanding that the Brits were using our bodies to break us' (cited in Feldman 1991: 179).

While the *meaning* of these bodily practices of protest may be vigorously debated, as evidenced by the heated exchange between Feldman and Jenkins over the latter's review (Feldman 1992; Jenkins 1992a, 1992b), that the body can become a form of protest and subjection is hardly in dispute. What makes the body so potent a symbol is the way in which it *naturalises* power. Instrumental uses of the body have 'metaphorical correspondences which link personal, social and natural *bodies*' (Jackson 1983, cited in Borneman 1986: 84, emphasis in original). The sexualised or gendered body seems a particularly powerful example of metaphorical convergence and 'naturalisation' of power, though it is evident too in ideas about diseased bodies as we noted earlier. In her analysis of the gendered imagery of the modern Turkish state, and drawing on David Schneider's discussion of the mediating role of sexual intercourse in establishing a homology between kinship and nationality in American kinship (see also Borneman 1986: 82), Delaney (1995) takes Stokes's discussion of Turkey's gendered national historiography a stage further. Atatürk's rhetorical construction of the nation-state depended not just on a notion of the 'father' whose procreative act brought Turkey into being, she suggests, but on the corresponding idea of the 'Motherland' (*Anavatan*). Symbolically associated with the land, women's bodies are in a sense, 'the ground over which national identity is played out' (Delaney 1995: 191). When Atatürk identified his own mother with the Motherland, portraying injuries to one as if they were injuries to the other, 'peasants did not have to understand the idea of a nation-state to be motivated to protect their own threatened soil if it was understood as their mother who was being raped and sold into captivity' (Delaney 1995: 186). As Delaney (1995: 182) is at pains to point out, what is being emphasised here is not just gender, however, 'but gender in the context of reproduction'. It is the coming together of sexualised bodies in a 'natural' act of political procreation that gives rise to the 'birth' of modern Turkey as a body politic.

Just as the strengthening of the state limits the room for internal political agency, so too the birth and growth of modern states put pressure on the space and political agency of their neighbouring states. As we discussed in chapter one, there is a continuing debate about the resiliency of the nation-state in the world today, a world in which some perceive a diminution in the power of states and in their borders. If borders no longer act as the agents of control and violence as they once did, then perhaps new forms of personal and state politics may emerge in this global, postmodern era, a possibility we examine in the conclusion.

−8−

Conclusion: Border Cultures and the Crisis of the Nation-State

The ideas that every nation should have its own state and that every state should be a single nation may not have much solid merit either as normative or as practical proposals. But between them they have made a great deal of the political history of the twentieth century.

Dunn, 'Introduction: Crisis of the Nation-State'

This book has examined culture and community at a variety of international borders in order to advance the notion that anthropology is ideally suited to provide cultural analyses of political and economic relations in modern nation-states. Although in the past anthropology has been principally known for its methodological contribution to comparative social science, primarily through its use of ethnographic field research, we agree with Gledhill (1994: 7) that it also has much to offer theoretically to the other social sciences through the cross-cultural comparison of social and political realities. Gledhill (1994: 225) argues that to succeed in this endeavour, however, anthropology must continue to try to break free from its particular historicity as a western form of knowledge, shedding western models of society and polity which constrain its view of other places. Similar efforts, he suggests, must be made in political anthropology. Yet try as they might, political anthropologists cannot escape the particular polity of the nation-state. Although the nation-state may be found everywhere in the world, its forms and structure are not universal (cf. Kapferer 1988: 3, who makes this point regarding nationalism), for it is constructed institutionally and symbolically in myriad ways across the global landscape.

Thus, it has been our view in this book that, whatever else it must do, political anthropology cannot and should not absolve itself from analysing the nation-state. Nevertheless, just as many anthropologists have attempted to avoid the methodological problems and ethical issues inherent in a western social science devoted to the comparative study of cultures, so many political anthropologists attempt to avoid examining the pre-eminent political entities of modernity: the nation and the state. There have been many reasons for this, from anthropology's roots in imperialism which emphasised non-western and non-state politics, to disciplinary boundaries which evolved in ways which allowed other academic disciplines to stake their claims to different forms of polity, to the methodological difficulties involved in trying to study the personnel and forces of the state from the preferred anthropological vantage point of that most local of levels, such as village or campsite, usually in a very peripheral part of the state among a relatively powerless group of people. As Michael Herzfeld has noted, 'anthropologists have hitherto largely shunned the state as a hostile and invasive presence in local social life and have seen nationalism as an embarrassing first cousin to the discipline itself, one distinctly prone to public excesses of essentialism and reification' (1997: 1). Even nationalism is discussed by political anthropologists 'with little or no reference to the institutional context of modern politics' (Spencer 1997: 3). Paradoxically, the very ubiquity of the state would seem to have made it all but invisible in the work of many ethnographers (cf. Gupta 1995: 375; Kertzer 1988: 6).

This is not to say that all anthropologists have eschewed opportunities to analyse the state and the nation, at local levels of society and beyond. Many of the works of these pioneering anthropologists have been noted and some summarised in this book. Taken together, in fact, their analyses are impressive for their depth and breadth, and have ranged over a variety of topics which are all crucial to the understanding of contemporary nations and states. Important examples include anthropological studies of myths, rituals and ideologies of nationalism (Handelman 1990; Handler 1988; Kapferer 1988); world and state religion and nationalism (Tambiah 1976, 1986); national unification (Borneman 1992); comparative European nationalism (Jenkins 1997); local and national perspectives on state socialism (Nagengast 1991; Verdery 1991); nation- and state-building (Fox 1985; D. Nugent 1994); bureaucracy (Herzfeld 1992); and transnationalism and internationalisation (Borneman 1998; Kearney 1995). There have also been a number of insightful analyses of the historical development of political anthropology to which this book is indebted (Eriksen 1993; Gledhill 1994; Vincent 1990).

We choose these examples as representative of a strong and growing presence in anthropology of scholars who have attempted to marry perspectives on the local and the national, within a political anthropology that privileges the state as a principal and integral political element of all levels of society. What sets these studies apart from those conducted by other social scientists, however, is that anthropologists have been less concerned with studying state structures and formal methods of governance. Many anthropologists 'have at last begun to do what most appropriately falls within their competence, directing their interests to the experiences of citizens and functionaries rather than to questions of formal organization' (Herzfeld 1997: 1). This developing interest is no coincidence, in that it parallels the deepening crisis of the nation-state itself.

As we noted in chapter one, scholars, journalists and government leaders, particularly in Europe, have been proclaiming for some time now a crisis in the nation-state (see Milward 1992; Wallace 1994). In some views the modern nation-state is weathering the storms of cultural globalisation, economic and political internationalisation, and social transnationalism, processes which are seen to be weakening the organs of the state, transforming notions of citizenship, and eroding state control over economic performance. Wallace (1994: 55) warns that although questions and answers regarding the loss of state power and the undermining of state functions must ultimately depend on one's perception of the role and function of the state itself, a perception shaped by the historical development of the nation, 'we have to recognize that there is *no* permanently-valid corpus of sovereign powers and state authority' (1994: 61, emphasis in original).

One of the key problems that has contributed to the loss of confidence in nation-states, and which has helped to create the criteria by which states are judged, is the presumed confluence of nation and state which Dunn criticises in the quotation with which we began this chapter. In their ideal form states serve and represent nations, groups of people whose relationship to each other is putatively based on notions of common culture and descent, and who legitimise the states to which they give rise. This one-to-one relationship, often assailed in a substantial scholarly literature which debates how states build nations and nations create states, is integral to any definition of the ideal nation-state, even though the nation-state is an artificial construct dependent on the historical experience of only two states, Britain and France (Wallace 1994: 61). While the origins and evolution of the nation-state are hotly debated, there can be little doubt that the twin concepts of nation and state sit uneasily with each other. This is due in large part to the appeal each concept has for its members. In fact, the crisis of the state may be due as much to shifts in people's perceptions of the importance and efficiency of the state as it is due to the state's loss of real control and power. As Dunn suggests (1994: 4–5):

> the present sense of crisis in the efficacy of the nation state comes from a resonance between two very different types of shift: a fading in all but the most extreme settings (typically those of armed conflict) in the normative appeals of the idea of the nation state, and a brusque rise in awareness of a series of new and formidable challenges (economic, ecological, military, political, even cultural) the scope of which plainly extends far beyond national boundaries and effectively ensures that they cannot be successfully met within such boundaries.

In these terms, the crisis of the nation-state is in fact a crisis in the efficacy of political action, in which the state is perceived to be failing in its primary role as the provider and guarantor of internal and external sovereignty. The state is an organisation which provides essential services. Its relationship to a nation, to *its* nation, gives it purpose and meaning beyond these services, but ultimately it is judged on its ability to deal with those internal and external pressures which threaten to impede its provision of the national and international order necessary for the working of its politics and economics.

This crisis of the nation-state is attracting some modest anthropological attention, of which this book is an example, but in tackling the state a number of accepted anthropological models need to be challenged. Anthropologists by and large have treated the state as an 'unanalyzed given' (Nagengast 1994: 116), adopting the Weberian notion that it has territorial integrity, commands the legitimate monopoly of the means of force, and is 'an autonomous structure of power in its own right, with distinct properties of its own, that cannot be reduced to any single set of social interests outside the state' (D. Nugent 1994: 334). But now new perspectives on the nation-state are coming forward, modifying and expanding the definitions of its forms and functions, and placing the emphasis on the dialectical relations between the state as an institution and all of its internal social groups and regions. Instead of proceeding as if the state operates as a cohesive and unitary whole, we should examine empirically the circumstances under which it acts as such (Gupta 1995: 392). This new political anthropology of the nation and the state recognises that

> the state is not just a set of institutions staffed by bureaucrats who serve public interest. It also incorporates cultural and political forms, representations, discourse, practices and activities, and specific technologies and organizations of power that, taken together, help to define public interest, establish meaning, and define and naturalize available social identities (Nagengast 1994: 116).

Furthermore, states are increasingly entering into supranational political and economic arrangements, international organisations and regional trading blocs which call into question the territorial integrity and monopoly of force which for so long have been hallmarks of the nation-state.

The crisis of nation-states today has become part of the crisis of the model of the nation-state in political anthropology. Anthropologists are increasingly gazing on the state in ways that were not foreshadowed in the history of the field, which has been long dominated by analyses of local politics in peasant and non-state settings, for anthropologists are looking beyond the formal apparatuses of institutional power in order to focus on politics and power as found in the everyday practices of social life (Abélès 1992; Gledhill 1994). And what this has increasingly revealed, as many of the examples in this book show, is that the state is often marked by internal inconsistencies and contradictions, not least those between the local-level officers of the state and those who formulate its central policies.

The point here is a simple one, but one which bears repeating. Political power is no longer found solely in the organs and processes of formal politics, if it ever was, nor even just in conjunction with the informal relations inherent in the other aspects of political culture which adhere to the institutions of the state and other political bodies. 'Power actually rests on the everyday social practices which are the concrete form taken by relations between the governing and the governed. These relations are not simply expressed in forms of social action we could explicitly label "political"' (Gledhill 1994: 22). Although this book has reviewed examples of political action in and by formal structures of the state, it has concentrated more on how power is demonstrated, projected, and contested in the social, economic and political practices of quotidian life at international borders.

We think it useful to consider here the various ways in which anthropologists might recognise and analyse notions of power in the social practice of daily life, whether it be in the realm of the more formal politics of state and other juridical institutions, or in other areas of social and economic life which become political at the times when, and in the places where, power is articulated. Eric Wolf (1990) sees four different modes of power at work in society, in a schema which provides a useful starting point in the attempt to distinguish power in everyday practice. Power is an attribute of a person; it is the capability of a person to act. But this form of *personal power* does not indicate the type or direction of action. The second mode of power is the ability of one person to affect another person. This is *interpersonal power*, and is based on transactions among people, but this type of power gives no information about the arena in which it occurs. The third kind of power for Wolf is *tactical* or *organisational power*, which allows an individual or a group to structure the actions of others within certain settings, but which has no necessary control over the setting itself. The fourth mode of power organises the settings and arenas themselves, and is *structural power*, which 'shapes the social field of action so as to render some kinds of behavior possible, while making others less possible or impossible' (Wolf 1990: 587).

For Wolf, this last type of power is a rephrasing of the social relations of production as one way to describe the power to allocate social labour. This Marxian approach is indicative of a political economy perspective which to some extent has fallen from favour in anthropology, but one which we have proffered throughout this book none the less. Lest the reader conclude that this attention to materialist factors in the relationships of power and exploitation, by the state, within the state and in relation to the state, is a denial of the symbolic areas of culture to which we have devoted much of this book, and which we have put forward as one of the distinctive areas of scholarship that anthropology can offer to the comparative study of borders, nations and states, we return to one more simple premise. 'All capital and labor, like all hegemony and exploitation, are symbolic because all human activity is conceived, imagined, and carried out in and amidst symbolic units and relations' (Friedrich 1989: 298).

In this volume we have reviewed anthropological studies of symbols and meaning, in rituals, as narrated in the form and actions of the body, and in the discursive practices of activities which are subversive of the state. We have also attempted to integrate this discussion with studies of formal and informal politics and economics, in an effort to present the range of possibilities inherent to the study of power in social action, within the contexts of nation and state. In our view there is no better place to do this than at the international borders between states. In our concluding remarks we review why this is so, and we suggest some ways in which anthropologists might develop international border studies in order to make a contribution to political anthropology in particular and to the comparative social science of borders, nations and states more generally.

National and state borders play significant roles at a time of crisis in the nation-state precisely because national boundaries can no longer fulfil their roles as protection and gateway, at least not in ways which were considered appropriate in the past. As Dunn has suggested, the challenges to the modern nation-state come chiefly in the awareness among its citizens that the economic, environmental, political and social problems with which they are faced in a changing global system can no longer be successfully handled within a state's territorial limits, nor even through a state's apparatuses wherever they may be found. As we noted earlier in the book, the state is often too big to be sensitive to the needs of local settings, and yet often too small to address those issues that stretch beyond its territorial confines. Because international borders have served as both locuses and symbols of a state's sovereignty, territorial integrity, and power, and have done so since states have existed, they have now become places and symbols which mark the important transformations which states are undergoing.

While power in everyday social practice can be found throughout a state's domain, a useful standpoint from which to view its simultaneous national and international dimensions is at state borders. Because the international dimension to the crisis of the state is so important, especially in terms of its impact on notions of legitimacy, citizenship, social inclusion and exclusion, state security, and the ethnic and civic characteristics to nationalism, borders in their roles as the first if not pre-eminent zones of intercultural communication and adaptation in a state have become even more important to the definition of nation-state transformation. While it is clear that borderlands have always been areas where some people attempt to subvert the state, it is also becoming increasingly clear that in the present climate many activities by border peoples, which in the past might have appeared to be relatively local and innocent, today strike much more dissonant chords in the life of the nation-state due to the changes that have occurred in the foundations of states worldwide. More people, in more ways, not only have experience of others at and across international borders, but through this, as tourists, students, shoppers, smugglers, soldiers, merchants, refugees, migrants and day-labourers, they also have experienced many different forms of power in social practice. These experiences allow many more people than ever before to imagine communities beyond the national, in ways which fit very well into the framework put forward by Benedict Anderson (1983) in his influential study of the origins of modern nationalism. In today's world new technologies allow us a glimpse of international practices before we physically go to what we used to call 'abroad', and on return they allow us to keep in touch, to continue the conversation with those many groups of people who too often and too glibly have been termed 'the other' by scholars of culture, not least anthropologists.

The upshot of these new forms of imagined transnational communities is that international borders are frontier zones which are widening both physically and figuratively, in ways that are certainly transformative in borderlands themselves, but also in ways that we have suggested in this book are spurring on such changes within their wider nations and states. Border people, communities and cultures are certainly active and contributing members in states, though to return to Nugent's point quoted above, they too may not be reducible to any set of social interests outside of the state, or for that matter to social interests within the state. Yet many border peoples are also contributing members in other such units which are attempting to assert their own irreducibility and to stand as unitary actors on the world stage as institutions with one voice and one image among their members. These sovereign units are of course neighbouring states, but they are being increasingly challenged by supranational bodies, such as the European Union, by regions which are using their transnational and international connections and status to establish sovereign rights within states – or perhaps, as in the case of Northern Ireland, between states – and by multinational corporations. Sharing membership in more than one self-styled unitary global actor establishes complex and multilayered patterns of local international relations in borderlands which involve diverse values, meanings, ideas and social networks. Such patterns may be viewed as subversive to and by the state, but to border peoples they may very well seem to be the common-sense stuff of everyday life. It is the interaction between border cultures and the wider cultures of nation and state that gives definition to a political anthropology which seeks to understand the workings of power in the daily practices of society.

The social sciences have each developed an interest in international borders which regards borders as motive forces in the development of their nations and states, and which treats them as zones of culture contact that often extend some distance from a borderline. These disciplines, such as history, politics, geography and sociology, have increasingly perceived border culture as problematic, and a key way to understand the international dimensions to a borderlands' development. Anthropology has been slow to enter this debate, despite long being the academic field which has theorised culture. Nor is its understanding of culture the only contribution that anthropology can make to the comparative study of borders. It also offers a growing theoretical interest in the analysis of power, politics and policy in everyday life, in localities long considered to be the focus of the discipline, such as rural communities and in peripheral regions, as well as in the cosmopolitan centres of power and decision-making. Furthermore, anthropology continues to rely on long-term field research, a method without equal in the study of culture. As a result of years of ethnographic study at international borders, anthropology can provide a solid corpus of local-level analyses of border communities, a body of work which can potentially put the flesh of culture on the stickman frame of institutional and macro-level studies of nation and state. Though much has already been done by anthropologists in these areas, much remains to be studied at international borders, precisely because of the crisis nation-states are perceived to be in, and because of the novel external pressures which states are experiencing, often first in their borderlands.

Bibliography

Abélès, M. (1992), 'Anthropologie politique de la modernité', *L'Homme* vol. 32, no.1, pp. 15–30.

Adeyoyin, F. A. (1989), 'Methodology of the Multi-disciplinary Problem', in A. I. Asiwaju and P. O. Adeniyi (eds), *Borderlands in Africa*, Lagos: University of Lagos Press.

Allen, T. (ed.) (1996), *In Search of Cool Ground: War, Flight and Homecoming in Northeast Africa*, London: James Currey.

—— and Turton, D. (1996), 'Introduction: In Search of Cool Ground', in T. Allen (ed.), *In Search of Cool Ground: War, Flight and Homecoming in Northeast Africa*, London: James Currey.

Almaráz, Jr., F. D. (1976), 'The Status of Borderlands Studies: History', *The Social Science Journal* vol. 13, no. 1, pp. 9–18.

Almond, G. A., and Verba, S. (1963), *The Civic Culture: Political Attitudes and Democracy in Five Nations*, Princeton: Princeton University Press.

—— (eds) (1989), *The Civic Culture Revisited*, London: Sage.

Alvarez, R. R. (1991), *Familia: Migration and Adaptation in Baja and Alta California, 1800–1975*, Berkeley: University of California Press.

—— (1994), 'Changing Ideology in a Transnational Market: Chiles and Chileros in Mexico and the US', *Human Organization* vol. 53, no. 3, pp. 255–62.

—— (1995), 'The Mexican–US Border: The Making of an Anthropology of Borderlands', *Annual Review of Anthropology* vol. 24, pp. 447–70.

—— and Collier, G. A. (1994), 'The Long Haul in Mexican Trucking: Traversing the Borderlands of the North and the South', *American Ethnologist* vol. 21, no. 3, pp. 606–27.

Anderson, B. (1983), *Imagined Communities: Reflections on the Origin and Spread of Nationalism*, London: Verso.

Anderson, M. (1982a), 'The Political Problems of Frontier Regions', *West European Politics* vol. 5, no. 4, pp. 1–17.

—— (ed.) (1982b), *Frontier Regions in Western Europe*, London: Frank Cass.

—— (1996a), *Frontiers: Territory and State Formation in the Modern World*, Oxford: Polity.

—— (1996b), 'The Frontiers of Europe', in M. Anderson and E. Bort (eds), *Boundaries and Identities: The Eastern Frontier of the European Union*, Edinburgh: International Social Sciences Institute, University of Edinburgh.

—— and den Boer, M. (1994), *Policing Across National Boundaries*, London: Pinter.

Anzaldúa, G. (1987), *Borderlands/La Frontera: The New Mestiza*, San Francisco: Aunt Lute Books.

Aretxaga, B. (1993), 'Striking with Hunger: Cultural Meanings of Political Violence in Northern Ireland', in K. B. Warren (ed.), *The Violence Within: Cultural and Political Opposition in Divided Nations*, Boulder, CO: Westview Press.

Aronoff, M. (1974), *Frontiertown: The Politics of Community Building in Israel*, Manchester: Manchester University Press.

Arreola, D. D. and Curtis, J. R. (1993), *The Mexican Border Cities: Landscape Anatomy and Place Personality*, Tucson: University of Arizona Press.

Asad, T. (1972), 'Market Model, Class Structure and Consent: A Reconsideration of Swat Political Organisation', *Man* vol. 7, pp. 74–94.

—— (1975), 'Anthropological Texts and Ideological Problems: An Analysis of Cohen on Arab Villages in Israel', *Review of Middle East Studies* vol. 1, pp. 1–40.

Asiwaju, A. I. and Adeniyi, P. O. (eds) (1989), *Borderlands in Africa*, Lagos: University of Lagos Press.

Bailey, E. and Reza, H. G. (1988), 'An Alien Presence', *Los Angeles Times*, 5 June, 1: 36.

Bailey, F. G. (1983), *Tactical Uses of Passion: An Essay on Power, Reason and Reality*, Ithaca: Cornell University Press.

Baker, S. (1996), 'Punctured Sovereignty, Border Regions and the Environment within the European Union', in L. O'Dowd and T. M. Wilson (eds), *Borders, Nations and States: Frontiers of Sovereignty in the New Europe*, Aldershot: Avebury.

Banks, M. (1996), *Ethnicity: Anthropological Constructions*, London: Routledge.

Barth, F. (1969), 'Introduction', in F. Barth (ed.), *Ethnic Groups and Boundaries: The Social Organization of Culture Difference*, London: George Allen and Unwin.

Basch, L., Schiller, N. G., and Blanc, C. S. (1994), *Nations Unbound: Transnational Projects, Postcolonial Predicaments and Deterritorialized Nation-states*, Amsterdam: Gordon and Breach.

Bath, C. R. (1976), 'The Status of Borderlands Studies: Political Science', *The Social Science Journal* vol. 13, no. 1, pp. 55–67.

Baud, M. (1992), *A Border of Refuge: Dominicans and Haitians against the State, 1870–1930*, Centre of Border Studies, Occasional Paper 2, Erasmus University, Rotterdam.

—— (1993), 'Una frontera para cruzar: la sociedad rural a traves de la frontera Dominico–Haitiana (1870–1930)', *Estudios Sociales* vol. 26, no. 94, pp. 5–28.

—— (1994), *A Border to Cross: Rural Society across the Dominican–Haitian*

Border, 1870–1930, Centre of Border Studies, Occasional Paper 3, Erasmus University, Rotterdam.

—— and van Schendel, W. (1997), 'Toward a Comparative History of Borderlands', *Journal of World History* vol. 8. no. 2, pp. 211–42.

Behar, R. (1993), *Translated Woman: Crossing the Border with Esperanza's Story*, Boston: Beacon.

Belk, R. (1988), 'Possessions and the Extended Self', *Journal of Consumer Research* vol. 15, pp. 139–68.

Birkbeck, C. (1979), 'Garbage, Industry, and the "Vultures" of Cali, Colombia', in R. Bromley and C. Gerry (eds), *Casual Work and Poverty in Third World Cities*, Chichester: Wiley.

Blacking, J. (1975), 'Comment on J-K. Ross, "Social Borders: Definitions of Diversity"', *Current Anthropology* vol. 16, no. 1, pp. 62–3.

Bohannan, P. (1967), 'Introduction', in P. Bohannan and F. Plog (eds), *Beyond the Frontier: Social Process and Cultural Change*, New York: The Natural History Press.

—— and Plog, F. (eds) (1967), *Beyond the Frontier: Social Process and Cultural Change*, New York: The Natural History Press.

Boos, X. (1982), 'Economic Aspects of a Frontier Situation: The Case of Alsace', *West European Politics* vol. 5, no. 4, pp. 81–97.

Borneman, J. (1986), 'Emigres as Bullets/Immigration as Penetration: Perceptions of the Marielitos', *Journal of Popular Culture* vol. 20, no. 3, pp. 73–92.

—— (1992), *Belonging in the Two Berlins: Kin, State, Nation*, Cambridge: Cambridge University Press.

—— (1998), *Subversions of International Order: Studies in the Political Anthropology of Culture*, Albany: State University of New York Press.

Bouquet, M. (1986), '"You Cannot be a Brahmin in the English Countryside": The Partitioning of Status, and its Representation within the Farm Family in Devon', in A. P. Cohen (ed.), *Symbolising Boundaries: Identity and Diversity in British Cultures*, Manchester: Manchester University Press.

Bowman, G. (1989), 'Fucking Tourists: Sexual Relations and Tourism in Jerusalem's Old City', *Critique of Anthropology* vol. 9, no. 2, pp. 77–93.

—— (1996), 'Passion, Power and Politics in a Palestinian Tourist Market', in T. Selwyn (ed.), *The Tourist Image: Myths and Myth Making in Tourism*, Chichester: Wiley.

Brah, A. (1996), *Cartographies of Diaspora: Contesting Identities*, London: Routledge.

Bronfman, M. and Moreno, S. L. (1996), 'Perspectives on HIV/AIDS Prevention among Immigrants on the US–Mexico Border', in S. I. Mishra, R. F. Conner and J. R. Mangaña (eds), *AIDS Crossing Borders: The Spread of HIV among Migrant Latinos*, Boulder, CO: Westview Press.

Bryan, D. and Jarman, N. (1997), 'Parading Tradition, Protesting Triumphalism: Utilising Anthropology in Public Policy', in H. Donnan and G. McFarlane (eds), *Culture and Policy in Northern Ireland: Anthropology in the Public Arena*, Belfast: Institute of Irish Studies.

Burton, F. (1979), 'Ideological Social Relations in Northern Ireland', *British Journal of Sociology* vol. 30, pp. 61–80.

Butt Philip, A. (1991), 'European Border Controls: Who Needs Them?', *Public Policy and Administration* vol. 6, no. 2, pp. 35–54.

Chambers, I. (1990), *Border Dialogues: Journeys in Postmodernism*, London: Routledge.

—— (1994), *Migrancy, Culture, Identity*, London: Routledge.

Chavez, L. R. (1991), 'Outside the Imagined Community: Undocumented Settlers and Experiences of Incorporation', *American Ethnologist* vol. 18, pp. 257–78.

—— (1992), *Shadowed Lives: Undocumented Immigrants in American Society*, Orlando: Harcourt Brace Jovanovich College Publishers.

Cheater, A. P. (1998), 'Transcending the State? Gender and Borderline Constructions of Citizenship in Zimbabwe', in T. M. Wilson and H. Donnan (eds), *Border Identities: Nation and State at International Frontiers*, Cambridge: Cambridge University Press.

Christian, C. (1961), *Some Sociological Implications of Government VD Control*, unpublished Masters thesis. Austin: University of Texas.

Clifford, J. (1988), *The Predicament of Culture*, Cambridge, MA: Harvard University Press.

Coakley, J (1982), 'National Territories and Cultural Frontiers: Conflicts of Principle in the Formation of States in Europe', *West European Politics* vol. 5, no. 4, pp. 34–49.

Cohen, A. (1965), *Arab Border-Villages in Israel: A Study of Continuity and Change in Social Organization*, Manchester: Manchester University Press.

—— (1969), *Custom and Politics in Urban Africa: A Study of Hausa Migrants in Yoruba Towns*, Berkeley: University of California Press.

—— (1974), *Two-Dimensional Man: An Essay on the Anthropology of Power and Symbolism in Complex Society*, Berkeley: University of California Press.

Cohen, A. P. (ed.) (1982a), *Belonging: Identity and Social Organisation in British Rural Cultures*, Manchester: Manchester University Press.

—— (1982b), 'Belonging: The Experience of Culture', in A. P. Cohen (ed.), *Belonging: Identity and Social Organisation in British Rural Cultures*, Manchester: Manchester University Press.

—— (1985), *The Symbolic Construction of Community*, London: Tavistock Publications.

—— (ed.) (1986a), *Symbolising Boundaries: Identity and Diversity in British Cultures*, Manchester: Manchester University Press.

Bibliography

—— (1986b), 'Of Symbols and Boundaries, or, Does Ertie's Greatcoat Hold the Key?', in A. P. Cohen (ed.), *Symbolising Boundaries: Identity and Diversity in British Cultures*, Manchester: Manchester University Press.

—— (1987), *Whalsay: Symbol, Segment and Boundary in a Shetland Island Community*, Manchester: Manchester University Press.

—— (1994), *Self Consciousness: An Alternative Anthropology of Identity*, London: Routledge.

Cohen, Y. A. (1969), 'Social Boundary Systems', *Current Anthropology* vol. 10, no. 1, pp. 103–26.

Cole, J. W. and Wolf, E. (1974), *The Hidden Frontier: Ecology and Ethnicity in an Alpine Valley*, New York: Academic Press.

Colley, L. (1997), 'The Frontier in British History', The Wiles Lectures, Queen's University of Belfast, 20–23 May 1997.

Collins, J. D. (1976), 'The Clandestine Movement of Groundnuts across the Niger–Nigeria Boundary', *Canadian Journal of African Studies* vol. 10, no. 2, pp. 259–78.

—— (1984), 'Partitioned Culture Areas and Smuggling: The Hausa and the Groundnut Trade across the Nigeria–Niger Border from the mid-1930s to the mid-1970s', in A. I. Asiwaju (ed.), *Partitioned Africans*, Lagos: University of Lagos Press.

Comaroff, J. (1996), 'The Empire's Old Clothes: Fashioning the Colonial Subject', in D. Howes (ed.), *Cross-Cultural Consumption: Global Markets, Local Realities*, London: Routledge.

Courtwright, D. T. (1996), *Violent Land: Single Men and Social Disorder from the Frontier to the Inner City*, Cambridge, MA: Harvard University Press.

Curtis, J. R. and Arreola, D. D. (1991), 'Zonas de Tolerancia on the Northern Mexican Border', *Geographical Review* vol. 81, pp. 333–46.

Curzon of Kedleston, Lord (1907), *Frontiers: The Romanes Lectures*, Oxford: Oxford University Press.

de Certeau, M. (1988 [1974]), *The Practice of Everyday Life*, Berkeley: University of California Press.

Delaney, C. (1995), 'Father State, Motherland, and the Birth of Modern Turkey', in S. Yanagisako and C. Delaney (eds), *Naturalizing Power*, New York: Routledge.

Delli Zotti, G. (1982), 'Transnational Relations of a Border Region: The Case of Friuli–Venetia Julia', in R. Strassoldo and G. Delli Zotti (eds), *Cooperation and Conflict in Border Areas*, Milan: Angeli.

—— (1996), 'Transfrontier Co-operation at the External Borders of the EU: Implications for Sovereignty', in L. O'Dowd and T. M. Wilson (eds), *Borders, Nations and States: Frontiers of Sovereignty in the New Europe*, Aldershot: Avebury.

DeMarchi, B. and Boileau, A. M. (1982a), 'Introduction', in B. Demarchi and A. Boileau (eds), *Boundaries and Minorities in Western Europe*, Milan: Angeli.

—— (eds) (1982b), *Boundaries and Minorities in Western Europe*, Milan: Angeli.

Demaris, O. (1970), *Poso del Mundo: Inside the Mexican American Border from Tijuana to Matamoros*, Boston: Little, Brown.

Derby, L. (1994), 'Haitians, Magic, and Money: *Raza* and Society in the Haitian–Dominican Borderlands, 1900–1937', *Comparative Studies in Society and History* vol. 36, pp. 488–526.

Desowitz, R. (1997), 'Ebola in Epsom, Lassa in Luton?', *Times Higher Education Supplement*.

do Amaral, I. (1994), 'New Reflections on the Theme of International Boundaries', in C. H. Schofield (ed.), *Global Boundaries: World Boundaries, Volume 1*, London: Routledge.

Donnan, H. and McFarlane, G. (1983), 'Informal Social Organisation', in J. Darby (ed.), *Northern Ireland: The Background to the Conflict*, Belfast and New York: Appletree Press and Syracuse University Press.

—— (1986), '"You Get On Better With Your Own": Social Continuity and Change in Rural Northern Ireland', in P. Clancy, S. Drudy, K. Lynch and L. O'Dowd (eds), *Ireland: A Sociological Profile*, Dublin: Institute of Public Administration.

Donnan, H. and Wilson, T. M. (1994a), 'An Anthropology of Frontiers', in H. Donnan and T. M. Wilson (eds), *Border Approaches: Anthropological Perspectives on Frontiers*, Lanham, MD: University Press of America.

—— (eds) (1994b), *Border Approaches: Anthropological Perspectives on Frontiers*, Lanham, MD: University Press of America.

Douglas, M. (1970 [1966]), *Purity and Danger: An Analysis of Concepts of Pollution and Taboo*, Harmondsworth: Penguin.

Douglass, W. A. (1977), 'Borderland Influences in a Navarrese Village', in W. A. Douglass, R. W. Etulain and W. H. Jacobsen, Jr. (eds), *Anglo–American Contributions to Basque Studies: Essays in Honor of Jon Bilbao*, Reno, NV: Desert Research Institute.

—— (1998), 'A Western Perspective on an Eastern Interpretation of where North Meets South: Pyrenean Borderland Cultures', in T. M. Wilson and H. Donnan (eds), *Border Identities: Nation and State at International Frontiers*, Cambridge: Cambridge University Press.

Driessen, H. (1992), *On the Spanish–Moroccan Frontier: A Study in Ritual, Power and Ethnicity*, Oxford: Berg.

—— (1998), 'The "New Immigration" and the Transformation of the European–African Frontier', in T. M. Wilson and H. Donnan (eds), *Border Identities: Nation and State at International Frontiers*, Cambridge: Cambridge University Press.

—— (n.d.), 'Smuggling as a Border Way of Life: A Mediterranean Case', unpublished paper.

Dunn, J. (1994), 'Introduction: Crisis of the Nation State?', *Political Studies* vol. 62, pp. 3–15.

Dupuy, P. (1982), 'Legal Aspects of Transfrontier Regional Co-operation', *West European Politics* vol. 5, no. 4, pp.50–63.

Eriksen, T. H. (1993), *Ethnicity and Nationalism: Anthropological Perspectives*, London: Pluto Press.

Evers, H-D. (1991), 'Shadow Economy, Subsistence Production and Informal Sector: Economic Activity Outside of Market and State', *Prisma* vol. 51, pp. 34–46.

Eyre, R., Gordimer, N., Hamilton, N., Hitchens, C., Raphael, F., Rodriguez, R., Swain, J. and Wells, J. (1990), *Frontiers*, London: BBC Books.

Feldman, A. (1991), *Formations of Violence: The Narrative of the Body and Political Terror in Northern Ireland*, Chicago: University of Chicago Press.

—— (1992), 'On "Formations of Violence"', *Current Anthropology* vol. 33, no. 5, pp. 595–6.

—— (1995), 'Ethnographic States of Emergency', in C. Nordstrom and A. Robben (eds), *Fieldwork Under Fire*, Berkeley: University of California Press.

Fernández-Kelly, M. P. (1983), *For We Are Sold, I and My People: Women and Industry in Mexico's Frontier*, SUNY Series in the Anthropology of Work, Albany: State University of New York Press.

Fitzgerald, J. D., Quinn, T. P., Whelan, B. J. and Williams, J. A. (1988), *An Analysis of Cross-Border Shopping*, Dublin: Economic and Social Research Institute.

Flynn, D. K. (1997), '"We are the Border": Identity, Exchange, and the State along the Bénin–Nigeria Border', *American Ethnologist* vol. 24, no. 2, pp. 311–30.

Foucault, M. (1979), *Discipline and Punish: The Birth of the Prison*, New York: Vintage.

Fox, R. G. (1985), *Lions of the Punjab: Culture in the Making*, Berkeley: University of California Press.

—— (ed.) (1990), *Nationalist Ideologies and the Production of National Culture*, Washington, DC: American Ethnological Society.

Frankenberg, R. (1957), *Village on the Border: A Social Study of Religion, Politics and Football in a North Wales Community*, Manchester: Manchester University Press.

French, L. (1994), 'The Political Economy of Injury and Compassion: Amputees on the Thai–Cambodia Border', in T. J. Csordas (ed.), *Embodiment and Experience: The Existential Ground of Culture and Self*, Cambridge: Cambridge University Press.

—— (1996), 'Border Trade: Thailand/Cambodia, 1996', paper presented to the American Anthropological Association Annual Meeting, San Francisco, 20–24 November 1996.

Friedrich, P. (1989), 'Language, Ideology, and Political Economy', *American Anthropologist* vol. 91, pp. 295–312.

Frost, H. G. (1983), *The Gentlemen's Club: The Story of Prostitution in El Paso*, El Paso: Mangan Books.

Geertz, C. (ed.) (1963), *Old Societies and New States: The Quest for Modernity in Asia and Africa*, New York: The Free Press.

—— (1973), *The Interpretation of Cultures*, New York: Basic Books.

Gessner, V., and Schade, A. (1990), 'Conflicts of Culture in Cross-border Legal Relations: The Conception of a Research Topic in the Sociology of Law', *Theory, Culture & Society* vol. 7, pp. 253–77.

Gildersleeve, C. R. (1976), 'The Status of Borderlands Studies: Geography', *The Social Science Journal* vol. 13, no. 1, pp.19–28.

Giroux, H. (1992), *Border Crossings: Cultural Workers and the Politics of Education*, London: Routledge.

Gledhill, J. (1994), *Power and Its Disguises: Anthropological Perspectives on Politics*, London: Pluto Press.

Gluckman, M. (1957), 'Introduction', in R. Frankenberg *Village on the Border: A Social Study of Religion, Politics and Football in a North Wales Community*, Manchester: Manchester University Press.

—— (1964), *Closed Systems and Open Minds: The Limits of Naivety in Social Anthropology*, Edinburgh: Oliver and Boyd.

Goody, J. (1970), 'Inheritance, Social Change and the Boundary Problem', in J. Pouillon and P. Maranda (eds), *Échanges et communications*, The Hague: Mouton.

Gordimer, N. (1990), 'The Ingot and the Stick, The Ingot and the Gun: Mozambique–South Africa', in R. Eyre et al., *Frontiers*, London: BBC Books.

Green, S. (1998a), 'Relocating Persons and Places on the Greek–Albanian Border', in C. Papa, G. Pizza and F. M. Zerilli (eds), *Incontri di etnologia Europea*, Napoli: Edizioni Scientifiche Italiane.

—— (1998b), 'A proposito della dimensione corporea del conflitto al confine greco–albanese' ('On the Corporeality of Conflict on the Greek–Albanian Border'), *Etnosistemi* vol. 5.

Gross, F. (1978), *Ethnics in a Borderland*, Westport, CT: Greenwood Press.

Gupta, A. (1995), 'Blurred Boundaries: The Discourse of Corruption, The Culture of Politics, and the Imagined State', *American Ethnologist* vol. 22, no. 2, pp. 375–402.

—— and Ferguson, J. (1992), 'Beyond "Culture": Space, Identity, and the Politics of Difference', *Cultural Anthropology* vol. 7, no. 1, pp. 6–23.

Gupta, S. (ed.), (1993), *Disrupted Borders: An Intervention in Definitions of Boundaries*, London: River Oram Press.

Handelman, D. (1990), *Models and Mirrors: Towards an Anthropology of Public Events*, Cambridge: Cambridge University Press.

Handler, R. (1988), *Nationalism and the Politics of Culture in Quebec*, Madison: University of Wisconsin Press.

Bibliography

Hann, C. and Bellér-Hann, I. (1998), 'Markets, Morality and Modernity in North-East Turkey', In T. M. Wilson and H. Donnan (eds), *Border Identities: Nation and State at International Frontiers*, Cambridge: Cambridge University Press.

Hann, C. and Hann, I. (1992), 'Samovars and Sex on Turkey's Russian Markets', *Anthropology Today* vol. 8, no. 4, pp. 3–6.

Hannerz, U. (1975), Comment on J-K. Ross, 'Social Borders: Definitions of Diversity', *Current Anthropology* vol. 16, no. 1, pp. 65–6.

—— (1996), *Transnational Connections: Culture, People, Places*, London: Routledge.

—— (1997), 'Borders', *International Social Science Journal* vol. 154, pp. 537–48.

Hansen, A. (1993), 'African Refugees: Defining and Defending their Human Rights', in R. Cohen, G. Hyden and W. Nagan (eds), *Human Rights and Governance in Africa*, Gainesville, FL: Universities of Florida Press.

—— (1994), 'The Illusion of Local Sustainability and Self-sufficiency: Famine in a Border Area of Northwestern Zambia', *Human Organization* vol. 53, no. 1, pp. 11–20.

Hansen, N. (1981), *The Border Economy*, Austin: University of Texas Press.

Harris, R. (1972), *Prejudice and Tolerance in Ulster: A Study of Neighbours and 'Strangers' in a Border Community*, Manchester: Manchester University Press.

Hart, D. (ed.) (1991), *Border Country: Poems in Process*, Birmingham: Wood Wind Publications.

Hastrup, K. and Olwig, K. F. (1997), 'Introduction', in K. F. Olwig and K. Hastrup (eds), *Siting Culture: The Shifting Anthropological Object*, London: Routledge.

Hein, J. (1993), 'Refugees, Immigrants, and the State', *Annual Review of Sociology* vol. 19, pp. 43–59.

Helman, C. (1991), *Body Myths*, London: Chatto and Windus.

Henry, S. (1978), *The Hidden Economy: The Context and Control of Borderline Crime*, London: Martin Robertson.

Herzfeld, M. (1985), *The Poetics of Manhood: Contest and Identity in a Cretan Mountain Village*, Princeton: Princeton University Press.

—— (1992), *The Social Production of Indifference: Exploring the Symbolic Roots of Western Democracy*, Oxford: Berg.

—— (1997), *Cultural Intimacy: Social Poetics in the Nation-State*, New York: Routledge.

Herzog, L. A. (1990), *Where North Meets South: Cities, Space, and Politics on the U.S.–Mexico Border*, Austin: University of Texas Press.

Heyman, J. (1991), *Land, Labor, and Capital at the Mexican Border*, Flagstaff: University of Arizona Press.

—— (1994), 'The Mexico–United States Border in Anthropology: A Critique and Reformulation', *Journal of Political Ecology* vol. 1, pp. 43–65.

—— (1995), 'Putting Power in the Anthropology of Bureaucracy: The Immigration and Naturalization Service at the Mexico–United States Border', *Current Anthropology* vol. 36, no. 2, pp. 261–87.

Hicks, E. (1991), *Border Writing: The Multidimensional Text*, Minneapolis: University of Minnesota Press.

Holmes, D. (1989), *Cultural Disenchantments: Worker Peasants in Northeast Italy*, Princeton: Princeton University Press.

Horsman, M. and Marshall, A. (1995), *After the Nation-State: Citizens, Tribalism and the New World Disorder*, London: HarperCollins.

House, J. W. (1982), *Frontier on the Rio Grande: A Political Geography of Development and Social Deprivation*, Oxford: Clarendon Press.

Howe, L. (1985), 'The "Deserving" and the "Undeserving": Practice in an Urban, Local Social Security Office', *Journal of Social Policy* vol. 14, pp. 49–72.

Howes, D. (ed.) (1996), *Cross-Cultural Consumption: Global Markets, Local Realities*, London: Routledge.

Jackson, M. (1983), 'Thinking Through the Body: An Essay on Understanding Metaphor', *Social Analysis* vol. 14, pp. 127–48.

James, W. (1979), *'Kwanim Pa. The Making of the Uduk People: An Ethnographic Study of Survival in the Sudan–Ethiopian Borderlands*, Oxford: Clarendon Press.

—— (1988), *The Listening Ebony: Moral Knowledge, Religion, and Power among the Uduk of Sudan*, Oxford: Clarendon Press.

—— (1996), 'Uduk Resettlement: Dreams and Realities', in T. Allen (ed.), *In Search of Cool Ground: War, Flight and Homecoming in Northeast Africa*, London: James Currey.

—— (1997), 'The Names of Fear: Memory, History and the Ethnography of Feeling among Uduk Refugees', *Journal of the Royal Anthropological Institute* vol. 3, no. 1, pp. 115–31.

Jarman, N. (1997), *Material Conflicts: Parades and Visual Displays in Northern Ireland*, Oxford: Berg.

Jenkins, R. (1992a), 'Doing Violence to the Subject', *Current Anthropology* vol. 33, no. 2, pp. 233–5.

—— (1992b), 'Reply', *Current Anthropology* vol. 33, no. 5, pp. 596–7.

—— (1997), *Rethinking Ethnicity: Arguments and Explorations*, London: Sage.

Kapferer, B. (1988), *Legends of People Myths of State: Violence, Intolerance, and Political Culture in Sri Lanka and Australia*, Washington, DC: Smithsonian Institution Press.

Kasperson, R. E. and Minghi, J. V. (1969a), 'Structure: Introduction', in R. E. Kasperson and J. V. Minghi (eds), *The Structure of Political Geography*, Chicago: Aldine.

—— (eds) (1969b), *The Structure of Political Geography*, Chicago: Aldine.

Kavanagh, W. (1994), 'Symbolic Boundaries and "Real" Borders on the Portuguese–

Spanish Frontier', in H. Donnan and T. M. Wilson (eds.), *Border Approaches: Anthropological Perspectives on Frontiers*, Lanham MD: University Press of America.

Kearney, M. (1995), 'The Local and the Global: The Anthropology of Globalization and Transnationalism', *Annual Review of Anthropology* vol. 24, pp. 547–65.

—— (1996), *Reconceptualizing the Peasantry: Anthropology in Global Perspective*, Boulder: Westview Press.

—— (1998a), 'Transnationalism in California and Mexico at the End of Empire', in T. M. Wilson and H. Donnan (eds), *Border Identities: Nation and State at International Frontiers*, Cambridge: Cambridge University Press.

—— (1998b), 'The Transfer of Economic Value Across the USA–Mexico Border', unpublished paper, American Anthropological Association Meetings, Philadelphia, December 1998.

Keith, M. and Pile, S. (eds), (1993), *Place and the Politics of Identity*, London: Routledge.

Kelleher, B. (1990), 'Text meets Culture: Anatomizing a Death on the Irish Border', Paper presented to American Anthropological Association meetings, New Orleans, 1990.

Keller, S. (1975), *Uprooting and Social Change: The Role of Refugees in Development*, Delhi: Manohar.

Kelsky, K. (1996), 'Flirting with the Foreign: Interracial Sex in Japan's "International": Age', in R. Wilson and W. Dissanayake (eds), *Global/Local: Cultural Production and the Transnational Imaginary*, Durham, NC: Duke University Press.

Kertzer, D. (1988), *Ritual, Politics, and Power*, New Haven: Yale University Press.

Kessler, C. S. (1978), *Islam and Politics in a Malay State*, Ithaca: Cornell University Press.

Klein, A. M. (1997), *Baseball on the Border: A Tale of Two Laredos*, Princeton: Princeton University Press.

Kopytoff, I. (1987), 'The Internal African Frontier: The Making of African Political Culture', in I. Kopytoff, *The African Frontier*, Bloomington: Indiana University Press.

Kristof, L. K. D. (1969 [1959]), 'The Nature of Frontiers and Boundaries', in R. E. Kasperson and J. V. Minghi (eds), *The Structure of Political Geography*, Chicago: Aldine.

Kroeber, A. L. (1953), *Cultural and Natural Areas of Native North America*, Berkeley: University of California Press.

La Fontaine, J. A. (1985), *Initiation: Ritual Drama and Secret Knowledge Across the World*, Harmondsworth: Penguin.

Lask, T. (1994), '"Baguette Heads" and "Spiked Helmets": Children's Constructions of Nationality at the German–French Border', in H. Donnan and T. M. Wilson (eds), *Border Approaches: Anthropological Perspectives on Frontiers*, Lanham MD: University Press of America.

Lattimore, O. D. (1968 [1956]), 'The Frontier in History', in R. A. Manners and D. Kaplan (eds), *Theory in Anthropology: A Sourcebook*, London: Routledge and Kegan Paul.

Lavie, S. (1990), *The Poetics of Military Occupation: Allegories of Bedouin Identity under Israeli and Egyptian Rule*, Berkeley: University of California Press.

—— (1992), 'Blow-ups in the Borderzones: Third World Israeli Authors' Gropings for Home', *New Formations* vol. 18, pp. 84–106.

Leach, E. R. (1960), 'The Frontiers of "Burma"', *Comparative Studies in Society and History* vol. 3, pp. 49–68.

—— (1972 [1964]), 'Anthropological Aspects of Language: Animal Categories and Verbal Abuse', in W. A. Lessa and E. Z. Vogt (eds), *Reader in Comparative Religion: An Anthropological Approach*, New York: Harper and Row.

Leizaola, A. (1996), 'Muga: Borders and Boundaries in the Basque Country', *Europæa* vol. 2, no. 1, pp. 91–102.

Letamendía, F., Gomez Uranga, M. and Etxebarria, G. (1996), 'Astride Two States: Cross-border Co-operation in the Basque Country', in L. O'Dowd and T. M. Wilson (eds), *Borders, Nations and States: Frontiers of Sovereignty in the New Europe*, Aldershot: Avebury.

Limón, J. E. (1994), *Dancing with the Devil*, Madison: University of Wisconsin Press.

Littlewood, R. (1997), 'Military Rape', *Anthropology Today* vol. 13, no. 2, pp. 7–16.

Lugo, A. (1997), 'Reflections on Border Theory, Culture, and the Nation', in S. Michaelsen and D. E. Johnson (eds), *Border Theory: The Limits of Cultural Politics*, Minneapolis: University of Minnesota Press.

Lyons, M. (1996), 'Foreign Bodies: The History of Labour Migration as a Threat to Public Health in Uganda', in P. Nugent and A. I. Asiwaju (eds), *African Boundaries: Barriers, Conduits and Opportunities*, London: Pinter.

MacGaffey, J. (1988), 'Evading Male Control: Women in the Second Economy in Zaire', in S. Stichter and J. Parpart (eds), *Patriarchy and Class*, Boulder, CO: Westview Press.

Machado, M. A. (1982), 'Booze, Broads, and the Border: Vice and U.S.–Mexican Relations, 1910–1930', in C. R. Bath (ed.), *Change and Perspective in Latin America*, El Paso: Center for Inter-American and Border Studies.

Malkki, L. (1992), 'National Geographic: The Rooting of Peoples and the Territorialization of National Identity among Scholars and Refugees', *Cultural Anthropology* vol. 7, no. 1, pp. 24–44.

—— (1995a), 'Refugees and Exile: From "Refugee Studies" to the National Order of Things', *Annual Review of Anthropology* vol. 24, pp. 495–523.

—— (1995b), *Purity and Exile: Violence, Memory, and National Cosmology among Hutu Refugees in Tanzania*, Chicago: University of Chicago Press.

—— (1997), 'Speechless Emissaries: Refugees, Humanitarianism, and Dehistoricization', in K. F. Olwig and K. Hastrup (eds), *Siting Culture: The Shifting Anthropological Object*, London: Routledge.

Mann, M. (1993), 'Nation-states in Europe and Other Continents: Diversifying, Developing, Not Dying', *Daedalus* vol. 122, pp. 115–140.

Margolis, M. L. (1994), *Little Brazil: An Ethnography of Brazilian Immigrants in New York City*, Princeton: Princeton University Press.

Mars, G. (1983), *Cheats at Work: An Anthropology of Workplace Crime*, London: Counterpoint.

Martínez, O. J. (1988), *Troublesome Border*, Tucson: University of Arizona Press.

—— (1994a), *Border People: Life and Society in the U.S.–Mexico Borderlands*, Tucson: The University of Arizona Press.

—— (1994b), 'The Dynamics of Border Interaction', in Clive H. Schofield (ed.), *Global Boundaries: World Boundaries, Volume 1*, London: Routledge.

Marx, K. (1967), *Capital: A Critique of Political Economy* (3 volumes), F. Engels (ed.), New York: International Publishers.

McFarlane, G. (1986), '"It's Not as Simple as That": The Expression of the Catholic and Protestant Boundary in Northern Irish Rural Communities', in A. P. Cohen (ed.), *Symbolising Boundaries: Identity and Diversity in British Cultures*, Manchester: Manchester University Press.

McMaster, G. R. (1995), 'Borderzones: The 'Injun-uity' of Aesthetic Tricks', *Cultural Studies* vol. 9, no. 1, pp. 74–90.

McNamara, P. H. (1971), 'Prostitution along the U.S.–Mexico Border: A Survey', in E. R. Stoddard (ed.), *Prostitution and Illicit Drug Traffic on the U.S.–Mexico Border* Occasional Papers No. 2, El Paso: Border-State University Consortium for Latin America.

Meléndez, T. (1982), 'Coyote: Towards a Definition of a Concept', *Aztlan: International Journal of Chicano Studies Research* vol. 13, no. 1–2, pp. 295–307.

Miller, D. (1998), *A Theory of Shopping*, Cambridge: Polity Press.

Milward, A. (1992), *The European Rescue of the Nation State*, London: Routledge.

Minghi, J. V. (1969 [1963]), 'Boundary Studies in Political Geography', in R. E. Kasperson and J. V. Minghi (eds), *The Structure of Political Geography*, Chicago: Aldine.

—— (1991), 'From Conflict to Harmony in Border Landscapes', in D. Rumley and J. V. Minghi (eds), *The Geography of Border Landscapes*, London: Routledge.

Minh-ha, T. T. (1996), 'An Acoustic Journey', in J. C. Welchman (ed.), *Rethinking Borders*, London: Macmillan.

Mishra, S. I. and Conner, R. F. (1996), 'Evaluation of an HIV Prevention Program among Latino Farmworkers', in S. I. Mishra, R. F. Conner and J. R. Mangaña (eds), *AIDS Crossing Borders: The Spread of HIV among Migrant Latinos*, Boulder, CO: Westview Press.

Mishra, S. I., Conner, R. F. and Mangaña, J. R. (eds) (1996), *AIDS Crossing Borders: The Spread of HIV among Migrant Latinos*, Boulder, CO: Westview Press.

Mlinar, Z. (1996), 'New States and Open Borders: Slovenia between the Balkans and the European Union', in L. O'Dowd and T. M. Wilson (eds), *Borders, Nations and States: Frontiers of Sovereignty in the New Europe*, Aldershot: Avebury.

Moore, H. L. (1994), *A Passion for Difference: Essays in Anthropology and Gender*, Cambridge: Polity Press.

Nader, L. (1974), 'Up the Anthropologist – Perspectives Gained from Studying Up', in D. Hymes (ed.), *Reinventing Anthropology*, New York: Vintage

Nagengast, C. (1991), *Reluctant Socialists, Rural Entrepreneurs: Class, Culture, and the Polish State*, Boulder, CO: Westview Press.

—— (1994), 'Violence, Terror, and the Crisis of the State', *Annual Review of Anthropology* vol. 23, pp. 109–36.

Needham, R. (1958), 'A Structural Analysis of Purum Society', *American Anthropologist* vol. 60, no. 1, pp. 75–101.

—— (1962), *Structure and Sentiment: A Test Case in Social Anthropology*, Chicago: University of Chicago Press.

Norman, K. (1997), 'Young Girls Dressing: Experiences of Exile and Memories of Home among Kosovo-Albanian Refugees in Sweden', in D. Baxter and R. Krulfeld (eds), *Beyond Boundaries: Selected Papers on Refugees and Immigrants, Volume V*, Arlington, VA: American Anthropological Association.

Nugent, D. (1994), 'Building the State, Making the Nation: The Bases and Limits of State Centralization in "Modern" Peru', *American Anthropologist* vol. 96, no. 2, pp. 333–69.

Nugent, P. (1996), 'Arbitrary Lines and the People's Minds: A Dissenting View on Colonial Boundaries in West Africa', in P. Nugent and A. I. Asiwaju (eds), *African Boundaries: Barriers, Conduits and Opportunities*, London: Pinter.

—— (n.d.), 'Power Versus Knowledge: Smugglers and the State along Ghana's Eastern Frontier, 1920–1992', unpublished paper.

—— and Asiwaju, A. I. (eds), (1996), *African Boundaries: Barriers, Conduits and Opportunities*, London: Pinter.

O'Dowd, L. and Corrigan, J. (1995), 'Buffer Zone or Bridge: Local Responses to Cross-border Economic Co-operation in the Irish Border Region', *Administration* vol. 42, no. 4, pp. 335–51.

—— (1996), 'Securing the Irish Border in a Europe without Frontiers', in L. O'Dowd and T. M. Wilson (eds), *Borders, Nations and States: Frontiers of Sovereignty in the New Europe*, Aldershot: Avebury.

O'Dowd, L., Corrigan, J. and Moore, T. (1995), 'Borders, National Sovereignty and European Integration', *International Journal of Urban and Regional Research* vol. 19, no. 2, pp. 272–85.

O'Dowd, L. and Wilson, T. M. (eds) (1996), *Borders, Nations and States: Frontiers of Sovereignty in the New Europe*, Aldershot: Avebury.

O'Hearn, D. (1994), *Free Trade or Managed Trade? Trading Between Two Worlds*, Belfast: Centre for Research and Documentation.

Okely, J. (1983), *The Traveller-Gypsies*, Cambridge: Cambridge University Press.

Paasi, A. (1996), *Territories, Boundaries and Consciousness: The Changing Geographies of the Finnish–Russian Border*, Chichester: John Wiley and Sons.

Paredes, A. (1993), *Folklore and Culture on the Texas–Mexican Border*, Austin: University of Texas Press.

Park, R., Burgess, E. and McKenzie, R. (1967 [1925]), *The City*, Chicago: University of Chicago Press.

Pettigrew, J. (1994), 'Reflections on the Place of the Border in Contemporary Sikh Affairs', in H. Donnan and T. M. Wilson (eds), *Border Approaches: Anthropological Perspectives on Frontiers*, Lanham MD: University Press of America.

Pratt, M. L. (1992), *Imperial Eyes: Travel Writing and Transculturation*, London: Routledge.

Preis, A. S. (1997), 'Seeking Place: Capsized Identities and Contracted Belonging among Sri Lankan Tamil Refugees', in K. F. Olwig and K. Hastrup (eds), *Siting Culture: The Shifting Anthropological Object*, London: Routledge.

Prescott, J. R. V. (1978), *Boundaries and Frontiers*, London: Croom Helm.

—— (1987), *Political Frontiers and Boundaries*, London: Unwin Hyman.

Price, J. A. (1971), 'International Border Screens and Smuggling', in E. R. Stoddard (ed.), *Prostitution and Illicit Drug Traffic on the U.S.–Mexico Border* Occasional Papers No. 2, El Paso: Border-State University Consortium for Latin America.

—— (1973), 'Tecate: An Industrial City on the Mexican Border', *Urban Anthropology* vol. 2, no. 1, pp. 35–47.

—— (1974), *Tijuana: Urbanization in a Border Culture*, Notre Dame/London: University of Notre Dame Press.

Rabinow, P. (1987), *The Foucault Reader*, Toronto: Peregrine Books.

Rabinowitz, D. (1994), 'To Sell or Not to Sell? Theory Versus Practice, Public Versus Private, and the Failure of Liberalism: The Case of Israel and its Palestinian Citizens', *American Ethnologist* vol. 21, no. 4, pp. 827–44.

—— (1998), 'National Identity on the Frontier: Palestinians in the Israeli Education System', in T. M. Wilson and H. Donnan (eds), *Border Identities: Nation and State at International Frontiers*, Cambridge: Cambridge University Press.

Rodman, M. C. (1992), 'Empowering Place: Multilocality and Multivocality', *American Anthropologist* vol. 94, pp. 640–56.

Roebuck, J. R. and McNamara, P. H. (1973), 'Ficheras and Free-lancers:

Prostitution in a Mexican Border City', *Archives of Sexual Behavior* vol. 2, no. 3, pp. 231–44.

Rosaldo, R. (1988), 'Ideology, Place and People without Culture', *Cultural Anthropology* vol. 3, pp. 77–87.

—— (1989), *Culture and Truth: The Remaking of Social Analysis*, Boston: Beacon Press.

Ross, J-K. (1975), 'Social Borders: Definitions of Diversity', *Current Anthropology* vol. 16, no. 1, pp. 53–72.

Ross, S. R. (1978), 'Introduction', in S. R. Ross (ed.), *Views Across the Border: The United States and Mexico*, Albuquerque: University of New Mexico Press.

Rouse, R. (1991), 'Mexican Migration and the Social Space of Postmodernism', *Diaspora* vol. 1, no. 1, pp. 8–23.

Roussou, M. (1986), 'War in Cyprus: Patriarchy and the Penelope Myth', in R. Ridd and H. Callaway (eds), *Caught Up in Conflict: Women's Responses to Political Strife*, Basingstoke: Macmillan Education.

Ruane, J. and Todd, J. (1996), *The Dynamics of Conflict in Northern Ireland: Power, Conflict and Emancipation*, Cambridge: Cambridge University Press.

Rumley, D. and Minghi, J. V. (1991a), 'Introduction: The Border Landscape Concept', in D. Rumley and J. V. Minghi (eds), *The Geography of Border Landscapes*, London: Routledge.

—— (eds) (1991b), *The Geography of Border Landscapes*, London: Routledge.

Sahlins, P. (1989), *Boundaries: The Making of France and Spain in the Pyrenees*, Berkeley: University of California Press.

—— (1998), 'State Formation and National Identity in the Catalan Borderlands during the Eighteenth and Nineteenth Centuries', in T. M. Wilson and H. Donnan (eds), *Border Identities: Nation and State at International Frontiers*, Cambridge: Cambridge University Press.

Samora, J. with Bustamante, J. A. and Cardenas, G. (1971), *Los Mojados: The Wetback Story*, Notre Dame: University of Notre Dame Press.

Sandos, J. A. (1980), 'Prostitution and Drugs: The United States Army on the Mexican–American Border, 1916–1917', *Pacific Historical Review* vol. 49, pp. 621–45.

Saris, J. A. (1996), 'Mad Kings, Proper Houses, and an Asylum in Rural Ireland', *American Anthropologist* vol. 98, no. 3, pp. 539–54.

Sayer, S. (1982), 'The Economic Analysis of Frontier Regions', *West European Politics* vol. 5, no. 4, pp. 64–79.

Scott, J. C. (1985), *Weapons of the Weak: Everyday Forms of Peasant Resistance*, New Haven: Yale University Press.

Scott, J. W. and Collins, K. (1997), 'Inducing Transboundary Regionalism in Asymmetric Situations: The Case of the German–Polish Border', *Journal of Borderlands Studies* Vol. 12, Nos. 1 and 2, pp. 97–121.

Seremetakis, C. N. (1996), 'In Search of the Barbarians: Borders in Pain', *American Anthropologist* vol. 98, no. 3, pp. 489–91.

Shanks, A. (1994), 'Cultural Divergence and Durability: The Border, Symbolic Boundaries and the Irish Gentry', in H. Donnan and T. M. Wilson (eds), *Border Approaches: Anthropological Perspectives on Frontiers*, Lanham, MD: University Press of America.

Shohat, E. (1989), *Israeli Cinema: East/West and the Politics of Representation,* Austin: University of Texas.

—— and Stam, R. (1996), 'From the Imperial Family to the Transnational Imaginary: Media Spectatorship in the Age of Globalization', in R. Wilson and W. Dissanayake (eds), *Global/Local: Cultural Production and the Transnational Imaginary*, Durham, NC: Duke University Press.

Skalník, P. (1989), 'Outwitting the State: An Introduction', in P. Skalník (ed.), *Outwitting the State*, Political Anthropology, Volume 7, New Brunswick, NJ: Transaction Publishers.

Sørensen, B. R. (1997), 'The Experience of Displacement: Reconstructing Places and Identities in Sri Lanka', in K. F. Olwig and K. Hastrup (eds), *Siting Culture: The Shifting Anthropological Object*, London: Routledge.

Spencer, J. (1990), *A Sinhala Village in a Time of Trouble: Politics and Change in Rural Sri Lanka*, Delhi: Oxford University Press.

—— (1997), 'Post-Colonialism and the Political Imagination', *Journal of the Royal Anthropological Institute* vol. 3, pp. 1–19.

Spyer, P. (ed.), (1998a), *Border Fetishisms: Material Objects in Unstable Spaces*, London: Routledge.

—— (1998b), 'The Tooth of Time, or Taking a Look at the "Look" of Clothing in Late Nineteenth-Century Aru', in P. Spyer (ed.), *Border Fetishisms: Material Objects in Unstable Spaces*, London: Routledge.

Steedly, M. M. (1996), 'Border Violations: A Case of Sexual Misconduct on the Van Mook Line, North Sumatra, 1949', paper presented to American Anthropological Association meetings, San Francisco, 1996.

Stein, B. N. (1981), 'The Refugee Experience: Defining the Parameters of a Field of Study', *International Migration Review* vol. 15, no. 1, pp. 320–30.

Stein, H. F. (1984), 'The Scope of Psycho-Geography: The Psychoanalytic Study of Spatial Representation', *The Journal of Psychoanalytic Anthropology* vol. 7, no. 1, pp. 23–73.

Stoddard, E. R. (1975), 'The Status of Borderlands Studies: Sociology and Anthropology', *The Social Science Journal* vol. 12, no. 3, pp. 29–54.

—— (1976), 'Illegal Mexican Labor in the Borderlands: Institutionalized Support of an Unlawful Practice', *Pacific Sociological Review* vol. 19, no. 2, pp. 175–210.

—— (1983a), 'Mexican Migration and Illegal Immigration', in E. R. Stoddard, R.

L. Nostrand and J. P. West (eds), *Borderlands Sourcebook: A Guide to the Literature on Northern Mexico and the American Southwest*, Norman: University of Oklahoma Press.

—— (1983b), 'Illegal Drug Traffic', in E. R. Stoddard, R. L. Nostrand and J. P. West (eds), *Borderlands Sourcebook: A Guide to the Literature on Northern Mexico and the American Southwest*, Norman: University of Oklahoma Press.

—— (1989), 'Developmental Stages of U.S.–Mexico Borderlands Studies', in A. I. Asiwaju and P. O. Adeniyi (eds), *Borderlands in Africa*, Lagos: University of Lagos Press.

Stokes, M. (1994), 'Local Arabesk, the Hatay and the Turkish Syrian Border', in H. Donnan and T. M. Wilson (eds), *Border Approaches: Anthropological Perspectives on Frontiers*, Lanham, MD: University Press of America.

—— (1998), 'Imagining "the South": Hybridity, Heterotopias and Arabesk on the Turkish–Syrian Border', in T. M. Wilson and H. Donnan (eds), *Border Identities: Nation and State at International Frontiers*, Cambridge: Cambridge University Press.

Strassoldo, R. (ed.) (1973), *Boundaries and Regions*, Trieste: Edizioni.

—— (1982a), 'Boundaries in Sociological Theory: A Reassessment', in R. Strassoldo and G. Delli Zotti (eds), *Cooperation and Conflict in Border Areas*, Milan: Franco Angeli.

—— (1982b), 'Frontier Regions: Future Collaboration or Conflict?', *West European Politics* vol. 5, no. 4, pp. 123–35.

—— (1989), 'Border Studies: The State of the Art in Europe', in A. I. Asiwaju and P. O. Adeniyi (eds), *Borderlands in Africa*, Lagos: University of Lagos Press.

—— and Delli Zotti, G. (eds.), (1982), *Cooperation and Conflict in Border Areas*, Milan: Angeli.

Strating, A. (1997), *De Lijnrijders van Rijnsburg: een antropologische Studie van Bloemenhandel, Verwantschap en Identiteit* (The Lijnrijders of Rijnsburg: An Anthropological Study of the Flower Trade, Kinship and Identity), University of Amsterdam.

Synnott, A. (1993), *The Body Social: Symbolism, Self and Society*, London: Routledge.

Tägil, S. (1982), 'The Question of Border Regions in Western Europe: An Historical Background', *West European Politics* vol. 5, no. 4, pp.18–33.

—— Gerner, K., Henrikson, G., Johansson, R., Oldberg, I., and Salomon, K. (1977), *Studying Boundary Conflicts: A Theoretical Framework*, Lund: Esselte Studium.

Tambiah, S. (1976), *World Conqueror and World Renouncer: A Study of Buddhism and Polity in Thailand Against a Historical Background*, Cambridge: Cambridge University Press.

—— (1986), *Sri Lanka: Ethnic Fratricide and the Dismantling of Democracy*, Chicago: Chicago University Press.

Bibliography

Tapper, R. (1997), *Frontier Nomads of Iran: A Political and Social History of the Shahsevan*, Cambridge: Cambridge University Press.

Taylor, J. R. (1976), 'The Status of Borderlands Studies: Economics', *The Social Science Journal* vol. 13, no. 1, pp. 69–76.

Thomassen, B. (1996), 'Border Studies in Europe: Symbolic and Political Boundaries, Anthropological Perspectives', *Europæa* vol. 2, no. 1, pp. 37–48.

Thuen, T. (1998), 'Borders as Resource and Impediment in East European Transition Processes', in C. Papa, G. Pizza, and F. M. Zerilli (eds), *Incontri di Etnologia Europea*, Napoli: Edizioni Scientifiche Italiane.

Tobias, P. M. (1982), 'The Socioeconomic Context of Grenadian Smuggling', *Journal of Anthropological Research* vol. 38, pp. 383–400.

Turner, F. J. (1977 [1920]), 'The Significance of the Frontier in American History', in F. J. Turner, *The Frontier in American History*, Franklin Center, PA: The Franklin Library.

Turner, V. (1974), *Dramas, Fields and Metaphors: Symbolic Action in Human Society*, Ithaca: Cornell University Press.

—— (1967), *The Forest of Symbols: Aspects of Ndembu Ritual*, Ithaca: Cornell University Press.

—— (1982), *From Ritual to Theater*, New York: Performing Arts Journal Publications.

Turton, D. (1996), 'Migrants and Refugees: A Mursi Case Study', in T. Allen (ed.), *In Search of Cool Ground: War, Flight and Homecoming in Northeast Africa*, London: James Currey.

van Schendel, W. (1993), 'Easy Come, Easy Go: Smugglers on the Ganges', *Journal of Contemporary Asia* vol. 23, no. 2, pp. 189–213.

Verdery, K. (1991), *National Ideology Under Socialism: Identity and Cultural Politics in Ceausescu's Romania*, Berkeley: University of California Press.

Vereni, P. (1996), 'Boundaries, Frontiers, Persons, Individuals: Questioning "Identity" at National Borders', *Europæa* vol. 2, no. 1, pp. 77–89.

Vincent, J. (1990), *Anthropology and Politics: Visions, Traditions and Trends*, Tucson: University of Arizona Press.

Wallace, W. (1994), 'Rescue or Retreat? The Nation State in Western Europe, 1945–93', *Political Studies* vol. 62, pp. 52–76.

Wallman, S. (1978), 'The Boundaries of "Race": Processes of Ethnicity in England', *Man* vol. 13, no. 2, pp. 200–17.

Weaver, T. (1988), 'The Human Rights of Undocumented Workers in the United States–Mexico Border Region', in T. E. Downing and G. Kushner (eds), *Human Rights and Anthropology*, Cultural Survival Report 24, Cambridge, MA: Cultural Survival.

Welchman, J. C. (1996), *Rethinking Borders*, London: Macmillan.

Whiteford, L. M. (1979), 'The Borderland as an Extended Community', in F.

Camara and R. Van Kemper (eds), *Migration Across Frontiers: Mexico and the United States* Contributions of the Latin American Anthropology Group (AAA) Vol. 3, Albany: State University of New York.

Wilson, T. M. (1993a), 'Frontiers Go But Boundaries Remain: The Irish Border as a Cultural Divide', in Thomas M. Wilson and M. Estellie Smith (eds), *Cultural Change and the New Europe: Perspectives on the European Community*, Boulder and Oxford: Westview Press.

—— (1993b), 'Consumer Culture and European Integration at the Northern Irish Border', in W. Fred van Raaij and Gary J. Bamossy (eds), *European Advances in Consumer Research, volume 1*, Provo, UT: Association for Consumer Research.

—— (1994), 'Symbolic Dimensions to the Irish Border', in H. Donnan and T. M. Wilson (eds), *Border Approaches: Anthropological Perspectives on Frontiers*, Lanham, MD: University Press of America.

—— (1995), 'Blurred Borders: Local and Global Consumer Culture in Northern Ireland', in J. A. Costa and G. J. Bamossy (eds), *Marketing in a Multicultural World: Ethnicity, Nationalism and Cultural Identity*, London: Sage.

—— (1996), 'Sovereignty, Identity and Borders: Political Anthropology and European Integration', in L. O'Dowd and T. M. Wilson (eds), *Borders, Nations and States: Frontiers of Sovereignty in the New Europe*, Aldershot: Avebury.

Wilson, T. M. and Donnan, H. (1998a), 'Nation, State and Identity at International Borders', in T. M. Wilson and H. Donnan (eds), *Border Identities: Nation and State at International Frontiers*, Cambridge: Cambridge University Press.

—— (eds) (1998b), *Border Identities: Nation and State at International Frontiers*, Cambridge: Cambridge University Press.

Wolf, E. R. (1974), 'American Anthropologists and American Society', in D. Hymes (ed.), *Reinventing Anthropology*, New York: Vintage.

—— (1982), *Europe and the People Without History*, Berkeley: University of California Press.

—— (1990), 'Distinguished Lecture: Facing Power – Old Insights, New Questions', *American Anthropologist* vol. 92, no. 3, pp. 586–96.

Index

Index